Human Communication
The Process of Relating

Human Communication
The Process of Relating

George A. Borden
University of Delaware

John D. Stone
Auburn University

Cummings Publishing Company
Menlo Park, California • *Reading, Massachusetts*
London • *Amsterdam* • *Don Mills, Ontario* • *Sydney*

Copyright © 1976 by Cummings Publishing Company, Inc.
Philippines Copyright 1976

Library of Congress Catalog Number 75-27821

ISBN 0-8465-0615-7
ABCDEFGHIJKL-AL-79876

Cummings Publishing Company
2727 Sand Hill Road
Menlo Park, California 94025

Contents

Part 3: The Context for Humanistic Communication

Part 5: On Becoming a Humanistic Communicator

Table of Inventories

Preface

Good interpersonal communication is one of the most important skills we can develop. Every facet of our lives from birth until death is affected by our ability to relate to other people, which in turn is affected by how well we know ourselves. Traditionally, psychologists have been concerned mainly with the problem of human behavior. But in recent years a new school of psychology— humanistic psychology—has dealt with the problem of knowing ourselves, both in intra- and interpersonal relationships. Thus, humanistic psychology offers a cognitive model of human nature which is significantly different from that of the behaviorist with whom we have grown up and into whose philosophy we have been indoctrinated by psychologists, advertisers, and teachers. In this book we shall explore humanistic psychology's assumptions about human nature and the ramifications of these assumptions in interpersonal communication.

Human Communication: The Process of Relating is intended for undergraduate students in any course for which an understanding of human communicative behavior is desirable. The book is divided into five parts. Part 1 describes the basic models of human nature presented by the three leading schools of psychology, together with their underlying assumptions about human behavior. Part 2 applies the assumptions of humanistic psychology to a model of human communication. Part 3 looks in on where psychologists think we are today and where we are going—both our present position and our potential. Part 4 discusses the three basic constructs of humanistic psychology as essentials to human communication, and Part 5 applies the humanistic assumptions about human communication to the practical problems of becoming a humanistic communicator. The main thread running through each part is the relevance of the humanistic approach to interpersonal communication.

We have selected several previously published articles by leaders in humanistic psychology and several original essays around which to weave our conception of human communication. These readings are used primarily as references, but are essential to the development of our theme. Therefore, they are an integral part of the book and should be so considered by the reader.

Each major idea in the text is preceded by an inventory which will help you discover how you feel about that particular subject and which thus will help you know yourself better. There are seventeen of these inventories (Scales A-Q). All of them have more than one use, and if you duplicate them before you fill them out, you can use them to ascertain other people's feelings about you and to see if they agree with your perceptions.

Some of the concepts presented are quite abstract, but we have tried to explain them in enough detail and present enough examples and activities to make them understandable. Both experiential and theoretical activities are provided for both group and individual participation. Nevertheless, you should be prepared to encounter language different from the language of the usual basic speech or psychology text. We have tried to use nonsexist language, which in some cases may sound unfamiliar. Also, the language of humanistic psychology itself differs from that of behavioristic psychology, in which most present-day texts are written. One of the most distinctive aspects of humanistic psychology's language is that it uses common everyday terms and not the highly objective, structured language of "science." Therefore, we urge you to be patient if at first the language seems confusing. Once you become immersed in it, things will begin to clear up.

We wish to thank the following people for their assistance in bringing forth this book: our many colleagues with whom we discussed the ideas in this text, particularly Carol Puhl and Bob Eubanks; our students who have suffered through our evolution from behavioristic to humanistic persons; our critics who have given valuable recommendations for changes in the manuscript; and most of all our editor, Larry Wilson, who we found to be an example of the humanistic characteristics we have written about.

George A. Borden
John D. Stone
Newark, Delaware,
and Auburn, Alabama
December 1975

x

Acknowledgments

For permission to reprint material in this textbook, grateful acknowledgment is made to the following sources* :

Beyond Freedom and Dignity, by B. F. Skinner. Copyright © 1971 by Alfred A. Knopf, Inc. (p. 9)

"Humanistic Theory: The Third Revolution in Psychology," by Floyd W. Matson. This article first appeared in the March/April 1971 issue of *The Humanist* and is reprinted by permission. (pp. 19-27)

Introduction to Humanistic Psychology, by Charlotte Buhler and Melanie Allen. Copyright © 1972 by Brooks/Cole Publishing Co. (pp. 37, 154-55, 228)

"A Brief Introduction to Personal Construct Theory," by George A. Kelly, in *Perspectives in Personal Construct Theory*, edited by D. Bannister. Academic Press, London, New York, 1970. (pp. 38, 74, 88-89, 161)

Don't Say Yes When You Want to Say No, by Herbert Fensterheim, Ph. D., and Jean Baer. Copyright © 1975 by Herbert Fensterheim, Ph. D., and Jean Baer. Published by the David McKay Co. Inc. Reprinted with permission of the publisher. (pp. 75, 234-35)

The Prophet, by Kahlil Gibran. Reprinted with permission of the publisher, Alfred A. Knopf, Inc. Copyright 1923 by Kahlil Gibran; renewal copyright

* The numbers in parentheses following each entry refer to pages in this book on which quoted material appears.

*To all those who have facilitated
fulfilling communicative relationships*

Prologue

Know thyself.
Socrates

Who am I? What do I want out of life? What is a friend? Why do I feel lonely? Why do I think of the things I do? What makes me tick? Questions, questions, questions! Beginning with the human potential movements of the sixties, it has become popular to ask such questions, and hundreds of gurus have arisen to answer them. One movement after another comes into vogue, gaining adherents from all walks of life, only to be replaced by another. The encounter groups, T-groups, Jesus freaks, various maharishis, the schools of psychotherapy, behavior mod groups, the swingers, women's liberation, the right-to-life groups—each takes a somewhat different approach to the central question of being human; namely, Who am I?

In this book we will piece together, from all the movements, what we feel are the essentials of being human. To begin with, let us say that to find out who we are we must do more than have someone observe us and give us a label (paranoid, dummy, weirdo). Because many of us suffer from this type of labeling by others, we need to know more about why such behavior occurs and why it affects us so. This means that we must understand more about the communication process. The old adage "Sticks and stones may break my bones, but names will never hurt me" is a bold-faced lie. As human beings, we live in a glass world of words. We are symbolic animals, and our greatest use of symbols is in the language we use to communicate. To find out who we are, we must find out by what symbols we represent ourselves and are represented by others. To do this we must become aware of ourselves from the inside out (self-awareness through introspection) and from the outside in (self-awareness through honest communication with significant others). The first process we call intrapersonal communication, and the second, interpersonal communication. The purpose of this book is to facilitate both of these types of communication.

First of all, we would like to clarify our approach. Many of the activities you are asked to do in this book are psychologically and communicatively quite heavy. We are not interested in teaching you how to play communicative games that only titillate your humanistic sense. Rather, we present you with opportunities to get to know the *real* you, by talking about, giving examples of, and presenting exercises for the development of a fully conscious human being. We always leave you with the choice of reading or not reading, feeling or not feeling, doing or not doing. If an instructor *demands* that you, the student, complete activities that you are not willing or able to do, you should assert yourself and respectfully decline. After all, you and your instructor are locked into one of the potentially most dehumanizing communication situations society has yet devised. The student-instructor relationship is designed to be objective and rigorous. The instructor's behavior, and yours, in such a situation will tell you a great deal about the humanness of both of you.

We do not want to give you a wrong impression, however. We do not ask you to join us in a nude encounter group, nor make love with your instructor. Sex is not the only way to become aware of your humanness; nor is participation in encounter groups or consciousness-raising groups. We don't suggest any of these activities. We do ask you to find out why you communicate the way you do, and in doing this, you have to determine your own philosophy of life whether you want to or not. To know yourself means knowing not only who you are, but where you are going and why you are going in that direction. We will give you many opportunities to make explicit choices about your communicative behavior — choices that you may have been making implicitly for some time. We will ask you to describe your feelings about yourself and others, to evaluate yourself and others, and to determine the differences between who you feel you are and who you want to be.

To do this we will ask you to participate in group activities and individual self-searching sessions. We will give you the opportunity to fill out a number of scales (inventories) to measure *your* feelings and evaluations of yourself and others. Remember that this is your book. No one else need ever see it. Before you fill out a scale, you should tear it from the book, duplicate it, fill out the copy, and keep the original blank for future use. Don't throw your completed scales away, however; keep them in a folder somewhere so you can refer to them at a later date to see how you have changed. You may be amazed at how quickly you become the person you want to be.

In all of the activities you will be asked to do, you will be communicating with others, in dyads (groups of two), in small groups, or even in public discourse. These activities will help you understand how you and others communicate and will show you how human you and others are in your communication. It is important that you realize that all these behaviors are communicative behaviors, for many times we do not make explicit mention of the communicative behavior we are expecting in these activities. Further, we are not about to tell you how, why, or when to communicate. Since you are a unique person, these decisions must come from you. Any strategies we might set up would be just that—our strategies—so if you used them you would be trying to "play us." We do not believe in games.

We would like you to find out what you think most people think about communication. In the following inventory (Scale A), if you think most other people strongly disagree with the statement, put a 1 in the blank; if you think they disagree, put a 2; if you think they agree, put a 3; and if you think they strongly agree, put a 4. *Remember*, these are *your feelings right now*. Don't be surprised if they change.

SCALE A

Feelings about Communication

PEOPLE IN GENERAL FEEL THAT:

_____ 1. male-female communication is the most important communication situation.

_____ 2. to empathize with the person you are communicating with will interfere with efficient communication.

_____ 3. all of our communication should facilitate growth in the other person.

_____ 4. the most important skill one can develop is the ability to communicate.

_____ 5. people who need to talk about ideas are weird.

_____ 6. a beautiful woman may be a hindrance to "real" human communication.

_____ 7. we should all learn how to communicate because the better we communicate, the more control we will have over other people.

_____ 8. a good party person can usually communicate well.

_____ 9. letting your feelings show is a sign of immature communicative behavior.

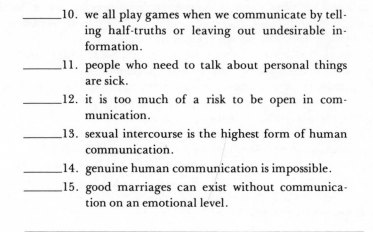

_____10. we all play games when we communicate by telling half-truths or leaving out undesirable information.

_____11. people who need to talk about personal things are sick.

_____12. it is too much of a risk to be open in communication.

_____13. sexual intercourse is the highest form of human communication.

_____14. genuine human communication is impossible.

_____15. good marriages can exist without communication on an emotional level.

Now, with a different-colored pen, fill out this inventory as *you feel* it should be (I FEEL THAT). You can see how *your feelings* about the communication process differ from how *you think others feel* about it. Are there many differences? If there are, can you live with them? As you progress through the rest of this book, you will find many more of these inventories. We hope you will fill them out and keep them for future reference. Now let's find out what we think it means to be a humanistic communicator.

Invictus

Out of the Night that covers me,
Black as the pit from pole to pole,
I thank whatever gods may be
For my unconquerable soul.

In the fell clutch of circumstance
I have not winced nor cried aloud;
Under the bludgeonings of chance
My head is bloody, but unbow'd.

Beyond this place of wrath and tears
Looms but the Horror of the shade,
And yet the menace of the years
Finds and shall find me unafraid.

It matters not how strait the gate,
How charged with punishments the scroll,
I am the master of my fate:
I am the captain of my soul.

William Ernest Henley

Part 1

Three Views
of Human Nature

Upon completion of this section you should be able to:
1. List the assumptions about people inherent in the humanistic psychological point of view.
2. List the assumptions about people inherent in the psychoanalytic point of view.
3. List the assumptions about people inherent in the behavioristic point of view.
4. Differentiate among the three major approaches to the study of human beings: psychoanalytic, behavioristic, and humanistic.
5. Compare the communicative behavior of the internally controlled person and the externally controlled person.

Henley's bold profession of control over his destiny seems naive in the world of mass education, mass media, and a shrinking universe. The constant cry of students, consumers, and employees that they are only a computer number and therefore have no personal control over their destiny is one of the most rudimentary complaints facing our society today. Some psychological studies have posited that people can be sorted into two categories: those who feel they are in control of their behavior, and those who feel they are controlled by other forces (Rotter 1966).*

The existence of these two types of people is not just academic, but has far-reaching effects. In fact, we can see both types at work in the personnel management of our great industrial-military complex. Some supervisors feel that their employees must be stimulated, motivated, and controlled on all levels, else their effectiveness deteriorates and production declines. Others feel that if the person is left to work out his or her own strategies for accomplishing a task it will be done more effectively and production will increase. This differentiation is known as the theory of X and Y (Athos and Coffey 1968, p. 299). The same principles are often applied to students at all levels of education, and it is obvious that, since both types of people exist, both examples can be shown to be correct.

The assumption that people must be motivated by external means versus the assumption that people are self-motivated exemplifies a basic difference between the main branches of psychology—the behavioristic and psychoanalytic schools of psychology on the one hand, and the humanistic school of psychology on the other. Its implications for the human communication process may be seen in the women's liberation movement, in which consciousness-raising groups are trying to change woman's image of herself from that of a passive, dependent being (needing and getting her stimulation and motivation from her environment [males]) to that of an active, assertive being (needing only freedom to do, because she is self-motivated).

How do you feel about this difference? How do you think others feel? Do you think most people believe we need external motivation, or do most people believe human beings are self-motivated? We have included an inventory of basic beliefs about human nature (Scale B), which you may complete to get an answer to these questions. To fill it out, put a 1 for strongly disagree, a 2 for disagree, a 3 for agree, or a 4 for strongly agree in front of each of the statements. Remember, you are filling out this inventory on the basis of how you feel *society* views human behavior. In other words, you are stating what you feel the norms of society are.

---

* In contrast to Henley's poem we have Herman Melville's Ahab saying, "This whole act's immutably decreed! 'Twas rehearsed by thee and me a billion years before this ocean rolled. Fool! I am Fates' lieutenant. I act under orders" (*Moby-Dick: Or, The Whale* 1948, p. 410).

SCALE B

Basic Characteristics of Human Nature

SOCIETY (ADVERTISERS, POLITICIANS, MANAGEMENT) THINKS PEOPLE ARE:

_____ 1. rather mechanistic—doing things by habit rather than by choice.

_____ 2. passive responders who must be motivated by external stimuli.

_____ 3. apathetic—not wanting to get involved with other people.

_____ 4. assertive—doing what they really want to do in most situations.

_____ 5. actively pursuing their own goals.

_____ 6. internally controlled—feel they can be and do what they really want to.

_____ 7. externally controlled—feel society dictates what they must do in each situation.

_____ 8. autonomous—look to themselves for their reasons for doing things.

_____ 9. conditioned not to think for themselves.

_____10. cognitive beings—making choices on the basis of reason rather than emotion.

_____11. aware of themselves—knowing what their choices are in most situations.

_____12. self-motivated and not needing external motivation.

_____13. irrational—subject to unconscious sexual and aggressive forces.

_____14. products of their environment with no means of counteracting this.

_____15. pleasure seekers—cannot be altruistic.

_____16. conditioned to be happiest when they fulfill the norms of society.

_____17. rational because they make choices that are expressions of themselves.

_____18. predictable because they adhere to the norms of society.

_____19. not responsible for their behavior.

_____20. motivated by unconscious sexual and aggressive forces.

_____21. unpredictable because they are free to choose their behavior.

_____22. rational because they make choices that are in line with society.

_____23. able to adapt creatively to any situation.

_____24. aware of their responsibilities to society and committed to helping others.

_____25. responsible for their own behavior.

_____26. capable of meaningful relationships through involvement with others.

_____27. open, honest communicators.

_____28. above using other people for their own gain.

_____29. in control of their own destiny.

_____30. dependent on others for support in making their own decisions.

Now that you have indicated what you feel society's view of people is, go back through this scale and, using a different-colored pen, evaluate how you think people are (I THINK PEOPLE ARE). Are there any differences? Discuss these characteristics with friends to see if they agree with you or what you thought the norm was.

Now that you have some feelings about the basic characteristics of human nature, we would like to give you some further insights into the assumptions about human nature peculiar to each of the three major schools of psychology. To differentiate clearly among these schools, the extreme positions will be expressed, but you should realize that in stating these assumptions very few, if any, psychologists will hold exclusively to one particular position. It can probably be said only that one has leanings toward one of these models (see Figure 1).

As you read through Part 1 of this book you may find yourself agreeing and disagreeing with parts of each of these models of human behavior. We hope you do, but we also hope you will discuss these three approaches to human nature with those who differ with you and thus sharpen your own understanding of human nature.

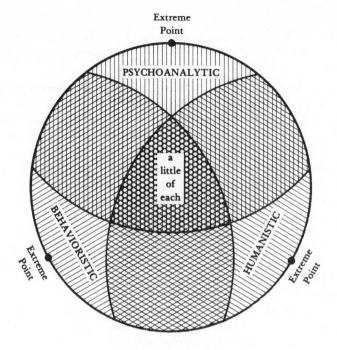

Figure 1 The overlapping nature of the three schools of psychology.

Behavioristic Assumptions

The model of human nature arising from the behavioristic approach to psychology stems from a point of view shared by several psychologists, notably, John Watson, Clark Hull, and B. F. Skinner. Its basic assumptions grew out of a desire to make the study of human behavior a pure science. The goal of the behaviorists has been to develop a simple, sovereign theory of human behavior, which they have tried to achieve by imitating the physical sciences in every way. They began by seeking

> to apply the mathematical physicist's exact and deductive methods to man and society. The endeavor bred a belief in the possibility of finding a few simple laws governing the actions of men as they governed the movements of the heavenly bodies. The connecting link was Matter, of which man was made and which held

the clue to phenomena. From this assumption the social sciences, like the physical, have not departed, even though Matter has been variously redefined. (Barzun and Graff 1970, p. 219)

The basic law that arose from this endeavor is that of stimulus-response. It essentially says that objects (human beings included) only respond to external stimuli and that these responses cluster around certain types of behaviors called *norms*. If we can control the stimuli and measure the responses, we can find out what the normative behavior will be for a given stimulus. The behavior can then be predicted whenever that stimulus occurs (e.g., a good-looking person of the opposite sex walks by (stimulus) and you turn your head to watch (response)—this behavior is predictable with nearly 100 percent accuracy). In essence, the behaviorist is treating the human being like an object that has no choice in how it is to respond to the stimulus. This is a direct carry-over from the physical sciences, where the same type of experimenting is done with chemicals and other nonliving substances. The law of stimulus-response seems as basic to psychology as Newton's laws are to the physical sciences.

In an attempt to make their research more "scientific," the behaviorists generally have attempted to objectify their human subjects by referring to them not as persons or individuals but as organisms—the same term they use to refer to rats and pigeons. By using one term to refer to all living things, one can, theoretically, remove oneself from involvement with the object of research. Just as the physical scientists would not become personally involved with a lump of coal, so behaviorists would not likely have a relationship with an organism—but they might want to with a person.

The laws, rules, or hypotheses resulting from this type of research are concerned with the sameness of individuals and may be used to predict normative behavior. Given a particular stimulus (such as a smile), what is the normal response? If we can define what *normal* behavior is, we can then identify those who deviate from it. (The normal family has 2.3 children, 1.2 pets, and 1.7 cars.) This type of research leads to a "concern with traits that are characteristic of all individuals or to categories into which people can be grouped" (Pervin 1970, p. 62), thereby de-emphasizing the uniqueness of the individual. Its concern is with the observable stimulus and the normative response. We see this as overlooking the fact that the differences between people may be greater and/or more important than their similarities.

The behaviorists' model of human nature is basically a learning theory model, which holds that through reinforcement of acceptable behaviors you adopt (learn) the structures of society and they become your own. There are three basic assumptions about human nature around which this process functions (Pervin 1970). The first is the assumption that "behavior is learned by the building up of associations." These associations may be called "habits, reflexes or relationships between responses and reinforcement contingencies in the environment" (p. 441). Whatever they are called, they assume some sort of internal connection between external stimuli and resulting responses. They are assumed to be accumulative; that is, a large change in behavior can be accomplished by the realization of many small ones, and human behavior is assumed to be like that of a machine, with many interdependent parts enabling the stimulation of one part to produce a response from another part (blow in my ear and I'll follow you anywhere).

The second assumption is that humans are basically hedonistic, "seeking to obtain pleasure and avoid pain" (p. 441). Basically, it is a "what's in it for me" model ruling out charitable behavior, love, or altruism. It works on the basis of reinforcement; the more desirable feedback we get, the more prone we are to continue the behavior. People learn to maximize their gains and minimize their losses — a fairly simple economic model (if I am nice to people, they will give me what I want).

The third assumption, following from the first two, is that "behavior is basically environmentally determined" (p. 441). Since behavior is a function of associations between an act and a reinforcement for the act, and all reinforcement comes from the environment, then by manipulating the environment one can eventually produce the behavior one wants. The resulting assumption is that, since behavior is learned and can be produced, it can also be controlled. A person "grows to be what he is made to be by his environment" (Langer 1969, p. 4). (Can you think of examples of both the truth and the falsity of the above assumption?)

Though the behaviorists' model of human nature is a learning theory model, it seeks to do away with any reference to mental concepts such as will, ideas, thoughts, and intentions.* This model views a person as a rational being whose mind is originally void of any structure (tabula rasa) but which, like a piece of clay, receives the impressions of environmental structure. The mind does have the ability to associate the simple ideas imprinted by society into more complex ones, but since we cannot observe this process, we can only infer it from observable behavior. Therefore, behaviorists seek to understand human beings by studying those behaviors which can be observed and measured.

The objectification of the human being is a basic tenet of the behavioristic school of psychology. Behaviorism has been defined as "a psychological approach in which investigation is limited to objective, observable phenomena and to methods of natural science — a revolt against functionalism and introspection" (Goldenson 1970, p. 149). One can only measure what can be observed. Even though the observing may be done by an instru-

---

* The present trend is for all schools of psychology to move in the direction of accepting some form of cognitive activity to exist in their models of human nature, even though these activities can only be inferred.

ment that is much more sensitive than our natural senses, one is still dealing with observable phenomena. Since introspective processes cannot be observed directly, they can play no role in the description of human behavior. The underlying assumption is that a direct cause-effect relationship exists between the event (stimulus) and the behavior (response) of the organism.

Paralleling this belief is an even more crucial assumption that the behavior of an organism always occurs in response to a stimulus from the environment. Any behavior, then, is the result of forces in the environment acting upon the organism. Behavioral analysis establishes the relationship between behavior and the environmental context and then uses this knowledge to further control behavior. These developments are the outgrowth of Watson's statement that "psychology as the behaviorist views it is a purely objective, experimental branch of natural science. Its theoretical goal is the prediction and control of behavior " (Pervin 1970, p. 62). He further states that

> all complex forms of behavior, including reasoning, habit, and emotional reactions are at bottom composed only of simple stimulus-response events which can be seen, measured, and therefore known. . . . Moreover, once we have isolated the stimuli that produce responses, whether normal or abnormal, we can use them to predict an individual's behavior and, if the stimuli are within our control, to control his behavior completely. (Goldenson 1970, pp. 149–150)

The behaviorist holds that all behavior is observable and consequently can be explained in terms of environmental variables. Even self-control is under the control of external forces. Skinner gives this explanation :

> It appears, therefore, that society is responsible for the larger part of the behavior of self-control. If this is correct, little ultimate control remains with the individual. A man may spend a great deal of time designing his own life — he may choose the circumstances in which he is to live with great care, and he may manipulate his daily environment on an extensive scale. Such activity appears to exemplify a high order of self-determination. But it is also behavior, and we account for it in terms of other variables in the environment and history of the individual. It is these variables which provide the ultimate control. (Southwell and Merbaum 1971, p. 130)

A basic question we would raise at this point is one of responsibility. Who is responsible for one's behavior? If not the individual, then society? And who is to determine how and for what reason society will establish a certain kind of environment? If we are under the control of environmental forces, who is controlling these forces? Following this model, one soon begins to see people as robots, programmed by society to function in such a way that they will maintain the status quo. Shades of 1984.

We feel that aside from the fact that the language of the behaviorist sounds very nonhuman — featuring words like "conditioning," "control," and "organism" — the thought that something out there is controlling our behavior is very upsetting to many human beings. We don't like to admit to being manipulated. We would like to believe that something inside our heads is responsible for the way we behave. When the behaviorists are questioned about this they will agree that there may be something going on inside the head, but they argue that it is more important to understand a person's behavior in conjunction with the environment in which it occurs, inferring a cause-effect relationship between environment and behavior, than to assume that one is free to behave as one wills, regardless of the situation. The scientific objectivity with which behaviorists work is exemplified by the following:

> An experimental analysis shifts the determination of behavior from autonomous man to the environment — an environment responsible both for the evolution of the species and for the repertoire acquired by each member. Early versions of environmentalism were inadequate because they could not explain how the environment worked, and much seemed to be left for autonomous man to do. But environmental contingencies now take over functions once attributed to autonomous man, and certain questions arise. Is man then "abolished"? Certainly not as a species or as an individual achiever. It is the autonomous inner man who is abolished, and that is a step forward. But does man not then become merely a victim or passive observer of what is happening to him? He is indeed controlled by his environment, but we must remember that it is an environment largely of his own making. The evolution of a culture is a gigantic exercise in self-control. It is often said that a scientific view of man leads to wounded vanity, a sense of hopelessness, and nostalgia. But no theory changes what it is a theory about; man remains what he has always been. And a new theory may change what can be done with its subject matter. A scientific view of man offers exciting possibilities. We have not yet seen what man can make of man. (Skinner 1971, pp. 214–215)

From the foregoing statement one gets the feeling that, in the behaviorists' model of human nature, the individual is both the controlled and the controller, and that they have not worked out the details as to who controls whom. (Perhaps God is really the top behaviorist and we are all prisoners in his laboratory!)

In summarizing this brief review of the underlying assumptions of behavioristic psychology, we may say that the behavioristic model of human nature is a learning theory model. A person begins with a passive, blank mind having only the ability to be activated by some internal but primarily external stimuli and to associate with these stimuli the responses one makes to them. We are hedonistic (seeking pleasure and avoiding pain), so we will do things that are positively reinforced. The incoming stimuli leave an "impression" on the mind that can be compared with past and future impressions and are associated with similar responses. Thus, we are conditioned to behave in certain ways in certain situations because we are a reflection of the environment and predictable in the normativeness of our behavior. This is a deterministic model in that stimuli from the environment are said to be the cause of human behavior. The human being is a machine whose mental processes are merely the associations between stimulus and response.

We are said to be rational beings because we only respond to external stimuli the way we have been conditioned to respond. Even self-control is environmentally conditioned, so we are not autonomous beings but products of our environment. Therefore, we are not responsible for our behavior, even though we are known by it alone. We are economically oriented, seeking only positive reinforcement, and thus are incapable of doing anything altruistic. We cannot transcend ourselves. A human being is basically perceived as "merely another type of animal, with no essential differences from animals and with the same destructive, anti-social tendencies" (Goble 1970, p. 8). Thus, a person can be objectified and divided into traits that are observable and measurable. Stimulation, control, and, therefore, responsibility are all rooted in the environment.

BEHAVIORISTIC ACTIVITIES

1. Does the environment control your behavior? If you are a college student living away from home, probably the most dramatic example of such a "control" comes into play when you return home from college on your vacations.
    a. List ten examples of your behavior in each environment (home and college) and indicate how these behaviors differ. What do these behaviors have to do with communication?
    b. Structure some of these examples into an oral report focusing on the parts of the environments that "cause" these different behaviors.
    c. Form a group of four to six members and discuss the different behaviors that occur in the two environments with the goal of finding the normative behavior in each environmental setting.
    d. Evaluate either the oral report or the group discussion and determine the similarities and differences of the behaviors reported in these two environments.
2. Can one person control another's behavior without the second person's being aware of being controlled? In this exercise you will have to use your own ingenuity. Try to set the mood for an encounter with a friend. Can you increase or decrease the possibility of having the day or evening go the way you want it to? Do the clothes you wear or how you fix your hair have an impact or influence over such control? Does your language or other behavior have an influence over the behaviors of friends? Of strangers?
    a. Create your own experiment to test the effect you can have on a communication event and report it to the class.

   b.   Form a group of four to six persons and create a communication situation involving friends or the class in which you can predict some of the behaviors that will result. Report your successes or failures.
3.   Analyze the environment in which you live.
   a.   What elements affect your behaviors over which you have no (or very little) control?
   b.   What elements in your environment affect your behaviors because you choose to let them do so?
   c.   Are there any elements in your environment whose influence you cannot report? Explain this to your classmates. (This may serve as a stimulus for group discussion, as others may be made aware of similar things in their environments.)
4.   Discuss with a group of your classmates the general type of "system" upon which Western culture operates. Is the "free enterprise" economic system basically behavioristic? Is the educational system? The social system? If the society is fundamentally behavioristic, when do we learn how to act in this system?

Psychoanalytic Assumptions

Unlike the behavioristic approach to psychology, the psychoanalytic approach has a single founder, Sigmund Freud. Though other leaders of the movement, such as Alfred Adler, Carl Jung, and Erik Erikson, differed with him in some ways, they all accepted the basic model of human nature that Freud developed. His model shows strong influences from the developments in the physical sciences at that time, in that it is essentially a hydraulic model with a set amount of fluid. Since it is a closed system, pressure exerted on the system will manifest itself at the point of least resistance (as in a hydraulic jack, cake decorator, or blowing up a balloon). Pervin (1970, pp. 216-217) says it this way:

> What is at the heart of the psychoanalytic view of man is that man is an energy system. There is the sense of a hydraulic system in which energy flows, gets side-tracked, or becomes dammed-up. In all, there is a limited amount of energy, and if it gets discharged in one way, there is that much less energy to be discharged in another way. The energy that man employs for cultural purposes he withdraws from the energy available for sexual purposes, and vice-versa. If the energy is blocked from one channel of expression, it finds another, generally

along the path of least resistance. Human behavior may take many forms, but basically all behavior is reducible to common forms of energy, and the goal of all behavior is pleasure, meaning the reduction of tension or the release of energy.

Freud was the first to popularize the idea that mental forces, unseen and existing only through inference, were in control of human behavior. His statement of this belief was in direct contrast with the "scientific" views of reality which held that all objects to which cause could be attributed had to be both observable and measurable with some scientific instruments. Such internal cognitive functioning was, obviously, not observable. "It seems like an empty wrangle over words to argue whether mental life is to be regarded as coextensive with consciousness or whether it may be said to stretch beyond this limit, and yet I can assure you that the acceptance of unconscious mental processes represents a decisive step towards a new orientation in the world and in science." (Freud 1943, p. 23).

The psychoanalytic model of human nature, then, is one that is primarily internal, based on inference, and quite different from that of the behaviorists. However, motivated or driven by unseen mental forces, an individual is as much at the mercy of these forces as the behaviorists' organism is to the forces in his or her environment. Freud delimited two basic forces: sex and aggression. If these two urges are not gratified, the pressures generated by them may show up in disguise in other forms of human behavior, such as artistic or scholarly expression. The energy of sexual impulses (the most primitive force) is called the *libido* and plays the primary role in the Freudian view of human nature. Freud, having grown up under the strict sexual constraints of Victorian parents, undoubtedly felt that the sexual prohibitions taught at that time had a great deal to do with human problems. Since he found this to be true in his therapy, it became the core of his theory.

But how do sex and aggression fit into the psychoanalytic model? Freud hypothesized three levels of mental processes: the unconscious thoughts, which have been repressed and are not able to be brought into consciousness; the preconscious thoughts, which may be brought into consciousness when needed; and conscious thought processes. Besides these levels of mental processes, there are also two modes of thinking: primary and secondary. The primary thought processes are the more primitive of the two and are characteristic of unconscious thoughts. Their most familiar manifestation is in dreams. Because of their primary nature, however, they exert an influence over our behavior in all aspects of life. These thought processes are free floating and, in accordance with the hydraulic model, they take the path of least resistance, being condensed and combined with other equally permissible thoughts. These ideas are "guided solely by a desire for immediate wish fulfillment—with no concern for logic, morality, time sequence, causal connections, or the demands of external reality. Thinking at this level obeys the *pleasure principle* — the seeking of pleasure and the avoidance of pain. Doubt, uncertainty, and contradiction have no place in the primary process. Typically, pictures, which are prior to words developmentally, represent unconscious thoughts" (Blum 1966, p. 2).

The secondary mental processes are those most characteristic of preconscious and conscious thought. They develop along with the symbolic processes and lend structure to one's world. Speech is the most common manifestation of these processes. As we mature, we become better able to relate past experiences with anticipated events in a coherent, rational, and organized way. We begin to use symbols to apprehend and manipulate experience, both internal and external, and "the capacity to distinguish environmental from internal stimuli permits the operation of the *reality principle* — the regulation and control of behavior according to the demands of the outside world. Anticipation of probable changes in the environment and of consequences of acts leads to the ability to delay gratification by relinquishing immediate satisfaction in favor of a better-adjusted and adaptive long-range plan of action" (Blum 1966, p. 3).

Freud's model now begins to take shape. We see the human being as a system motivated by the pleasure principle through unconscious thought processes to seek unbridled gratification of all his or her desires. Since these are usually not the goals of society and our environment, we are at the same time developing a secondary thinking process, using language, by which we can manipulate both our own behavior and the external environment to relieve as much tension as possible. Thus, we are in a constant struggle with ourselves, usually not knowing why, but realizing that we must find a socially acceptable behavior through which we can relieve our internal tensions.

The drives, or forces, that energize a human being (i.e., sex and aggression) are said to have a source, an intensity, an aim, and an object. Freud felt the source was a "state of excitation within the body" (Blum 1966, p. 4), and though the physiological source of sexual forces is the genitals, the real source is any erotic behavior, including most affiliative interaction (touching, kissing, or other affectionate interaction). The source for aggression is frustration, which may result from the inability to solve internal or external problems. When our tolerance limits are surpassed, we strike out to relieve our tensions. The outburst may be verbal or physical and may be disguised to appear as the result of some other drive (e.g., is rape the product of the sex drive or aggression?).

The intensity of a drive refers to the amount of psychic energy it contains and can only be inferred from the resulting behavior. The number and kinds of obstacles that one overcomes in achieving gratification are an indication of the intensity of the drive. The aim of a drive is its gratification. When one has satisfied an urge (such as by eating to relieve hunger), the psychic system returns to equilibrium and remains there under the control of its own regulatory mechanisms. The drive is always toward some object through which its aim can be realized. These objects may be anything internal or external to the person, are developed through the person's experiences, and are dependent on the immediate situation. Homosexual behavior, for example, may develop if heterosexual outlets are not available for the "normal" gratification of the sex drive.

The model of human nature that Freud proposed is basically a mental balance model. In his later writings he developed it more completely by identifying the parts of the system (divisions of personality) as the id, ego, and superego. The id is the source of psychic energy and the storehouse for unconscious ideas. As such it serves as the container for the libido. It has no structure, being dominated by the primary mode of thinking and the guidance of the pleasure principle. All sexual and aggressive ideas originate here, and it is pictured as a "cauldron of seething excitement" (Blum 1966, p. 5). The id may be stimulated by internal or external forces, but the results are neither predictable nor observable; they can only be inferred. Thus, one component of personality is an unpredictable force operating at an unconscious level, seeking maximum gratification for its sexual and aggressive urges. (You may have felt these forces while seeing an X-rated movie or when feeling thoroughly frustrated and wanting to lash out at something or someone.)

Pitted against the id is the superego, which develops as the person matures and contains the internalized structures of right and wrong found in the environment — including family, peer groups, and society. The superego is concerned with "moral standards" and deals with "self-criticism, prohibitions, and guilt feelings" (Blum 1966, p. 6). It develops by a process of reinforcement not unlike that described by the behaviorists. It operates at all three levels of consciousness, but its structures are sometimes repressed into the unconscious level, where it cannot be modified by new developments. When the superego dominates the personality, the person usually feels an increase in self-esteem; when it is overriden, the person feels apologetic and inadequate for the situation.

The third division of personality is the ego. ("Ego" is popularly used to refer to "self" but that is quite dissimilar from the meaning employed here.) The ego is the governor of the system and has the task of balancing the forces of the id with the structure the superego seeks to impose. To do this it may side with either one against the other, but most often sides with the superego. It operates at all three levels of consciousness and its functions include "perception, conscious thought, memory, learning, choice, judgment, and action" (Blum 1966, p. 5). At the unconscious level it tries to control the sexual and aggressive urges of the id to keep them from coming to the surface. The ego is guided by the reality principle and is constantly seeking to test reality. What is fact, fiction, wish, or need? When a course of action is chosen, it must decide what actions the person should take to maximize pleasure and minimize pain.

To maintain equilibrium within the psychic system, the ego must often stop the rash impulses of the id as well as deal with genuine threats from the outside world. The ego has its own psychic energy, but, as with the others, there is only a limited amount. One can see, then, why the ego more often sides with the superego to help contain the irresponsible impulses of the id by imposing the inculcated moral structures of society. It is only when these structures become too confining that the ego forces the superego to relinquish its control of the psychic system. The three divisions of personality, the id, ego, and superego, all with their own supply of psychic energy, are in constant battle — the id and superego striving for control of the psychic system and the ego striving to maintain equilibrium.

Freud's model of human nature, then, is a psychodynamic model patterned after a hydraulic system, with three divisions (the id, ego, and superego) operating on three levels of consciousness (unconscious, preconscious, and conscious), under two principles of behavior (pleasure and reality), and driven by two primary urges (sex and aggression). Freud goes on to make it very clear that in his view there is no room for chance behavior. All behavior is determined, and although much of it is determined by forces outside our awareness, all of it can be traced back to an impulse from one of the two primary urges. Though explanations of behavior must be based on inference, there is nothing mystical about these explanations. Overt behavior can be traced back to its source through a chain of cause-effect units by a sufficiently skilled therapist with adequate knowledge of the patient's history (i.e., psychiatric analysis). Most of these cause-effect units are the results of struggle and compromise among motives, drives, needs, and conflicts, but there is no one-to-one relationship between behavior and cause. A behavior may result from very complex interactions among these forces and, of course, either of the basic urges may be expressed in any number of different ways, depending on the state of the individual and the immediate situation (sexually frustrated people may be extremely creative, very inhibited, or neither).

According to the psychoanalyst, a person's behavior results from the basic conflict between the gratification of the two basic impulses and society's norms. Thus, life is seen as a struggle to bring one's desires in line with socially acceptable behavior. This results in the repression of sexual-aggressive energy or its sublimation into more socially acceptable behavior than is actually desired. It is this rerouted psychic energy that is behind creative efforts, whether they are artistic, scientific, diplomatic, or anything else. However, if this psychic energy does not find culturally acceptable outlets, it leads to a neurotic personality.

Because of the continual conflict within our psyche, Freud did not see humans as basically gentle, friendly, loving beings who only fight when compelled by outside forces. Instead, we may seek occasions in which to gratify aggressive and sexual impulses. To find out how psychic energy is released through this behavior, Freud saw the need to consider the total personality and emphasized individual differences. It was the goal of the psychoanalyst to find the repressed desires in the "sick" individual so the psyche could establish the necessary homeostasis between the three divisions. This meant helping the ego decide whether it should side with the id or the superego to bring the psychodynamic forces into equilibrium.

Using this model in his therapy, Freud decided that a person goes through five psychosexual stages of development, based on the investment of sexual energy in different bodily zones. (These stages were designated as oral, anal, phallic, latency, and genital.*) He then used these classifications to designate the source of the pathological behavior of his patients as an inability to resolve the conflicts arising at a particular stage of development. Thus, a person is said to have fixations at a particular stage, which shapes the adult personality. The movement from stage to stage does not depend upon cognitive maturity at the present stage, but rather on what is called the *epigenetic principle*. "This principle states that anything that grows has a ground plan, and that out of this ground plan the parts arise, each part having its time of special ascendancy, until all parts have arisen to form a functioning whole" (Erikson 1968, p. 92). Thus, continual physical and mental growth is determined and no consideration is given to a "healthy" resolution of the conflicts that arise at each stage. Adequate mental health at each stage must be assured by insightful parents or psychoanalysis.

In summary, we may say that the psychoanalytic model of human nature states that a person is a "conflicted being who is driven to action and growth by his own passions or instincts and by external demands" (Langer 1969, p. 10). We are driven by unseen psychic forces that operate on our emotions, making us irrational and unpredictable. We are constantly reacting to and defending against both internal impulses and external demands. Being driven by internal forces, we are not responsible for our behavior and are seen as self-gratifying animals incapable of altruistic behavior.

Freud's model is mentalistic, based on a closed, hydraulic system. It is a balance model where the ego strives to maintain a homeostatic relationship between the id and the superego. It has three levels of mental processes: unconscious, preconscious, and conscious; and two modes of thinking: primary (emotional) and secondary (rational). The mental processes are developed during five psychosexual stages—oral, anal, phallic, latency, and genital—and their "health" depends on how well the individual is able to meet the requirements of social-psychic integration at each stage. These stages are biologically programmed around the harnessing of one's sexual urges, requir-

---

* See Gerald S. Blum, *Psychodynamics: The Science of Unconscious Mental Forces* (Monterey, Calif.: Brooks/Cole Publishing Co., 1966), pp. 7-13, for a short, detailed discussion of these stages.

ing the psyche to deal with each stage as it comes along whether it is ready to or not. Since there is no one-to-one relationship between our basic urges and our behavior, these forces — sex and aggression — may be the source of any kind of behavior. This makes each person unique and the product of the gratification of basic drives. The only way behavior can be investigated and understood is by searching out its dynamics and associating them with inferred psychosexual forces.

PSYCHOANALYTIC ACTIVITIES

1. In the area of sports, particularly individual sports like boxing or gymnastics, many feel that sexual intercourse during the twenty-four hours preceding an athletic event is detrimental to the performance of the individual. Do some research on this subject by talking to coaches and athletes, and report your findings to the class. Consider some of the following questions:
    a. How strongly do people feel about this subject?
    b. Do athletes take this as a fact or a superstition?
    c. What evidence is there to warrant this conclusion?
    d. Is it considered equally valid for male and female athletes?
    e. Explain your findings in terms of the Freudian model. *Note:* If you are an athlete, are dating one or married to one, you may have firsthand information on this subject. Your insight should be of great interest to the class.
2. There is some indication that sex and aggression play off on each other. During the protest marches of the 1960s it was claimed that much of the aggressive behavior built up in these confrontations was dissipated through sexual activity. The movie *Getting Straight* illustrates this theme. Perhaps this movie can be shown in class and the theme discussed. Find out as much as you can on this theme and report to the class.
3. What do you do when you are really frustrated? List the five things that frustrate you the most and try to explain your behavior using the Freudian model. What needs are you trying to fill when you encounter these frustrations?
4. Collect advertisements relating to sex; to aggression. Develop an oral report in which you analyze them according to the Freudian model. What choices do these ads allow you? How basic are their appeals?
5. In what ways do you orient your life around sexual relationships, goals, and intentions? List ten ways in which this orientation affects your communicative behavior. In a group, come to a consensus on the five most important communicative effects this orientation has on "normal" people. Are they the same for males and females?

Humanistic Assumptions

The third school to be considered is that of humanistic psychology, commonly called the Third Force in psychology. Abraham Maslow has been proclaimed the father of this school, but its model of human nature is not the work of any one person. Rather, it is the coming together of a number of movements and the search for the characteristics of the "healthy" person by a number of independent therapists. The integration of all of these forces has led to a picture of the ideal, well-adjusted human being. Colin Wilson (1972, p. 15) says of Maslow's contribution: "Some time in the late thirties, he [Maslow] had been struck by the thought that modern psychology is based on the study of sick people. But since there are more healthy people around than sick people, how can this psychology give a fair idea of the workings of the human mind? It struck him that it might be worthwhile to devote some time to the study of *healthy* people." There are a number of histories of humanistic psychology, notably, those by Charlotte Buhler and Melanie Allen, Albert Ellis, Frank Goble, Matson, and Wilson (see reference list at the end of Part 1). But since it is just now gaining status within the discipline of psychology, we can expect its future to bring about some important insights into the implications of this view of human nature.

We must differentiate immediately between the unprincipled behaviors sometimes associated with *humanism* and the idealistic structures of *humanistic psychology*. The humanism of the Renaissance served to release people's minds from the burden of the Church. With this freedom came undisciplined attempts to gain self-knowledge by unconventional and eccentric behavior. Experimentation with life and lack of moral standards and social responsibility were much like some of the modern-day activities propagated under the banner of humanism, as when people adhere to it as a cult of the self and preach against intellectualism, science, rationality, discipline, and work. Although "humanism" relieves us of our responsibility to society and the environment, humanistic psychology sees this responsibility as one of our basic obligations. The primary concepts contributed by Renaissance humanism are those of dignity and freedom and the ability to know and express our own feelings, thoughts, and experiences.

The existentialists provided humanistic psychology with some fundamental concerns about humans. These include their basic focus on "being" (personal development). Thus their concern for individuality and the role of individual ethics in decision making, allowing for integrity of choice as opposed to social utility. Their emphasis is on the absence of meaning, unless the perceiver is committed to involvement with the event; that is, an event is meaningful only to the extent that one is involved with it and is committed to this involvement. Thus, the concern becomes one of people's experiencing their environment. This leads to a central belief that life is to be lived subjectively as it takes place (an immediate as opposed to past or future orientation) and an image of the person as active and positive.

One can see the influence of other disciplines and movements on present-day humanistic psychology. General semantics and its concern for awareness during human communication highlights the importance of the person in any relationship. The neo-Freudian psychoanalytic movement that emphasized the concept of self and its development through human relationships underlines the interplay between internal and external variables in human growth. Child psychologists, such as Jean Piaget, lend their hypotheses about cognitive structures to this school to give it an acceptable cognitive framework within which to work. Individual therapists, such as Carl Rogers, Rollo May, Adler, and Maslow, show through clinical experience that the ideal person proposed by this school is an extrapolation of the characteristics they have discovered in people who are becoming fully functioning persons (see Rogers's article on page 137). Add to this the self-transcendence envisioned by theological existentialists, such as Martin Buber, Sören Kierkegaard, and Paul Tillich, and the humanistic psychological mode begins to take shape.

To give a more realistic orientation to this view, we should look at it in light of the two models proposed earlier in this part of the book. To do this we have reprinted an article by Floyd W. Matson in which he questions the behavioristic and the psychoanalytic views while presenting some of the ideals of humanistic psychology. We have italicized some key phrases and numbered sixteen passages in this article to which we will refer in the pages following it.

Humanistic Theory:
The Third Revolution in Psychology

Floyd W. Matson

The oft-used term "humanistic psychology" has the appearance of what semanticists call a "redundant tautology." After all, psychology is the science of mind, is it not? And is not mind the property of human beings? And is not all psychology then humanistic?

The answer to all of the questions is, in a word, no. Psychology is the study of more than mind, and of less than mind. It is the science of behavior, much of which is "mindless." Nor is the behavior studied by psychologists only that of humans: much of it, perhaps most, is that of animals. And where it is human behavior that is being studied, it is very often physiological rather than psychical. It would not be stretching the truth too far to observe that much of what goes on in psychology is not "psychological" at all. And that brings us to the reason for the third revolution — the renaissance of humanism in psychology.

1   *Humanistic psychology tries to tell it not like it is, but like it ought to be.* It seeks to bring psychology back to its source, to the *psyche,* where it all began and where it finally culminates. But there is more to it than that. Humanistic psychology is not just the study of 2 "human beings"; *it is a commitment to human becoming.*

It was a humanistic philosopher, Kurt Riezler, who said that "science begins with respect for the subject matter." Unfortunately that is not the view of all scientists, whether in the hard sciences of nature or in the softer sciences of man and mind. It is almost, as it seems to me, a defining characteristic of *behaviorist psychology that it begins with* disrespect *for the subject matter,* and therefore leads straightaway to what Norbert Wiener (a pretty hard scientist 3 himself) called the "inhuman use of human beings." At any rate, *I know of no greater disrespect for the human subject than to treat him as an object — unless it is to demean that object further* 4 *by fragmenting it into drives, traits, reflexes, and other mechanical hardware.* But that is the procedure of behaviorism, if not of all experimental psychology; it is a procedure openly admitted, indeed triumphantly proclaimed, in the name of Science and Truth, of Objectivity and Rigor, and of all else that is holy in these precincts. And it leads in a straight line out of the ivory tower into the brave new world of Walden Two.

Everyone remembers, I am sure, that curious utopian novel, *Walden Two,* written more than 20 years ago by the preeminent behaviorist of our generation, B. F. Skinner. His book presented such a stark scenario of behavioral engineering and mind manipulation, such a "conditional" surrender of autonomy and freedom on the part of its docile characters, that many readers at the time mistakenly supposed it to be a clever put-on, a satirical prophecy of the nightmare shape of things to come if ever a free society should relax its vigilant defense of the values of liberty and 5 responsibility — *especially the liberty and responsibility of choice.*

But that was what Skinner's novel openly defied and disparaged; the Elysian community it projected was a sort of crystal palace (or womb with a view) within which perfect peace and security might abide forever — tranquility without trauma, pleasure without pain, attainment without struggle — and *all at the trivial price of the freedom to make choices,* the right (as it were) to blunder. The key to the kingdom of Walden Two was operant conditioning; by this magical technique, applied to all residents from birth, the "Hamlet syndrome" (the anxiety of choice) was efficiently removed. Like that wonderful Mrs. Prothro in Dylan Thomas's Christmas story, who "said the right thing always," so the creatures of Skinner's novel were conditioned to make the right choices automatically. It was instant certitude, at the price of all volition. Like Pavlov's dogs, Skinner's people made only conditioned responses to the stimulus of their master's voice.

Let us recognize that such a homeostatic paradise, like the classless society and the heavenly city, has great seductive appeal for many, especially in an age of anxiety and a time of troubles. It appeals particularly to those with a low tolerance for ambiguity and a high rage for order. I believe it was Thomas Huxley who was so fearful of chance and choice as to declare that if he were offered a world of absolute security and certainty, at the price of surrendering his personal freedom, he would close instantly with the bargain. Unlike his grandson, Aldous, whose own futuristic novel made just the opposite point, the elder Huxley would surely have enjoyed the still life on Skinner's Walden Pond.

Let me recall now a different disposition, both existential and humanistic. It is Dostoevsky's underground man, struggling to be heard by the Establishment above. "After all," he says,

> I do not really insist on suffering or on prosperity either. I insist on my *caprice*, and its being guaranteed to me when necessary. Suffering would be out of place in vaudevilles, for instance; I know that. In the crystal palace it is even unthinkable; suffering means doubt, means negation, and what would be the good of a crystal palace if there could be any doubt about it? . . . You believe in a crystal edifice that can never be destroyed; that is, an edifice at which one would neither be able to stick out one's tongue nor thumb one's nose on the sly. And perhaps I am afraid of this edifice just because it is of crystal and can never be destroyed and that one could not even put one's tongue out at it even on the sly. (*The Short Novels of Dostoevsky*, Dial Press, New York, 1945, p. 152)

Now *there,* as Sartre might say, is an existentialism that is a humanism.

There have been, as I believe, three distinct conceptual revolutions in psychology during the course of the present century. The first, that of behaviorism, struck with the force of a revelation around 1913 and shook the foundations of academic psychology for a generation. Behaviorism arose in reaction to the excessive preoccupation of 19th-century psychology with consciousness, and with introspection as a way of getting at the data of conscious mental activity. The behaviorists reacted with a vengeance. *They threw out not only consciousness, but all the resources of the mind.* The mind, to them, was the ghost in the machine, and they did not believe in ghosts. The founding father of the movement, John B. Watson, declared in an early proclamation, a kind of behaviorist manifesto, that the behaviorist began "by sweeping aside all medieval conceptions. *He dropped from his scientific vocabulary all subjective terms such as sensation, perception, image, desire, purpose, and even thinking and emotion as they were subjectively defined"* (*Behaviorism* [1924], University of Chicago Press, Chicago, 1958, pp. 5-6).

Overt behavior, that which could be 6 *seen and measured, was all that counted.* And all that was needed to explain it was the simple and classical formula of *stimulus-response*—with one added refinement, that of the conditioned reflex. It was this concept of conditioning, borrowed from the Russian laboratories of Pavlov and Bechterev, that gave the real revolutionary impetus to Watson's behaviorist movement. Conditioning was power; it was control. This was no merely objective psychology, for all its scientific claims; it was an applied psychology—and what it was applied to, or rather against, was man. *"The interest of the behaviorist,"* said Watson, *"is more than the interest of a spectator; he wants to control man's reactions as physical scientists want to control and manipulate other natural phenomena"* (Ibid., p. 11). Just as man was simply "an assembled organic machine ready to run," so the behaviorist was no pure scientist but an engineer unable to keep from tinkering with the machinery. Pointing out that such sciences as chemistry and biology were gaining control over their subject matter, Watson inquired, "Can psychology ever get control? Can I make someone who is not afraid of snakes, afraid of them, and how?" The answer was clear: And how!

"In short," said Watson, "the cry of the behaviorist is, 'Give me the baby and my world to bring it up in and I'll make it crawl and walk; I'll make it climb and use its hands in constructing buildings of stone or wood; I'll make it a thief, a gunman, or a dope fiend.' The possibility of shaping in any direction is almost endless" (*The Ways of Behaviorism*, Harper, New York, 1926, p. 35).

That should be enough to suggest the general character (and authoritarian personality) of behaviorist psychology, the first of the three psychological revolutions that have taken place in our century. The second revolution was, of course, that of Freud. It is noteworthy that psychoanalysis and behaviorism made their appearance at roughly the same time, give or take a decade, and that both of them emerged in reaction against the accent on consciousness in traditional psychology. Apart from these coincidences, however, there was little in common between these two movements, and there was a great deal that put them at opposite poles.

Whereas *behaviorism placed all its stress upon the external environment* (that is, *upon stimuli from the outer world*) as the controlling factor in behavior, *psychoanalysis placed its emphasis upon the internal environment* (upon *stimuli from within, in the form of drives and instincts*). For Freud, man was very
7   much a creature of instinct — and in particular of two primary instincts, *those of life and death* (Eros *and* Thanatos). These two instincts were in conflict not only with each other but with the world, with culture. *Society was based,* said Freud, *on renunciation of the instincts via the mechanism of repression.* But the instincts did not give up without a

struggle. In fact, they never gave up; they could not be vanquished, only temporarily blocked. *Life,* then, *was a constant alternation between frustration and aggression.* Neither for the individual person nor for the culture was there a permanent solution or "happy ending"; there were only compromises, expedients, working adjustments. The price of civilization, indeed, was mass neurosis — the result of the necessary suppression of the natural instincts of man. But if that seems bad, the alternative was worse; whenever the repressive forces are for a moment relaxed, declared Freud, "we see man as a savage beast to whom the thought of sparing his own kind is alien" (*Civilization and Its Discontents,* Hogarth, London, 1930, p. 86).

Perhaps the most interesting, not to say frightening, concept advanced by Freud was that of *Thanatos*, the aggression or death instinct, which he regarded as an innate and irresistible drive toward the destruction of oneself and others. What is especially significant about this bleak conception of man's aggressive nature is the "comeback" it has been making in recent years after a long period of almost total eclipse. The current revival of the shadow side of Freud, the pessimistic musings of his later years, does not tell us so much about Freud as it does about the temper of our own time. I shall return to this point.

The main point I want to make immediately about the psychoanalytic movement, in its Freudian form, *is that it presents a picture of man as very much the "victim-spectator,"* as Gordon Allport has put it, of blind forces working through him. For all its differences with behaviorism, Freudian theory agrees in the fundamental image of man as a stimulus-response machine, although the stimuli that work their will upon the human being come from within rather than from without. *Freud's deter-*

8 *minism* was not environmental, like Watson's, but psychogenic; nevertheless, it was a determinism, and it *left little room for spontaneity, creativity, rationality, or responsibility.* The declared faith in conscious reason that underlay Freudian therapy (rather more than Freudian theory) did not prevent his insistently minimizing the role of reason as an actual or potential determinant of personality and conduct—nor, on the other hand, from maximizing the thrust of irrational forces that press their claims both from "below" (the id) and from "above" (the superego). In Freud's topographical map of the mind, the ego, itself only partially conscious, never achieves full autonomy but functions as a kind of buffer state between the rival powers of instinct and introjected culture, between animal nature and social nurture.

I have been deliberately hard on Freud in these remarks in order to emphasize those aspects of his theory and therapy that, by virtue of their pessimism and determinism, have called out over the years the critical and creative response that (for want of a better term) we may call "humanistic psychology." *This new psychology, the third revolution, represents a reaction against* both *behaviorism and orthodox psychoanalysis; it is for that reason that humanistic psychology has been called the "third force."* But perhaps the first thing to say about it is that, unlike the two movements of thought that precede and oppose it, humanistic psychology is not a single body of theory but a collection or convergence of a number of lines and schools of thought. If it owes nothing to behaviorism, it does owe much to psychoanalysis, although less perhaps to Freud himself than to the considerable number of Freudian heretics and deviationists, beginning with his own associates of the original Vienna Circle

and culminating in the so-called neo-Freudians (anti-Freudians, really) of the second generation.

For despite the many differences among them, those who broke away one by one from the side of Freud shared a number of crucial insights and commitments. Adler, Jung, Rank, Stekel, Ferenczi—all these early associates found themselves unable to accept Freud's theory of instinctual determinism (specifically, his libido theory) and his tendency to find the source of all difficulty and motivation in the remote past. These deviationists began to place equal or greater emphasis upon the present (that is, upon the here and now, the "presence" of the patient) and also upon the future (that is, upon the pull of aspiration and purpose, the goal or life-plan of the individual). What this implied was a **9** greater reliance upon the consciousness of the person in analysis or therapy: a new respect for his powers of will and of reason, his capacity to choose and to understand.

In Adler's work, this emphasis took the form of virtually converting the psychoanalytic therapy session into a dialogue or conversation on the conscious level—which of course enraged Freud, who thought that Adler had betrayed the basic postulate of unconscious motivation. In Jung's work, the new approach took the form of emphasizing what he called the "prospective factor," the pull of purpose as opposed to the push of instinct (and in particular the push of erotic instinct); it also took the form, in Jung's later years, of *increasing stress upon understanding the other, whether neurotic patient or normal individual, in his unique identity.* This involved a kind of intuitive and sympathetic understanding, which Jung distinguished from scientific knowledge and which led him finally to advocate abandoning the textbooks altogether in any venture into helping or healing. In the case of Otto Rank, another of the heretics of the original Freudian circle, the deviation took the form of an *emphasis* upon the existential will of the person, that is, *upon his capacity for self-direction and self-control.*

The common denominator in these various lines of theory and therapy was, I believe, *respect for the person, recognition of the other not as a case, or an object, or a field of forces, or a bundle of instincts, but as himself.* In terms of theory, it meant respect for his powers of creativity and responsibility; in terms of therapy, it meant respect for his values, his intentions, and, above all, his peculiar identity.

This recognition of man-in-person, as opposed to man-in-general, goes to the heart of the difference between humanistic psychology, in any of its forms or schools, *and scientific psychologies such as behaviorism.* Not only in psychoanalysis, but in other fields as well, increasing numbers of students have found themselves drawn to the unsettling conclusion that *the definitive features of a human being cannot be made out at all from a "psychological distance,"* but can be *brought into focus only by understanding* (literally, by "standing under") *the unique perspective of the individual himself.*

This emphasis upon the human person, upon the individual in his wholeness and uniqueness, is a central feature of the "psychology of humanism." But there is an important corollary without which this personalistic emphasis would be inadequate and distorted. *That corollary* is the recognition, to use a phrase of Rank, that *"the self needs the other."* This recognition is variously expressed: For the neo-Freudians, *it points to the importance of relationship in the growth of personality;* for the existentialists, it leads to emphasis on the themes of dia-

logue, encounter, meeting, intersubjectivity, and so on.

While this recognition is broadly shared by humanistic psychotherapists, analysts, personality theorists, perceptual psychologists and others, perhaps the most impressive and systematic development of the idea has been provided by existential thinkers, both in psychology and philosophy. There is a striking similarity in the formulation of this self-other relationship by various existentialists. Martin Buber's philosophy of dialogue, centering around the I-Thou relation, is probably the most influential and possibly the most profound. Among other fruitful effects, it has given rise to a "psychology of meeting" that finds its paradigm in the therapeutic encounter. The significance of Buber's general concept has been well described by Will Herberg:

> The term I-Thou points to a relation of person to person, of subject to subject, a relation of reciprocity involving "meeting" or "encounter," while the term I-It points to a relation of person to thing, of subject to object, involving some form of utilization, domination, or control, even if it is only so-called "objective" knowing. The I-Thou relation, which Buber usually designated as "relation" par excellence, is one in which one can enter only with the whole of his being, as a genuine person. (*The Writings of Martin Buber,* Meridian Books, New York, 1956, p. 14.)

It follows that the relationship of therapy in its ideal development represents an authentic encounter "on the sharp edge of existence" between two human beings, one seeking and the other helping. This mutual recognition, which is never immediate but only a possibility to be achieved, cuts through the conventional defenses and postures of both part-

13 ners *to permit each to reach out as a person to the other as a person.* What is demanded of the doctor in particular, says Buber, is that he "himself step forth out of his protected professional superiority into the elementary situation between one who asks and one who is asked" (Maurice Friedman, *Martin Buber: The Life of Dialogue,* Harper Torchbooks, New York, 1960, p. 190).

Apart from its uses by existential psychologists and psychoanalysts — such as Ludwig Binswanger, Viktor Frankl, Rollo May, and others — Buber's immensely fertile concept of I-Thou "meeting" finds parallels and reverberations in the work of other existential philosophers, especially those commonly referred to as the religious existentialists or existential theologians. For Gabriel Marcel, who came independently to the formula of I-and-Thou, the sense of genuine encounter is conveyed by the term "intersubjectivity," implying an authentic communication on the order of communion. "The fact is," writes Marcel, "that we can understand ourselves by starting from the other, or from others, and only by starting from them; . . . it is only in this perspective that a legitimate love of self can be conceived" (*The Mystery of Being,* Gateway, Chicago, 1960, Volume II, p. 9). This insight, quite similar to Fromm's concept of productive love and self-realization, implies a reciprocity of knowing in which what "I am" as well as what "Thou art" is made known only through the mutual experience of what "We are." Each communicant recognizes himself in the other.

In Paul Tillich's "therapeutic theology," this general appreciation of the enlightening role of engagement or meeting is applied directly to psychotherapy, which is regarded as the "community of healing." In common with other existentialists, Tillich believes that the personal troubles represented by *neurosis stem fundamentally from failures in relationships with others,* thereby resulting in self-alienation from any genuine contact with the world. The central therapeutic problem thus becomes one of "acceptance" or, more precisely, of successive stages of acceptance culminating in *acceptance of oneself and of the world of others.*

In this new kind of therapeutic encounter — and here is another humanistic tenet — there are no silent partners. The existential therapist (which is to say, the humanistic therapist) is no longer the blank screen or "mute catalyzer" that he was in Freud's day, but rather is a participant with the whole of his being. He 14 participates not only for the purpose of helping, but even more basically for the purpose of knowing or understanding. *"You must participate in a self,"* according to Tillich, *"in order to know what is.* By participation you change it" (*The Courage to Be,* Yale University Press, New Haven, 1959, p. 124). The inference is that the kind of knowledge essential to psychology and psychotherapy is to be gained not by detached observation but by participant-observation (to use Harry Stack Sullivan's phrase). It may be possible, through detachment, to gain knowledge that is "useful"; but *only through participation is it possible to gain the knowledge that is helpful.*

In any adequate account of the sources and forces that have nourished the movement of humanistic psychology (which this brief sketch does not pretend to be), much more would have to be said in acknowledgment of the contributions of individual theorists and therapists. Fortunately, there are a number of comprehensive surveys available; among them, James Bugental's *Challenges of Humanistic Psychology,* Anthony Sutich and Miles Vich's *Readings in Humanistic Psy-*

chology, and my own *The Broken Image* (especially Chapters 6 and 7). But even the present essay cannot avoid mention of at least a few of the movers and shakers behind the third revolution, notably: Abraham Maslow, who more than any other deserves to be recognized as the "spiritual father" of the humanistic movement in psychology; Gordon Allport, the great American personalist and heir to the mantle of William James; Rollo May, who introduced the existential approach to American psychology and has developed it creatively; Carl Rogers, whose therapeutic mandate of "unconditional regard" for the client resembles Tillich's philosophy of ultimate concern; Erich Fromm, the most influential of the neo-Freudians, who has long since moved from psychoanalysis to the higher ground of social philosophy and cultural criticism; Henry A. Murray, inspired teacher and exemplar of humanism; Charlotte Buhler, who has made us all aware of how important personal goal-values and the whole course of human life are to psychological understanding.

In conclusion — if I may be excused the puff of vanity — I wish to suggest something of the activist potential of humanistic psychology by repeating a few paragraphs from a talk I gave before the annual conference of the Association for Humanistic Psychology:

I'd like to propose one line of commitment, and of protest, that we might well undertake as humanistic psychologists. That course is, following Jefferson, to swear undying opposition to all forms of tyranny over the mind of man. I propose that we commit ourselves to the defense of psychological liberty. *For I believe that quite possibly the greatest threat to freedom in the world today (and tomorrow) is the threat to freedom of the mind — which is, at bottom, the power to choose.*

That freedom is threatened now on all sides. It is threatened by what Herbert Marcuse has called the "one-dimensional society," which seeks to reduce the categories of thought and discourse to a kind of consensual endorsement of the directives of an aggressive and acquisitive culture. It is threatened by the technology of mass society, mass culture and mass communication, which manufactures (*pace* Marshall McLuhan) a marshmallow world of plastic pleasures in which the bland lead the bland endlessly into the sea of tranquility.

Freedom of the mind is also threatened by the biological revolution and its psychological corollaries — not only by the familiar cuckoo's nest of lobotomies and shock treatments, over which no one can fly, but by the imminent breakthroughs in "genetic surgery" and kindred interventions that promise to make feasible the rewiring and reprogramming of the brain mechanism.

Perhaps most critically of all, *our psychological liberty is threatened by failure of nerve: by our inability to live up to and live out the democratic dogma, which rests upon faith in the capacity of* 15 *the ordinary human being to lead his own life, to go his own way and to grow his own way, to be himself and to know himself and to become more himself.* This failure of nerve is rampant in the field of education; it is a kind of occupational disease of social work, where the aided person becomes a client who is treated as a patient who is diagnosed as incurable. And it is a pervasive feature of the landscape of academic psychology and behavioral science in so many saddening ways that it would take a book (which I have already written) to enumerate them all.

But let me mention just one of the ways in which this failure of nerve manifests itself in the study of man. The old reactionary doctrine of Original Sin, of innate depravity, has lately been enjoying a very popular and large-scale revival. It takes the form of the hypothesis of aggression as a fixed instinctual endowment of man—a genetic taint in the blood, as it were, a dark stain in the double helix of each of us. The alleged discovery or rediscovery of this killer instinct is being hailed in the book clubs and popular journals as if it were the ultimate benediction, the final good news of man's redemption. How are we to account for the popularity of this darkly pessimistic thesis? How account for the best-seller status of Lorenz' *On Aggression,* Ardrey's *Territorial Imperative* and *African Genesis,* and Desmond Morris's *Naked Ape?*

I believe the answer is clear: mass failure of nerve. Nothing could be better calculated to get us off the uncomfortable hook of personal responsibility, of self-control and self-determination, than this doctrine of our innate aggressive pro-

pensities. That's why we fight; that's why we hate; that's why we cannot love one another or ourselves. People are no damn good—and there's an end of it.

Well, I do not believe that humanistic psychologists will accept that cop-out. I propose therefore that we place the full weight of our movement, the whole third force of it, against this and all other *threats to the freedom of the mind and* **16** *the autonomy of the person.* Let us become the active conscience of the psychological fraternity, searching out and exposing—and *condemning—each and every dehumanizing, depersonalizing and demoralizing force that* would move us further down the road to the Brave New World and the technocratic society—that social laboratory of the behaviorist's dreams and the humanist's nightmares.

For down that road lies not just the end of psychological freedom, but the death of humanity.

Although the preceding article gets a bit evangelistic, it makes some cogent points that should be emphasized at this time. The reader should notice the idealistic nature of the goals of humanistic psychology as pointed out in passages 1–4. The whole person becomes the model to be used, but not as an object of experimental science. Our freedom of choice (5) does not allow us to be studied using the deterministic models of behaviorism and psychoanalysis (6–8). The unfaithful followers of Freud began to see the necessity of considering the positive, active nature of man (9). This led to an in-depth consideration of man as a person (10, 11, 13, 16). The only way of knowing the person is through a personal relationship with him or her (12), and it is only through these relationships that we can learn to accept ourselves and others and grow toward maturity (14, 15).

Some of the basic components of the humanistic model of human nature have been alluded to in this article: respect for man as a whole person, as a being with free choice who is unpredictable but rational; and emphasis on personal relationships with others as a means of understanding oneself, developing the self, and growing toward maturity. These components will be expanded and others added as we continue to delve into the ideas of the humanistic psychologists. We shall also see that the concepts some would like to see as basic assumptions about humans have already been accepted by others. This will become evident as you read the next article and our comments on it.

The following article is an attempt by one humanistic psychologist to incorporate the works of another psychologist into the framework of humanistic psychology. As we stated before, this is a young movement, and as such it has a great deal of growing to do. No one is yet aware of all of the existing works that will lend themselves to this movement. Whenever a new member is found, his or her works will alter the basic assumptions in some way — usually by expansion. In the case of Adler, the subject of this essay, probably all of his basic assumptions have already been included in the tenets of humanistic psychology, but the following reflections on these assumptions help to clarify them for others and give us further insights into how humanistic psychology views human nature.

In this article, Heinz L. Ansbacher shows that the basic assumptions of Alfred Adler are also the basic assumptions of humanistic psychology, and suggests that humanistic psychology could profit from Adler's concept of social interest and usefulness. We have numbered his twelve major points and italicized several others.

Alfred Adler and Humanistic Psychology*

Heinz L. Ansbacher
University of Vermont

Our late, beloved friend Abe Maslow counted Alfred Adler from the beginning as part of the Third Force or humanistic psychology movement which he created, and during the last years before his death he turned increasingly toward Adler's ideas. "For me," Maslow said, "Alfred Adler becomes more and more correct year by year. As the facts come in, they give stronger and stronger support to his image of man" (Various, 1970).

What he meant by this specifically becomes in part evident from the 1970 revision of his *Motivation and Personality* (Maslow, 1970b). Through nearly all the new passages in this book Maslow comes closer to Adler. Of these, the most striking is the suggestion, "We should perhaps use Adler's term of the 'pampered style of life,' " in connection with a new "value pathology . . . a gratification-produced pathology." Maslow refers here to the phenomenon that with increasing affluence, *many, far from counting their blessings, tend to depreciate them and make increasingly unreasonable demands, like pampered children.*

It is indicative of the extraordinary timeliness of Adler that for the descrip-

* This article is reprinted, with permission, from the Spring 1971 issue of *The Journal of Humanistic Psychology.*

tion of a *new* pathology Maslow resorted to this homely term—the pampered life style, which, however is of central significance in Adler's theory of psychopathology (Adler, 1956, 1964). Adler meant by it essentially *a life style of expecting and demanding from others, while feeling incompetent to do things for oneself, let alone to make a real contribution.* This often results in retreat from the tasks of life, as found among criminals, suicides, neurotics, and drug-addicts (Adler, 1933).

Yet, Adler's relationship to humanistic psychology has never been shown in detail. To do so is the purpose of this paper which was offered as part of the commemoration of Adler's 100th birthday during 1970. Our point of departure will be the presidential address by Floyd W. Matson (1969) at the meeting of the Association for Humanistic Psychology, August 29, 1969.

In the first part we shall show that the basic premises of Adler's Individual Psychology are indeed essentially the same as those stated by Matson for today's humanistic psychology. Six key concepts can be derived from Matson's paper, and terms originated by Adler can be used for some of the headings. These are: (*a*) man's creative power, (*b*) anthropomorphic model of man, (*c*) purposes instead of causes, (*e*) holism and life style, (*f*) subjectivity, and (*g*) psychotherapy as good human relations.

In the second part we shall propose that Adler still has an important contribution to make. Matson described the urgent necessity for "a sense of purpose, and a sense of direction" to combat a threatening "failure of nerve," and to guide the future growth of humanistic psychology and humanity in general. It is exactly this which Adler (1964) offered through his concept of social interest, or community feeling, which he described specifically as "direction-giving."

BASIC PREMISES

Man's Creative Power— The Third Force

When humanistic psychology emerged some ten years ago as the Third Force, it was as an alternative to Freudianism and behaviorism as the two most influential intellectual currents in psychology. The term "force" in the phrase Third Force was used in the sense of a social force—a movement in psychology—through a grouping of like-minded psychologists.

In Matson's presentation, however, the term force takes on a second meaning—namely, as a primary determining agent in our lives, to which each of these three groupings of psychologists adheres. *The orthodox Freudians adhere to biological determinism through their emphasis on instincts; the behaviorists adhere to environmental determinism through conditioning; while the humanistic psychologists adhere to self-determination through the concept of an active self.* [1]

While Adler (1956) certainly subscribed to the concept of an active self, he designated the third force in man by a term which makes the concept of force explicit, namely, man's "creative power." Adler never used the term "creative self." This was introduced by Hall and Lindsey (1957) in their presentation of Adler. It is in a sense regrettable that their term has caught on so well, because Adler's original term, "creative power of the self" is much more dynamic and less conducive to static and elementaristic reification. It was in rejecting heredity and environment as decisive determining forces that Adler (1964) assumed *"the existence of still another force: the creative power of the individual."* And once, in reminding a student, Adler (1956) put it this way: *"Do not forget the most important fact that not heredity and not environment are determining factors—*

both are giving only the frame and the influence which are answered by the individual in regard to his styled creative power." Here we have then clearly expressed the *individual's own "creative power" as a third determining force, superordinated to nature and nurture as dominant determiners.*

2   This "creative power" is not something mysterious or unscientific, as it may at first appear. After all, the cultural and technological world in which we find ourselves is in fact the creation of man. For this reason alone it is justified to assume creative power in man and to enter this force into our calculations, especially also since we have a corresponding developed cortex with the power of abstraction and fiction formation, what Goldstein (1940) called the ability of an "attitude toward the abstract," and the merely possible. In Adler's sense such *creative power means ability to envisage goals and make decisions, choices, and all sorts of "arrangements consistent with the individual's purposes and values."*

Anthropomorphic versus Mechanomorphic Model of Man

Adler's (1964) attack on Freud was essentially aimed at the latter's mechanistic assumptions, and he wrote: "Freud was wholly confined in a mechanistic conception and used a mechanistic principle for the explanation of mind and psyche." Adler (1956) found many psychologists inclined, like Freud,

3   . . . to present their dogmas disguised in mechanistic or physical similes. At one time they use as a comparison a pump handle . . . at another a magnet . . . at another a sadly harassed animal struggling for the satisfaction of its elementary needs. From such a view, to be sure, little can be seen of the fundamental differences which human psychological life manifests.

Regarding environmentalism in particular, Adler (1956) asked: "Who seeks, who answers, who utilizes the impressions from the environment? *Is man a dictaphone or a machine?* There must be something else at play."

Adler was a pragmatist, an admirer of William James and John Dewey. His adherence to an anthropomorphic model was thus largely influenced by its greater therapeutic usefulness. For him it was not a question whether man is actually the center of the world; his intention was "to make him the center. In this way mankind attains a task and a goal which, although unattainable, points the way and the direction." We see how Adler was always concerned with aspects which would meet man's need for direction. In view of this need, *an adequate psychology must deal with values and norms.*

Purposes versus Causes

With *a model of man as active and self-determined,* the customary causalistic approach had to give way to a purposive or teleological approach. Adler's (1956) battle call here was:

The most important question of the healthy and the diseased mental life is not whence? but, whither? Only when we know the effective direction-giving goal of a person may we try to understand his movements. . . . In this whither? the cause is contained . . . we regard man as if nothing in his life   4 were causally determined and as if every phenomenon could have been different. . . . Individual Psychology insists on the indispensability of finalism for the understanding of all psychological phenomena. Causes, powers, instincts, impulses, and the like cannot serve as explanatory principles. The final goal alone can. Experiences, traumata, sexual development mechanisms cannot yield an explanation, but the perspective in which these are regarded . . . which subordinates all life to the final goal, can do so."

One of the attractions of causalistic thinking is, according to Adler (1956), *that it frees the person from responsibility and excuses him from blame.* Such freedom is exactly what all failures in life are seeking in order to safeguard their low self-esteem and high aspirations. Thus we find them very much engaged in causalistic reasoning. Very early in his career Adler called this the "life lie" of the neurotic. The neurotic's life plan ". . . demands categorically that if he 5 fails, it should be through someone else's fault and that he should be freed from personal responsibility; or that, if his triumph is prevented, it should be by a fatal detail only." For this purpose, anything can be the cause. Adler once made a list of such causes: "because of my parents; because I am the youngest; because I am too small, too weak; because I am cross-eyed, near-sighted; because I am not manly; because I am a girl; because I am stupid; because I have masturbated; because I have a long nose, too much hair, too little hair; because I have been pampered; and because I have been discriminated against."

Holism and Life Style

As a machine consists of parts, so we find — together with the machine model of man — a corresponding elementaristic conception. The organism, on the other hand, including the human organism, begins as one fertilized cell and remains through its life-span a unity. All parts have grown from this original unity.

6 For Adler, *the unity of the individual was most important.* In fact, when he chose for his school the name, Individual Psychology, it was for the reason that individual also means indivisible — that which cannot be divided. Thus, he was very sympathetic to Gestalt psychology and enthusiastic about Jan C. Smuts' *Holism and Evolution* (Ansbacher, 1961). Adler (1956) *considered the unity of the personality "an established fact, scientifically confirmed and illumined from many sides."*

Adler's concept of life style reflects his holistic view. All aspects of the person enter into his life style, which is really his style or his way of living, his individual striving in orientation toward a goal. In full agreement with Matson (1969) this is a unitary striving which includes all of the individual, that is, reason, "mechanisms," his heart, mind, will, and even spleen, but also all of the physique, the hereditary and environmental influences. Adler (1956) wrote: "Very early in my work, I found man to be a unity. The foremost task of Individual Psychology is to prove this unity in each individual — in his thinking, feeling, acting, in his so-called conscious and unconscious, in every expression of his personality. This unity we call the style of life of the individual. What is frequently labeled the ego is nothing more than the style of the individual." It includes of course also the values and goals of the individual as well as the use he makes of his heredity and environment — all of which, like the entirety, are individually unique. Every component is individualized with regard to the styled creative power of the person. Through such comprehensiveness the holistic psychologist actually becomes the truly eclectic psychologist (Thorne, 1970).

Subjectivity

Part of the humanistic conception of man is the recognition of man's individual uniqueness which rests on the individual's inner life, his "private world," his subjectivity. This must be respected and accepted as an important

7 part of the personality. The early behaviorists denied the value of subjectivity, while Freud considered it only as a guide to something else—objective conditions like traumata and repressions, general drive components, all nomothetic concepts. not idiographic ones, as Allport (1937) pointed out.

The psychologist tries to understand the subjectivity, not to reduce it to some hypothetical causes. The individual's goal of success which is so important in Adler's (1956) psychology is subjective and individually unique. *Early in life the individual develops a unique "schema of apperception," which includes his view of the world and of himself.*

As a simple illustration of the importance of subjectivity, Adler reminds us, "It has the same effect on me whether a poisonous snake is actually approaching my foot or whether I merely believe that it is a poisonous snake." In summary, "Each one organizes himself according to his personal view of things, and some views are more sound, some less sound." To this extent Adler can certainly be counted among the phenomenologists.

Psychotherapy as Good Human Relationship

Humanistic psychotherapy avoids formal technology and is not based on the diagnosis of an "illness" by which the patient is afflicted. Rather, according to Matson (1969), it has to do with caring, commitment, empathy, understanding, liberation, dialogue.

All these aspects of treatment and descriptions of mental health can be found in the Adlerian approach. According to Adler (1956), the therapist

has the task "to give the patient the ex- 8 perience of contact with a fellow man, and then to enable him to transfer this awakened social interest to others. This method . . . is strictly analogous to the function of the mother, whose social task it is to interpret society to the individual. . . . Since his is a belated assumption of the maternal function, the therapist must work with a corresponding devotion to the patient's needs."

Adler believed this was the common element in all schools of therapy, regardless of their theoretical orientation. "We are far from denying that other schools of psychiatry have their successes . . . , but in our experience they do so less by their methods than when they happen to give the patient a good human relationship . . . above all . . . encouragement." Yet, Adler also developed specific methods. These have been expanded particularly by Dreikurs (1967).

SOCIAL INTEREST

We now come to what Adler has primarily still to offer to humanistic psychology. Maslow (Various, 1970), in his brief message on Adler's Centennial from which we quoted initially, also said: "In one respect especially the times have not yet caught up with Adler. I refer to his holistic emphasis." We should like to add to this Adler's pragmatic emphasis, which also has not yet become common property.

Holistic and Pragmatic Emphases

Adler's holistic emphasis was indeed comprehensive. He saw man not only as a whole but also as part of larger wholes—his family, community, humanity, our planet, the cosmos. He consistently saw each individual in his most significant context. In a straightforward statement Adler (1956) expressed this position in the words: "Individual Psychology *regards and examines the individual as socially embedded. We refuse to recognize and examine an isolated human being.*"

9   Consistent with this principle, Adler also saw man endowed with an aptitude to understand this embeddedness in larger contexts, and to cope with it. This he called community feeling or social interest, an aptitude which, however, needs to be consciously trained and developed. Developed social interest is the criterion for mental health. It is "the true and inevitable compensation for all the natural weaknesses of individual human beings."

Again, like the concept of the "creative power," social interest is nothing mystical. The concept is based on the simple assumption that we have a natural aptitude for acquiring the skills and understanding to live under the conditions under which we are born as human beings. Maslow (1970b), in his paper on self-actualizers, retained the original German term, *Gemeinschaftsgefühl*. But a foreign term introduces an aura of remoteness and mystery, contrary to the spirit of Adlerian psychology, which emphasizes directness and concreteness. Therefore, although the German term has some further connotations, we prefer "social interest," the term Adler himself used in his English writings, or perhaps "community feeling."

At this point the pragmatic emphasis must be added. Adler (1929) established a behavioral criterion for social interest in the form of socially useful goal striving, and *he defined such useful conduct*
10   *as "in the interests of mankind generally."* This criterion is important because one might easily become "confused by the fact that some neurotics seem to be benevolent and wish to reform the whole world" (Adler, 1964). Yet their actions are not on the useful side of life. The test

for *true* social interest is that the actions correspond to the words. "We are closing our ears to professions and looking at achievements" (Adler, 1956).

Social interest is then direction-giving, as mentioned earlier. The direction it gives to action is one of synergy of the personal striving with that of others. It is a direction on the socially useful side, in line with the interests of others, of mankind in the long run. On the other hand, *all failures in life have in common their striving for a goal of success which has only personal meaning*—that is, no general validity, making it in the long run unsatisfactory even to the individual himself.

Humanistic psychology, as well as psychology in general, has so far not sufficiently developed such a conception. Humanistic psychology, as expressed by Matson (1969), *has stressed primarily the fight for "the freedom of the mind and the autonomy of the person . . .* exposing and condemning each and every dehumanizing, depersonalizing and demoralizing force." *But the tenor here is one of individual independence, rather than of interdependence and cooperation.*

True enough, Maslow's (1970b) "self-actualizing people" all displayed in fact a highly developed social interest and led lives of great usefulness to mankind (Ansbacher, 1968). But this is not made explicit. *While true self-actualization and fulfillment are in the end defined as facilitating the self-actualization of others as well, even purely semantically this takes second place. The concept of self-actualization remains formulated from the viewpoint of the self without regard to the larger whole.*

In the Adlerian view the self is structurally not so absolute. *The most important structural terms are the goal for which a person is striving and his manner of striving as a whole, his style of life.*   11

The self is not considered as an entity but only to the extent that it becomes evident in transactions with its surroundings. Thus Adler, one of the original self-psychologists, is far more than this. He is a transactional psychologist much like Cantril (Kilpatrick, 1969) and the pragmatists (Winetrout, 1968).

There is literally no self to actualize but through transactions with its world. *The self prospers psychologically to the extent that our interests are focused beyond the self—on our work, family, friends, a cause (including rebellion), anything beyond the self that represents a contribution to the progress of mankind* (Adler, 1964). This even includes taking care of ourselves because otherwise our general usefulness, our ability to contribute to life would certainly be impaired if not terminated.

Implications for Humanistic Psychology

In his presidential address, Matson (1969) expressed concern about the present situation of humanistic psychology. It seems to have become *"a haven for the irrational and the anti-intellectual—for all that is exotic, erotic, and psychotic."* Toward the end of his life, Maslow (1970a) was similarly concerned. "I share," he wrote, "with many other scholars and scientists a great uneasiness over some trends in Esalen-type education. For instance, in some of its less respectworthy adherents, I see trends toward anti-intellectualism, anti-science, anti-rationality, anti-discipline, anti-hard work, etc. I worry when competence and training are by some considered to be irrelevant."

To an Adlerian it is quite understandable that the humanistic movement in psychology should have attracted such "less respectworthy adherents." With self-actualization as the ideal, the move-ment can easily be mistaken for a cult of the self. It would thus attract self-seeking, immature persons who wish to avoid responsibility toward their fellow men, and who are not prepared to contribute to the whole, exemplifying the pampered style of life.

Matson's (1969) first recommendation reveals a further weakness in the theory of self-actualization. He recommends that "We had better take a sharp look at, and get a firm grip on, our real and authentic self." In all fairness we must point out that Matson speaks here metaphorically of the authentic self of the Association of Humanistic Psychology, not of an individual. But nevertheless, he uses concepts which are generally applied to individuals. As such, they cannot be visualized, let alone be operationalized. What are we concretely to do to get "a firm grip on our real self?" The concept is even more atomistic and static than that of the self. If anything, it centers again on the self and thus facilitates an attitude which according to Adler is common to all psychological disturbances.

Matson's (1969) recommended next step is in the right direction when he suggests, "Let us seek, not a Collective Unconscious à la Jung, but a collective consciousness: a sense of purpose, a sense of direction, and a sense of proportion." But he is unable to name the direction.

Here Adler's (1931) answer would be as indicated above—namely, to recognize that *"the true meaning of life is contribution,"* in accordance with a well-developed social interest. The sense of purpose and sense of direction which Matson is seeking could be found by accepting Adler's (1956) criterion for psychological soundness of any individual or group, namely social usefulness. "All social movements . . . should be judged only in accordance with their ability to further interest in our fellow men. There are many ways to help in increasing cooperation."

It should be possible to explain to those who are against science, rationality, discipline, hard work, etc. that in this way they may think they are actualizing themselves, but they are in fact denying in an arrogant manner the values and goals mankind has held throughout the centuries and to which we are indebted for the progress that has undeniably been achieved despite the fact that the world is still far from perfect. Let us confront them with the question, *"What effort are you making to perfect the world? Or are you satisfied with merely making demands on others in accordance with a pampered style of life?"*

In summary, it is our opinion that the concept of social interest with its corollary of social usefulness represents outstandingly the "holistic-dynamic" point of view which Maslow (1970b) was advocating in his last book. Moreover, since it forms the bridge from the individual to his world of which he is a part, the concept also has immediate therapeutic implications, inasmuch as mental health and disorders can be evaluated only from the way the individual relates himself to his world — as a cooperator, or as a self-seeker.

CONCLUSION

We have attempted to show in the first part of this paper the common premises on the basis of which Alfred Adler must truly be considered a humanistic psychologist. In the second part we have pointed out that Adler's holism took man never by himself but always in his social and general ecological context. Man's psychological soundness was seen as depending on his degree of community feeling with his context, and on his contributions to life, his social interest and usefulness.

It is in this respect that the movement of humanistic psychology as it has developed could profit from Adler. By its emphasis on the self and absence of the concept of social usefulness, it has recently tended to attract self-seeking groups to the dismay of its responsible leaders. By adopting the concept of social interest the movement would have a tool to remedy the situation and to find a clearer definition of its purpose and direction.

As far as Adler is concerned, we believe to have shown that he is not merely a historical figure, but that he has still a contribution to make, that he can still show the way.

REFERENCES

Adler, A. *Problems of neurosis* (1929). New York: Harper & Row, 1964.

———. *What life should mean to you* (1931). New York: Capricorn Books, 1958.

———. *Social interest: a challenge to mankind* (1933). New York: Capricorn Books, 1964.

———. *The Individual Psychology of Alfred Adler.* Ed. by H. L. & Rowena R. Ansbacher. New York: Basic Books, 1956.

———. *Superiority and social interest: A collection of later writings.* Ed. by H. L. & Rowena R. Ansbacher. Evanston, Ill.: Northwestern University Press, 1964.

Allport, G. W. *Personality.* New York: Holt, 1937.

Ansbacher, H. L. On the origin of holism. *Journal of Individual Psychology,* 1961, *17,* 142–148.

———. The concept of social interest. *Journal of Individual Psychology,* 1968, *24,* 131–149.

Dreikurs, R. *Psychodynamics, psychotherapy, and counseling: collected papers.* Chicago, Ill.: Alfred Adler Institute, 1967.

Goldstein, K. *Human nature in the light of psychopathology.* Cambridge, Mass.: Harvard University Press, 1940.

Hall, C. S., & Lindsey, G. *Theories of personality.* New York: Wiley, 1957.

Kilpatrick, F. P., Hadley Cantril (1906-1969): The transactional point of view. *Journal of Individual Psychology,* 1969, 25, 219-225.

Maslow, A. H. Humanistic education vs. professional education: Further comments. *New Directions in Teaching, Bowling Green University,* 1970, 2(2), 3-10. (a)

———. *Motivation and personality.* 2nd ed. New York: Harper & Row, 1970. (b)

Matson, F.W. What ever became of the Third Force? *American Association of Humanistic Psychology, Newsletter,* 1969, 6(1), 1 & 14-15.

Thorne, F. C. Adler's broad-spectrum concept of man, self-consistency, and unification. *Journal of Individual Psychology,* 1970, 26, 135-143.

Various. Tributes to Alfred Adler on his 100th birthday. *Journal of Individual Psychology,* 1970, 26, 10-16.

Winetrout, K. Adlerian psychology and pragmatism. *Journal of Individual Psychology,* 1968, 24, 5-24.

The preceding article was included for two reasons. First, it presents several concepts that illuminate some of the basic assumptions of humanistic psychology about human nature, and second, it illustrates how a whole movement (individual psychology) can be integrated into the framework of humanistic psychology. If we return to the basic thrust of humanistic psychology, that of characterizing the healthy person, we can probably find other movements that may augment its present structure. In this article we found the author juxtaposing Adler's theories with those of Matson, and, though the paper he refers to by Matson is not the one we reprinted (ours gives a more optimistic outlook than that referred to by Adler), the one you have read contains information on most of the topics Ansbacher discusses.

Ansbacher begins by contrasting the deterministic models of the behaviorists and psychoanalysts with the self-determinism of humanistic psychology (1). He then shows that Adler's term "creative power" is more descriptive than "creative self" (2). He rejects the mechanistic models of the other two schools in favor of an anthropomorphic model (3) and indicates that a person can only be understood if we consider the *purpose* of his or her action, not its *cause* (4). This means that we must consider the constraints of the situation, including environment and psychic state, but that we must ultimately be held responsible for our own behavior since we are the doers (5). The whole-person view of humans focuses on the indivisibleness of our personalities and the unity of our lifestyles (6). We can observe the lifestyle but cannot understand it unless we know the subjective inner life of the person (7).

The goal of therapy should be to facilitate the development of good human relationships (8). This type of relationship is not possible if a person has a weak self-concept. This is one of the reasons why humanistic psychology emphasizes the development of a healthy self-concept and stresses individual autonomy and responsibility. Yet Ansbacher shows how Adler's concept of social embeddedness (no man is an island) (9) makes it imperative that one's goals be acted upon as well as talked about (10). It is comparable to the humanistic concept of "intentionality," which "implies both a person's focusing on a subject which means something to him and his directing himself toward that subject" (Buhler and Allen 1972, p. 44). The healthy person must have a goal that transcends the "self" (11). This gives meaning to life (Buhler and Allen 1972, p. 69) and allows one to become a contributor to society (12).

We have included references to Buhler and Allen on intentionality and self-transcendence to indicate that, although Ansbacher presents these concepts as valuable for humanistic psychology to consider, others have already included them in their basic assumption about the nature of the healthy person. Our model has now grown to include the assumptions that a person's creative force is future oriented and that his or her goal has a social contribution. Only the person can know the "inner self" and understand it through an awareness of his or her embeddedness in society. We have intentionality in that we set goals and actively pursue them, and these goals are self-transcending in that they serve the good of society, not just the self.

Buhler and Allen (1972) give us several other distinguishing characteristics of humanistic psychology's view of human nature. First they emphasize "the image of man as active and positive, as experiencing his existence" (p. 52) —the subjective awareness of the previous article. They speak of "person" rather than "individual" or "organism," and they quote Maslow as saying, "I must approach a person as an individual, unique and peculiar, as the sole member of his class" (p. 10). The uniqueness of each individual does not mean that there is no such thing as normative behavior, but rather that each person's reason for behaving in that way is unique to that person. If we are only looking at behavior, we will not find the tendencies toward certain types of behavior that are universal to human beings. There appear to be four such tendencies:

> (1) the tendency to strive for personal *satisfaction* in sex, love, and ego recognition; (2) the tendency toward self-limiting *adaption* for the purpose of fitting in, belonging, and gaining security; (3) the tendency toward *self-expression* and creative accomplishments; and (4) the tendency toward integration or *order-upholding*. Conflicts in the individual's self-direction toward his end goals can be traced all through life to the interplay of these four basic tendencies." (Buhler and Allen 1972, p. 48)

They go on to say (p. 49) that "the healthy person will try to integrate the pursuits of pleasure-sex-love needs, his adaptive desire to fit in, and his need to accomplish creatively in the direction of self-realization and fulfillment. He will also strive for a balance between pursuit of his own needs and dedication to self-transcending contributions."

We have seen that the behavioristic view of human nature is basically external, dependent upon the environment, and that the psychoanalytic approach is basically internal, dependent upon psychic forces. We now see that the humanistic approach is both externally and internally oriented, in that it recognizes as one of a person's basic goals the healthy integration of one's internal structure with the external structures of society and environment. One of the humanistic assumptions about the human being is that one "develops to be what he makes himself by his own actions" (Langer 1969, p. 7). This is an *autogenetic thesis,* which holds that the "future organization of the organism is inherent in the seed out of which it develops" (Langer 1969, p. 7). The assumption of rational behavior is implicit here, and we shall now consider the process by which this behavior comes about.

Humanistic psychologists have assumed a model of human nature based on intellectual (cognitive) development. Although he may not admit to being a member of the humanistic school of psychology, Jean Piaget's work best exemplifies this model. In his review of Piaget, Hans Furth points out that a person is a biological structure and that "a biological structure implies functioning; it requires no source of motivation external to itself in order to function." He continues that "Piaget likens the internal scheme to a starving animal looking for food which the scheme finds in its interaction with the environment; the scheme assimilates the environmental stuff that provides the necessary food for its funciton" (Furth 1969 p. 45). Thus, the individual is an ongoing living process and should be considered as such when attempting to understand one's behavior. George Kelly (1970, p. 9) says it in a slightly different way:

> We start with a *person*. Organisms, lower animals, and societies can wait. We are talking about someone we know, or would like to know—such as you, or myself. More particularly, we are talking about that person as an event—the processes that express his personality. And, since we enter the system we are about to elaborate at the point of a process—or life—rather than at the point of a body or a material substance, we should not have to invoke any special notions, such as dynamics, drives, motivation, or force to explain why our object does not remain inert. As far as the theory is concerned, it never was inert.

The basic assumption of the humanistic approach, then, is that a human being is a process, and unless society has conditioned us to stop moving, we are continually changing. We are active seekers of stimuli, not passive responders to them. In this way we can grow into fully functioning human beings—individuals relying on an internal structure with which we are so well acquainted that we know *who* we are and *why* we are. We may interact with other human beings as free moral agents who are responsible for our own behavior and who understand the behavior of others. Because we are a process, we know that we are growing and that we must keep in touch with ourselves to maintain understanding and control of our own behavior. We must also communicate with others—experience events—to see if our anticipations of these events are confirmed or disconfirmed—to see if our perceptions and anticipations are consistent.

As we move through various stages of understanding both ourselves and others, where we are, in a cognitive sense, after we experience an event depends on where we were, cognitively, before we experienced the event. Thus, our cognitive growth may be said to be psychologically determined. It can also be assumed that the cognitive system is a cybernetic system, using internal and external feedback to regulate its activity and structure its growth (Borden 1971, pp. 50-55). (After you have once flunked a test you have different expectations and prepare differently for the next one.)

We have probably presented sufficient information about the humanistic school of psychology to summarize its basic assumptions about human nature. We should remember that humanistic psychology's model is basically a projection of what the ideal healthy person should be. It is an anthropomorphic model in that it is uniquely human. One cannot use the analogue of a hydraulic system or a piece of machiners; we must look at the human being as its own model. Furthermore, it is a rational, cognitive model, requiring a theory of cognitive development to make sense out of the assumptions about human nature. Because it directs itself to develop mental structures it is a self-controlled model; successive structures are determined by the preceding ones. The model is growth oriented, but the successive stages may be inhibited from developing.

These basic characteristics of the cognitive model imply other features of the human being. For one thing, we are active seekers of information, experiences, relationships, and fulfillment. By becoming actively involved in our experiences and being committed to their development, each of us builds a unique self. Being aware of the self, we realize that we are the mediators of our experiences—that the meaning we derive from them is uniquely ours—and, thus, that we are the ones who shape our self-concept. We are autonomous and responsible for our behavior. As a continuing process, we have intentionality and actively pursue the goals we have established. Realizing that since we are socially embedded our goals must be greater than mere self-satisfaction, we are self-transcendent and creative in our ability to adapt to social and environmental restrictions.

We are whole persons and cannot be subdivided into drives or motives, and we should treat others as whole persons also. Because we have freedom of choice and respond to both internal and external stimuli, we are unpredictable—not necessarily in our behaviors but in the reasons for such behaviors. We originate stimuli as well as respond to them. We are not inherently evil, and when allowed to develop naturally we are both positive and active. By understanding ourselves and our view of reality, we can change our internal structure, and therefore change our behavior. Thus, we control our own destiny. Since we are free to initiate our own interaction with others and our environment, we can truly share our experiences and ourselves with others, and we are able to accept others as processes in constant modification through experience. In short, we are "a process of potentialities being born" (Rogers and Stevens 1971, p. 18).

HUMANISTIC ACTIVITIES

1. Observe a young child (preschool age) in an unstructured situation (home, playground, etc.).
    a. Try to determine the percentage of time in which he was bored, with nothing to do. How many different things did the child do in about ten minutes?
    b. Talk to the child and see if he can tell you about life as he sees it (e.g., what he thinks about time [tomorrow, yesterday], relationships [parents, friends], etc). Does it fit the humanistic model?
2. Form a group of four to six persons and discuss what each one would do if she could do anything she wanted to.
    a. Why isn't she doing it? Does she *really* want to do it?
    b. What physical needs do you control? How do you do it?
    c. Do you cooperate with your body? Dominate it? Does it control you? When?
    d. Evaluate this discussion, focusing on what you feel are the underlying assumptions about human behavior exemplified by each person's reasons for doing or not doing what he or she wants to do.
3. Individually, list the ways you feel the human being differs from lower forms of animal life. Where does freedom of choice and control of the environment fit in? Join a group of five to seven persons and compare your lists while composing one master list.
4. We all have a number of relationships in our lives. Start keeping a journal (or log) which describes one such relationship. Discuss how intimate the relationship is, how much trust is involved in it, how much (and how deeply) disclosures take place, and the mutuality of the disclosures, and try to determine why such inequities of disclosure might take place.
5. Form a group of not more than five to seven persons and rank the following characteristics in the order you feel they are important, marking the most important 1, and the least important 16. Do not rank any of the terms on the same level.

Caring	Constructive	Energetic	Friendly
Compassionate	Discriminating	Capable	Courteous
Egocentric	Straightforward	Predictable	Reverent
Ambitious	Accomplished	Loyal	Goal Oriented

6. Form a group of five to seven persons and construct a list of the characteristics or attributes you *most admire* in a person (any person). Now, make a list of those characteristics or attributes you *like least* in a person. How do these two lists fit together? Can you evaluate yourself freely?

A Comparison of the Three Models

We have now examined the three major forces in contemporary psychological thinking. We have considered the assumptions underlying each model of human nature and have tried to keep the depth of analysis consistent. One could take the analysis deeper and arrive at another level of assumptions from which the models are built, but the present set of assumptions will suffice to show some basic differences among the three schools of psychology. The reader can get an overview of these differences by consulting the chart on pages 44–46.

There are at least twelve dimensions on which differences can be shown to exist among these three models. (1) The basic model of the behaviorists is a learning model analogous to a piece of machinery: there is input and output and some mechanical apparatus in between that we cannot get into, so we do not concern ourselves with it. The basic model of the psychoanalysts is a psychodynamic model patterned after a hydraulic system: energy in the form of unconscious sexual-aggressive drives is channeled into creative or disruptive behavior. The basic model of the humanists is a cognitive-affective model which is uniquely human (anthropomorphic) : we are assumed to develop intellectual and emotional structures of which we can be aware and in control.

(2) The behaviorist sees humans as basically passive organisms which differ very little from other animals (thus the term "organism") and which must be motivated (stimulated by external forces) to perform. Accordingly, we do not have a will of our own and can be adequately explained in terms of stimulus-response behavior. The psychoanalysts see humans basically as passive individuals differing very little from other animals who are driven by internal, unconscious, sexual-aggressive forces and react to external stimuli from the environment. There is constant conflict between such internal and external forces and our behavior can only be explained in terms of unconscious mental forces. The humanists see humans as basically active in that we have a will of our own, are aware of our self-concepts, and have a potential for growth. We differ from other animals in a number of ways and are thus referred to as persons rather than organisms. Our behavior can only be understood in relation to the whole person acting within a context.

(3) The behaviorists have a response-dominated view of humans and are interested primarily in how the environment functions to elicit desired responses from us. The psychoanalysts also maintain a response-dominated view of humans, but because such responses are due to unconscious mental forces in conjunction with external stimuli and can be disguised in many ways, one can only infer what the cause of specific behaviors may be. The humanists have a generative-dominated view of humans in that they believe

we can creatively adapt to any situation and not just respond to it. Further, we actively seek growth experiences by anticipating events, checking our perceptions of the event with our anticipations, and modifying our thinking to agree with these tests of reality. Only we know why we behave the way we do, because only we know our intentions.

(4) The behaviorists see humans as products of their environment. We are in a continual process of being conditioned by our environment through reinforcement of desirable behavior. Thus, we are environmentally determined. The psychoanalysts see humans as passing through five psychosexual stages (oral, anal, phallic, latency, and genital) which are biologically determined. We have no control over when we pass from one stage to another, and our adult behavior is the product of the completeness with which we have resolved the problems peculiar to each stage. The humanists see humans as developing through a sequence of cognitive stages that are psychologically determined but not time bound; we move through these stages at our own rate and may never pass through all of them. Some stages have ideal biological times when they are more appropriately accomplished, and all have the prerequisite of a successful completion of the previous stage before they can be actively engaged in.

(5) The behaviorists reason that it is unnecessary to speculate about cognitive processes, since one cannot observe them firsthand. Inferences are unscientific, and only that which can be observed and measured is of importance to their model of human nature. Freud astounded the world by asserting that unconscious mental forces were primarily responsible for an individual's behavior. Since then psychoanalysts have put great faith in their ability to infer what mental problems are responsible for certain behaviors. These have been explained in terms of the three divisions of personality: the id, ego, and superego. The humanists view the human being as developing through the cognitive growth of a self-directing system; that is, the cognitive structure of a person is built up through a process using feedback (as mentioned in (3), above). Since it is self-regulating, it is subject only to its own limitations and is responsible for the resulting mental structure.

(6) The behaviorists' model is of an organism conditioned to be in equilibrium with its environment, to behave so as not to disrupt the norms of society. The psychoanalysts' model is of an individual who has developed a homeostatic relationship between the id and the superego governed by the ego. In this way the individual can maintain some degree of conformity to social norms without too much internal strife. The humanistic model is of a person who may become aware of and move toward his or her fullest potential. This self-actualization is prompted by the humanistic conscience — the awareness of one's potential, as a human being, to mature as a person and contribute to the healthy growth of society.

(7) The behaviorists see a human being as a rational animal, a paradox, since they do not want to be concerned with the mind. Our rational behavior,

as opposed to the emotional, stems from the imprinting in our minds of the order in the environment through operant conditioning. The psychoanalysts see the human as irrational, driven by unconscious forces beyond one's complete control. Though we may behave rationally much of the time, we are always subject to irrational urges to gratify our basic drives. The humanistic view of human beings is that we are rational because we are aware of the self and of our social embeddedness. This implies that we must control our behavior with both of these factors in mind. Thus, we do not accentuate the one to the detriment of the other.

(8) The behaviorists' model is built on the pleasure-pain principle. We can be conditioned by our environment because we seek pleasure and avoid pain. The psychoanalysts' model sees humans as being driven towards unbridled gratification of their sexual-aggressive drives. This puts us in constant conflict with our environment, as society will not allow the full realization of these drives. The humanistic model is built on the ideal that a person will obtain greatest self-fulfillment through self-transcendence. This assumes a strong self-image, with an awareness of our potential, and means living in the present but being bigger than the moment, being able to give up some self-gratification for the betterment of others.

(9) According to the behaviorists, an organism responds positively to pleasurable stimuli and is therefore controlled by external forces in the environment. By reinforcing desired behavior, society can mold the organism into what it would like it to be. The psychoanalysts' model is quite the reverse, for it sees the individual as being controlled by internal forces; our unconscious sexual and aggressive drives. This takes us out of the control of our environment and puts our environment in an adversary position against which we must constantly fight. The humanistic view is that humans can control themselves and their environment through their own reasoning processes. We can be autonomous beings (self-governed and self-determined), neither driven by internal forces nor manipulated by external ones.

(10) The behaviorists' view of human nature leads them to believe that one's behavior is predictable. Being the mirror of our environment and in its control, our behavior patterns are normative in nature so that, given sufficient numbers of organisms, normative behavior can be predicted with reasonable accuracy. Further, behaviorists believe that in time they will know enough about one's behavior to be able to predict the behavior of specific individuals. The psychoanalysts' view that human nature is determined by internal forces leads to the conclusion that the prediction of one's behavior on a group basis is the result of the quantity of subjects participating in the study rather than the predictability of human behavior. Since we may (and often do, socially) disguise the behavior resulting from our sexual or aggressive urges, it is impossible to predict an individual's behavior in any given instance. The humanistic approach is that, although the normative behavior of masses of people may be predictable, an individual's behavior is not, because

of one's freedom of choice. The humanists' meaning of "predictable" is at a deeper level than the behaviorists': humanists believe many people may behave overtly the same way but that each will have a different reason for behaving that way. Thus, our choice (behavior) is not predictable. Further, since we are free to make choices, we may choose not to make the same choice the next time.

(11) For the behaviorists, since a person is molded and controlled by the environment, it follows that one is not responsible for one's behavior. The responsibility falls on the shoulders of society, for we can only behave as we have been conditioned. For the psychoanalysts, since overt behavior is the result of unconscious drives, the individual is not responsible for his or her behavior. The responsibility lies with our unconscious urges, of which we are victims. In opposition to these two views, the humanistic model sees the person as responsible for his or her behavior. If we are autonomous, aware of self and society, and have freedom of choice, then we must be responsible for our actions.

(12) Reexamining the assumptions of the behavioristic model of human nature, we can conclude that the behaviorists see us locked in a deterministic structure within which we function as we are reinforced. Thus, we are incapable of any altruistic behavior, including love. The psychoanalysts come to the same conclusion but for different reasons. Since we are at the mercy of our psychosexual-aggressive drives, we can only attempt to satisfy these drives. Thus, we cannot perform altruistically, but only for self-gratification. The humanistic model presents the ideal person as being able to transcend "self" to enter into meaningful relationships through involvement with others and commitment to a love greater than "self." In this ideal model we may seek the good of others with no thought of reward or gratification for ourselves.

TABLE 1

Three Views of Human Nature

Behavioristic	Psychoanalytic	Humanistic
1. A mechanistic learning model.	1. A hydraulic psychodynamic model.	1. An anthropomorphic cognitive emotional model.
2. A passive organism — must be motivated.	2. A passive individual driven by sexual and aggressive forces.	2. An active person aware of self and his/her potential.

TABLE 1 (cont.)

Behavioristic	Psychoanalytic	Humanistic
3. Responds to environmental stimuli.	3. Responds to unconscious impulses.	3. Generates and responds to external and internal stimuli — creative adaptation.
4. Organism develops through continuous conditioning — environmentally determined.	4. Individual develops through five psychosexual stages — biologically determined.	4. Person develops many stages of cognitive growth — psychologically determined.
5. Unnecessary to speculate on cognitive processes.	5. A mental-balance model with three divisions — id, ego, and superego.	5. Self-direction produces growth and cognitive structure.
6. Conditioned to be in equilibrium with the environment.	6. Develops homeostatic relationships among id, ego, and superego.	6. Self-actualization prompted by a humanistic conscience.
7. Rational — mirror of environmental structure.	7. Irrational — subject to unconscious urges.	7. Rational — aware of self and social embeddedness.
8. Seeks pleasure — avoids pain.	8. Seeks gratification of sexual-aggressive drives.	8. Seeks self-fulfillment through self-transcendence.
9. Externally controlled by the environment.	9. Internally controlled by psyche through sexual and aggressive drives.	9. Internally controlled — autonomous, self-determined.
10. Predictable because of environmental conditioning.	10. Unpredictable because of unconscious drives.	10. Unpredictable because of freedom of choice.
11. Environment is responsible for behavior.	11. Unconscious drives are responsible for behavior.	11. The person is responsible for his/her behavior.

TABLE 1 (cont.)

Behavioristic	**Psychoanalytic**	**Humanistic**
12. Incapable of altruistic behavior including love because it does things for rewards.	12. Incapable of altruistic behavior including love because it is reacting to sexual-aggressive drives.	12. Capable of meaningful relationships through involvement with others and commitment to a love greater than self (self-transcendence).

From the above twelve contact points, we may draw two obvious conclusions: there are good and bad aspects in all three views of human nature, and no one takes the extreme position of any one view. The primary difficulty for those who adopt the psychoanalytic view of human nature is that the use of inference to trace overt behavior back to its cause (a repressed sexual or aggressive urge) instills a sense of deviousness into the communication process. If human behavior is motivated by sexual and/or aggressive drives, then implicit in our communiqués is the attempt to move toward the gratification of these drives. It is difficult, then, for people to be genuine in their communication processes. According to the psychoanalytic philosophy, we may not even be aware of the ulterior motives (gratification of basic urges) underlying them, and even if we are, we have no control over them. Thus, the communication process becomes an artificial game played to obtain gratification of our unconscious desires.

The most obvious problem for those who take the humanistic view of human nature is that it is an idealistic view. If taken as the way we are (instead of how the humanists would like us to be), this approach leads to a naiveté about the communication process that results in perpetual "touchie-feelie" encounter groups where individuals are continually experiencing each other but making no provisions for the resultant knowledge to be incorporated into the ongoing processes of society. We do not argue against the experience, only the failure to incorporate the fruits of these experiences into the development of a mature individual. In this sense, such groups are as unnatural as the behaviorists' laboratory—neither can be duplicated in normal everyday living. This means that the communicative expectations developed by both of these schools (humanistic and behavioristic) are unrealistic. One cannot expect to find his or her fellow communicators either genuine and open or passive and closed (though the latter often seems more true than the former). Instead, *one must approach each communicative situation as an invitation to share in another person's experience.*

We have summarized the major assumptions of the three schools of psychology concerning human nature. We will now give you an opportunity to find out how you feel about these assumptions. Using Scale C, put an *x* on the dash closest (depending on the strength of your feelings) to the adjective in each pair that best describes the ideal communicator.

SCALE C

The Ideal Communicator

I FEEL THE IDEAL COMMUNICATOR IS:

Active __ __ __ __ __ __ __	Passive
Unaware of self __ __ __ __ __ __ __	Aware of self
Internally motivated __ __ __ __ __ __ __	Externally motivated
A responder __ __ __ __ __ __ __	A creator
Psychologically Determined __ __ __ __ __ __ __	Environmentally Determined
Objective __ __ __ __ __ __ __	Subjective
Dependent __ __ __ __ __ __ __	Independent
Irrational __ __ __ __ __ __ __	Rational
Altruistic __ __ __ __ __ __ __	Machiavellian
Externally Controlled __ __ __ __ __ __ __	Internally Controlled
Predictable __ __ __ __ __ __ __	Unpredictable
Not responsible __ __ __ __ __ __ __	Responsible

Now that you have found out what *you feel* the ideal communicator is like, you may want to find out how closely you approach that ideal. Go back through Scale C and use a   to indicate where *you feel you are* (I FEEL I AM) in relation to these adjectives. Remember, this test is only as accurate as you are honest, and it only reflects *your feelings. There are no norms.* See where the differences are between your ideal and yourself. The fact that *you* have been able to see them will automatically begin moving you toward your ideal.

Now if you have some friends you can talk to, you may want them to fill out Scale C indicating where they feel you are (I FEEL YOU ARE). Are there any differences? Where? Why?

Humanistic Concepts in Human Communicative Behavior

What insights can we get from the humanistic psychologists' view of human nature that might enhance our study of the processes inherent in human communication? As you might guess, in a book such as this we will try to highlight many characteristics that are dissonant with current approaches to human communication theory. In this way we will try to shape some new perceptions of the human communication process that may help us understand human interaction better. We admit to the fact that the humanistic view is an idealized view and therefore may not be any closer to reality than the behavioristic or psychoanalytic view. However, by considering some of the humanistic ideas, our attention may be focused on some areas of the human communication process that have been neglected by other views and thus may lead to a greater understanding of this process.

For example, the problem stated at the beginning of this section noted the difference between those who feel we are internally motivated and those who feel we are externally motivated. These two views are basic to the humanistic and behavioristic models of human nature, respectively. Think of the implications these views have on your communication processes. If we feel that people must be stimulated (motivated) by their environment, then we will feel responsible for directing and controlling the communicative event. On the other hand, if we feel people are (or can be) internally motivated, we will be more likely to let things happen as they will. The other person may be assertive and open or timid and closed, but in either case we will not feel responsible for their communicative behavior and we will make more progress toward finding out what the person is really like.

The most important aspect of the humanistic view of human nature is the concern that one be considered a *person*. We may be called an organism or an individual, but *we must first of all be a person*. The reason we emphasize this is because of all the attributes that go along with this concept. First, a person has a name, and immediately we begin to get "personal." Each of us has a personality and an appearance like no one else in this world. In short, we are unique, and our *uniqueness* is our most valuable attribute. We may communicate in many ways similar to other persons, even for similar reasons, but this is no reason to make of us a generalized, normative object. To understand us it would appear to be far more important to know how we differ from other persons than how similar we are to them. It may very well be that to find our uniqueness you will have to look behind our overt behaviors—communicate more intimately. On the surface (or in a laboratory) we may act like hundreds of others, but if you ask why and probe deeply enough, you may find that the reasons for our communicative behavior are quite different from those of our companions.

The above procedure (asking why) presupposes another important assumption (taken from the psychoanalysts but emphasized by the humanistic psychologists)—that a person can be understood only by understanding his or her *mental processes*. The consideration of mental processes in the analysis of communication processes has been a thorn for many communication researchers. Basically, they do not want to accept mental processes as an integral part of communication, but the concepts dealt with can not exist without these processes (e.g., attitudes, beliefs, fears, dissonance, and intention). Thus, many communication researchers have become schizophrenic, believing only in what they can see and measure but forced to explain these behaviors by allusions to cognitive processes. If we accept as a fact that human beings have mental processes, we may be able to develop our conceptualization of these processes in such a way as to open new areas of research and understanding.

Humanistic psychologists attach a very important characteristic to mental processes—that of being *active*. This assumption is the major difference between the humanistic and the other two schools of psychology. Essentially, it is saying that we are not merely responders to internal or external stimuli, but that as an active, ongoing system we can both respond to and create stimuli, whichever is appropriate to us. As active systems we may seek information as well as process that which naturally comes to us; we may instigate communication as well as respond to it. Thus, we may have goals for which we strive that have no external reward or internal ulterior motive. They may be purely cognitive goals, and fulfillment comes upon completion of and participation in the cognitive processes (e.g., creating, discovering, and learning just for themselves). Granted, in our present society these activities are soon conditioned out of most of us, but from the humanistic point of view we have the potential to find fulfillment in ourselves. We seek realization of our mental images and are satisfied, or fulfilled, when they are realized.

Another characteristic of humans as seen from the humanistic viewpoint is that we may become *aware of ourselves* and our *embeddedness in society*. The awareness of self is a highly controversial concept. It is a basic tenet of humanistic psychology, and as a factor in human communication theory it helps us to understand some of the facets of the human communication process. Awareness of self helps us realize that in any communication situation we have *choices* as to how we are to behave. A conditioned organism has no choice but those established by its environment. One who knows oneself and is aware of one's involvment with society can determine *why* he or she behaves as he or she does. We can determine our *intentions* and act on the dictates of our humanistic conscience. We are aware of the repercussions of our behavior on ourselves and our society and can choose what behavior we will exhibit.

Other characteristics result from the assumption of *choice*. Given the ability to choose our own behavior, we may then become internally, but rationally, controlled. We are not driven by unknown urges nor pulled by environmental reinforcement unless we allow it. The degree to which we are not in control of our actions becomes an important variable in the communication process and in our awareness of our own communicative behavior, as well as in understanding the behavior of others. Further, it places the *responsibility* of this behavior squarely on the person and thus focuses the attention of the communicator and the researcher there as well. In doing this it helps us *understand each other as persons* and *not as objects* pulled by the environment or driven by unseen internal urges. Humans are seen as *autonomous* beings able to make choices and take responsibility for their subsequent behaviors.

The above insights into our communicative behavior may help us to understand each other better. We shall elaborate more on them as we continue to look at the human communication process throughout this book. In the next part we will construct a humanistic model for the human communication process (basically interpersonal) and present some methods by which this process may be analyzed.

THOUGHT QUESTIONS

1. Is there a "difference that really matters" in the way we view man? Does it really matter if we view people as basically humanistically oriented, or behaviorally oriented? Do we communicate differently, depending on our view?

2. Is there a universal (or universally accepted) model of the way humans operate in relation to their work? In their relation to other people? In their relationships with loved ones? Consider the internal-external motivation model (pp. 3–4). Where does it fail to apply to the above relationships?

3. All of us seem to have a tendency to judge others in some way. If one persists in doing this, are "mistakes" possible? How might they show up in our communicative behavior? What might some of these errors be? What might the consequences of such errors in judgment be? What might we do to avoid making such errors?

4. Can you name times when you have attempted to gain control over your environment (including other people)? How have you gone about doing this? What means did you employ in gaining such control? Would you consider such means ethical? Did such means and methods take into consideration the uniqueness of each person involved in the situation, or did it tend to categorize people?

5. Why is it virtually impossible for a person who is humanistically-psychologically oriented to talk of people in terms of means (averages) or groups or use statistics to talk about people? Why does the person who is humanistically-psychologically oriented tend to avoid putting people into groups?
6. Discuss a major problem in the approach toward understanding human behavior of each of the three schools of psychology. Give some examples.
7. Speculate on what behaviors *might* result from the *extreme* positions of these three schools of psychology in a male-female encounter. Give examples.
8. How would these three psychological views explain the workings of authority in the military, academia, religion, or politics; where would they place responsibility, control, motivation, etc.? Give examples.
9. What is the significance of the terms used to designate the human being in each school of psychology (person, individual, organism)?
10. You as a lawyer must defend a woman on the charge of prostitution. What arguments (strategies) would you use if the judge were a humanist? Behaviorist? Freudian?

RESEARCH QUESTIONS

The following three questions are intended to be research questions. Besides the references supplied for this part of the book, you may also want to consult the following sources (as well as others of your own knowledge) :

Child, Irvin L. *Humanistic Psychology and the Research Tradition: Their Several Virtues.* New York: John Wiley & Sons, 1973.

Jourard, Sidney M. *Disclosing Man to Himself.* New York: Van Nostrand Reinhold Co., 1968.

Rogers, Carl R. *Freedom to Learn.* Columbus, Ohio: Charles E. Merrill Publishing Co., 1969.

————. *On Becoming a Person.* Boston: Houghton Mifflin Co., 1961.

Sherman, A. Robert. *Behavior Modification: Theory and Practice.* Monterey, Calif.: Brooks/Cole Publishing Co., 1973.

Skinner, B. F. *About Behaviorism.* New York: Alfred A. Knopf, 1974.

1. How do the researcher's assumptions about human nature affect the questions he might ask about the human communication process? Give examples.
2. The teacher-student relationship is one of the most pervasive communication situations in American society. Consider the behaviorists' view of the human being as a passive responder to environmental stimuli and the humanists' view of the human being as an active seeker of

cognitive stimulation as they relate to the communicative strategies developed in the student-teacher relationship.

3. Consider the possibility that the facilitative behavior of the humanist is just one of the many environmental situations that the behaviorist might create. Defend or refute this statement by definition and example.

REFERENCES

Ansbacher, Heinz L. "Alfred Adler and Humanistic Psychology." *Journal of Humanistic Psychology,* no. 1 (Spring 1971), pp. 53–63.

Athos, Anthony G., and Coffey, Robert E. *Behavior in Organizations: A Multi-dimensional View.* Englewood Cliffs, N.J.: Prentice-Hall, 1968.

Barzun, Jacques, and Graff, Henry F. *The Modern Researcher.* New York: Harcourt, Brace & World, 1970.

Blum, Gerald S. *Psychodynamics: The Science of Unconscious Mental Forces.* Monterey, Calif.: Brooks/Cole Publishing Co., 1966.

Borden, George A. *An Introduction to Human-Communication Theory.* Dubuque, Iowa: William C. Brown Co., Publishers, 1971.

Buhler, Charlotte, and Allen, Melanie. *Introduction to Humanistic Psychology.* Monterey, Calif.: Brooks/Cole Publishing Co., 1972.

Ellis, Albert. *Humanistic Psychotherapy.* New York: Julian Press, 1973.

Erikson, Erik H. *Identity: Youth and Crisis.* New York: W.W. Norton & Co., 1968.

Freud, Sigmund, *A General Introduction to Psychoanalysis.* Translated by Joan Riviere. Garden City, N.Y.: Garden City Publishing Co., 1943.

Furth, Hans G. *Piaget and Knowledge.* Englewood Cliffs, N.J.: Prentice-Hall, 1969.

Goble, Frank G. *The Third Force.* New York: Grossman Publishers, 1970.

Goldenson, Robert.*The Encyclopedia of Human Behavior, Psychology, Psychiatry, and Mental Health.* Vol. 1. New York: Doubleday & Co., 1970.

Kelly, George A. "A Brief Introduction to Personal Construct Theory," in *Perspectives in Personal Construct Theory,* edited by D. Bannister. New York: Academic Press, 1970.

Langer, Jonas. *Theories of Development.* New York: Holt, Rinehart & Winston, 1969.

Matson, Floyd W. "Humanistic Theory: The Third Revolution in Psychology." *The Humanist,* no. 2. (March/April 1971), pp. 7–11.

Melville, Herman. *Moby-Dick: Or, The Whale.* Great Books of the Western World, vol. 48. Chicago: Encyclopedia Britannica, 1948.

Nye, Robert. *Three Views of Man.* Monterey, Calif.: Brooks/Cole Publishing Co., 1975.

Pervin, Lawrence. *Personality: Theory, Assessment and Research.* New York: John Wiley & Sons, 1970.

Rogers, Carl R., and Stevens, Barry. *Person to Person: The Problem of Being Human.* New York: Pocket Books, 1971.

Rotter, Julian B. "Generalized Expectancies for Internal Versus External Control of Reinforcement." *Psychological Monographs,* 80 (1966): pp. 1–28.

Skinner, B.F. *Beyond Freedom and Dignity,* New York: Alfred A. Knopf, 1971.

Southwell, Eugene A., and Merbaum, Michael. *Personality: Readings in Theory and Research.* Monterey, Calif.: Brooks/Cole Publishing Co., 1971.

Wilson, Colin. *New Pathways in Psychology: Maslow and the Post-Freudian Revolution.* New York: Taplinger Publishing Co., 1972.

House Rules

*Do not step across this threshold unless you consider
yourself my friend.
Otherwise, I will be obliged to meet with you;
but not here.*

———————

*Take a deep breath before you knock — or take several —
until you can smell essence.
Touch this door; feel it until your body tingles.
Swallow and recycle yesterday and today.
Listen for the sounds of the present and imagine sounds
of past and future.
Look in my mirror until you can transform that aspect of
your personal appearance which you deem grotesque into an
awareness and arousal of a resolving sense of beauty.
If you can't do all this, then walk back outside.
Experience until you know how very important yet
unimportant you are.
Then, please come back.*

———————

*Know that if you enter, we will not always follow
conventionally defined social graces.
I will give you as much of my sense of being as I can,
but I will hold back enough to insure my own self concept.
Claim no holds on me — let me run free — and,
I will do my best to help you maximize your freedoms.*

———————

*Do not expect too much of me for I am often small
and need to be.
Do expect, however, that both you and I will be different
following your visit.
I will be more of you and you will be more of me.*

W. Fielden Nelson

Part 2

Some Aspects of a Humanistic Communication Model

Upon completion of this section you should be able to:

1. List and define five distinct types of "noise."
2. Construct a replica of the Shannon-Weaver model of communication and label each element.
3. Compare and contrast the humanistic communicator with the behavioristic communicator with regard to (a) concern for others, (b) awareness of feelings, (c) consideration of emotional responses, and (d) feelings of commitment.
4. Identify at least five major variables or characteristics which describe *human* relationships.
5. List and define the ten dimensions of human involvement.
6. Describe situations in which stroking behaviors seem to manifest themselves.
7. Understand your own communicative behavior better.

The Human Communication Process

Human contact changes us. Even nodding hello as we pass someone on the sidewalk acknowledges to the other that he or she is recognized as a human being and to us that we exist in a world of others. The statement set forth on page 54 makes it very clear that communication changes things. The author, Bill Nelson, is a personal friend of both of us and has had a major influence on both our lives, as we have had on his. Stop and think for a moment who has had a major influence on your life. Was it through a "good" communicative event or a "bad" one? Usually negative events are remembered longer and we may be more aware of their effect on our lives than positive ones, but you should be able to recall some of each. Hopefully, by the time you are through with this book you will be able to turn all communicative events into enriching experiences and see yourself growing as a result of them.

We have used the word "communication" several times now, and although we all "know" what it means, perhaps it would be helpful if we focused on a couple of definitions so we can build on them specifically later. We often precede the word "communication" with the word " human," thus excluding such processes as information flow between animals, plants, or computers. Some definitions of communication will function as well for these nonhuman processes as for human processes. We will start with such a general definition, but focus your attention on some communication variables that make it specifically human. The model we construct, then, will be a humanistic model of the communication process—humanistic because the communication occurring in these processes will be conducive to the development of the whole person.

We have presented a set of statements (Scale D) on page 57 to enable you to express some of your own feelings about communication. Put a 1 for strongly agree, a 2 for disagree, a 3 for agree, or a 4 for strongly agree on the line in front of each statement.

After you have filled out the scale, ask some friends to fill it out and discuss the statements with them. Try to figure out why you might change your reactions after your discussion. What difference does it make if you change your mind after talking with your friends? Is this what communication should do?

We will begin our model construction by looking at a very well known model of communication—that of Claude Shannon and Warren Weaver (1962). Although this model was developed for information flow through electronic equipment (radio, telephone, telegraph), it was shown to have some applications to human communication by Warren Weaver (1949). We have reprinted his article for you and numbered and italicized some of the major ideas you should note as you read it.

SCALE D

The Process of Communication

I FEEL THAT:

_____ 1. human communication is a process, not a product.

_____ 2. meaning resides in the words that we use.

_____ 3. information and meaning are the same.

_____ 4. ambiguity is always detrimental to communication.

_____ 5. redundancy makes communication boring.

_____ 6. we must be objective if we expect to understand what another person is saying.

_____ 7. the speaker has the responsibility to make the listener understand.

_____ 8. communication cannot occur without intent.

_____ 9. if you say what you mean, you don't have to worry about what your listeners get from it.

_____ 10. when we watch television, listen to radio, or read a book, we are *not* engaged in communication.

The Mathematics of Communication*

Warren Weaver

How do men communicate, one with another? The spoken word, either direct or by telephone or radio; the written or printed word, transmitted by hand, by post, by telegraph, or in any other way—these are obvious and common forms of communication. But there are many others. A nod or a wink, a drumbeat in the jungle, a gesture pictured on a television screen, the blinking of a signal light, a bit of music that reminds one of an event in the past, puffs of smoke in the desert air, the movements and posturing in a ballet—all of these are means men use to convey ideas.

The word *communication*, in fact, will be used here in a very broad sense *to include all of the procedures by which one*

1   *mind can affect another. Although the language used will often refer specifically to the communication of speech, practically everything said applies equally to music, to pictures, to a variety of other methods of conveying information.*

2   In communication there seem to be problems at three levels: 1) technical, 2) semantic, and 3) influential.

The technical problems are concerned with the accuracy of transference of information from sender to receiver. They are inherent in all forms of communication, whether by sets of discrete symbols (written speech), or by a varying signal (telephonic or radio transmission of voice or music), or by a varying two-dimensional pattern (television).

The semantic problems are concerned with the interpretation of meaning by the receiver, as compared with the intended meaning of the sender. This is a very deep and involved situation, even when one deals only with the relatively simple problems of communicating through speech. For example, if Mr. X is suspected not to understand what Mr. Y says, then it is not possible, by having Mr. Y do nothing but talk further with Mr. X, completely to clarify this situation in any finite time. If Mr. Y says "Do you now understand me?" and Mr. X says "Certainly I do," this is not necessarily a certification that understanding has been achieved. It may just be that Mr. X did not understand the question. If this sounds silly, try it again as "Cxy pan mnie rozumie?" with the answer "Hai wakkate imasu." In the restricted field of speech communication, the difficulty may be reduced to a tolerable size, but never completely eliminated, by "explanations." *They are presumably never more than approximations to the ideas being explained,* but are understandable when phrased in language that has previously been made reasonably clear by

usage. For example, it does not take long to make the symbol for "yes" in any language understandable.

The problems of influence or effectiveness are concerned with the success with which the meaning conveyed to the receiver leads to the desired conduct on his part. It may seem at first glance undesirably narrow to imply that the purpose of all communication is to influence the conduct of the receiver. But with any reasonably broad definition of conduct, it is çlear that communication either affects conduct or is without any discernible and provable effect at all.

One might be inclined to think that the technical problems involve only the engineering details of good design of a communication system, while the semantic and the effectiveness problems contain most if not all of the philosophical content of the general problem of communication. To see that this is not the case, we must now examine some important recent work in the mathematical theory of communication.

This is by no means a wholly new theory. As the mathematician John von Neumann has pointed out, the 19th-century Austrian physicist Ludwig Boltzmann suggested that some concepts of statistical mechanics were applicable to the concept of information. Other scientists, notably Norbert Wiener of the Massachusetts Institute of Technology, have made profound contributions. The work which will be here reported is that of Claude Shannon of the Bell Telephone Laboratories, which was preceded by that of H. Nyquist and R.V.L. Hartley in the same organization. This work applies in the first instance only to the technical problem, but the theory has broader significance. To begin with, *meaning and effectiveness are inevitably restricted by the theoretical limits of accuracy in symbol transmission.* Even more significant, a theoretical analysis of the technical problem reveals that it overlaps the semantic and the effectiveness problems more than one might suspect.

3 A communication system is symbolically represented in the drawing on pages 60 and 61. *The information source selects a desired message out of a set of possible messages.* (As will be shown, this is a particularly important function.) The transmitter changes this *message*
4 into a *signal* which is sent over the communication channel to the receiver.

The receiver is a sort of inverse transmitter, changing the transmitted *signal* back into a *message,* and handing this message on to the destination. When I talk to you, my brain is the information source, yours the destination; my vocal system is the transmitter, and your ear with the eighth nerve is the receiver.

In the process of transmitting the signal, it is unfortunately characteristic that certain things not intended by the information source are added to the signal. These unwanted additions may be distortions of sound (in telephony, for example), or static (in radio), or distortions in the shape or shading of a picture (television), or errors in transmission (telegraphy or facsimile). *All these changes in*
5 *the signal may be called noise.*

The questions to be studied in a communication system have to do with the amount of information, the capacity of the communication channel, the coding process that may be used to change a message into a signal and the effects of noise.

First off, we have to be clear about the rather strange way in which, in this theory, the word "information" is used; for it has a special sense which, among other things, must not be confused at all with meaning. It is surprising but true that, from the present viewpoint, two

messages, one heavily loaded with meaning and the other pure nonsense, can be equivalent as regards information.

In fact, in this new theory the word *in-*
6 *formation relates not so much to what you* do *say, as to what you* could *say. That is, information is a measure of your freedom of choice when you select a message. If you are confronted with a very elementary situation where you have to choose one of two alternative messages, then it is arbitrarily said that the information associated with this situation is unity.* The concept of information applies not to the individual messages, as the concept of meaning would, but rather to the situation as a whole, the unit information indicating that in this situation one has an amount of freedom of choice, in selecting a message, which it is convenient to regard as a standard or unit amount. The two messages between which one must choose in such a selection can be anything one likes. One might be the King James version of the Bible, and the other might be "Yes."

The remarks thus far relate to artificially simple situations where the information source is free to choose only among several definite messages—like a man picking out one of a set of standard birthday-greeting telegrams. A more natural and more important situation is that in which the information source makes a sequence of choices from some set of elementary symbols, the selected sequence then forming the message. Thus a man may pick out one word after another, these individually selected words then adding up to the message.

Obviously probability plays a major role in the generation of the message, and the choices of the successive symbols depend upon the preceding choices. Thus, if we are concerned with English speech, and if the last symbol chosen is "the," then the probability that the next word will be an article, or a verb form other than a verbal, is very small. After the three words "in the event," the probability for "that" as the next word is fairly high, and for "elephant" as the next word is very low. Similarly, the probability is low for such a sequence of words as "Constantinople fishing nasty pink." Incidentally, it is low, but not zero, for it is perfectly possible to think of a passage in which one sentence closes with "Constantinople fishing," and the next begins with "Nasty pink." (We might observe in passing that the sequence under discussion *has* occurred in a single good English sentence, namely the one second preceding.)

As a matter of fact, Shannon has shown that when letters or words chosen at random are set down in sequences dictated by probability considerations alone, they tend to arrange themselves in meaningful words and phrases *(see illustration on page 66).*

Now let us return to the idea of information. *The quantity which uniquely meets the natural requirements that one sets up for a measure of information turns out to be exactly that which is known in thermodynamics as entropy, or the degree of randomness, or of "shuffledness" if you will, in a situation.* It is expressed in terms of the various probabilities involved.

7

To those who have studied the physical sciences, it is most significant that an entropy-like expression appears in communication theory as a measure of information. The concept of entropy, introduced by the German physicist Rudolf Clausius nearly 100 years ago, closely associated with the name of Boltzmann, and given deep meaning by Willard Gibbs of Yale in his classic work on statistical mechanics, has become so basic and pervasive a concept that Sir Arthur Eddington remarked: *"The law that entropy always increases—the second law of thermodynamics—holds, I think, the supreme position among the laws of Nature."*

8

Thus when one meets the concept of entropy in communication theory, he has a right to be rather excited. That in-

A communication system may be reduced to these fundamental elements. In telephony the signal is a varying electric current, and the channel is a wire. In speech the signal is varying sound pressure, and the channel the air. Frequently things not intended by the information source are impressed on the signal. The static of radio is one example; distortion in telephony is another. All these additions may be called noise.

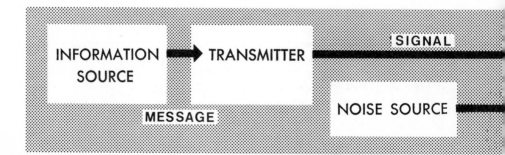

formation should be measured by entropy is, after all, natural when we remember that information is associated with the amount of freedom of choice we have in constructing messages. Thus one can say of a communication source, just as he would also say of a thermodynamic ensemble: *"This situation is highly organized; it is not characterized by a large degree of randomness or of choice—that is to say, the information, or the entropy, is low."*

We must keep in mind that in the mathematical theory of communication we are concerned not with the meaning of individual messages but with the whole statistical nature of the information source. Thus one is not surprised that the capacity of a channel of communication is to be described in terms of the amount of information it can transmit, or better, in terms of its ability to transmit what is produced out of a source of a given information.

The transmitter may take a written message and use some code to encipher this message into, say, a sequence of numbers, these numbers then being sent over the channel as the signal. *Thus one says, in general, that the function of the transmitter is to encode, and that of the receiver to decode, the message.* The theory provides for very sophisticated transmitters and receivers—such, for example, as possess "memories," so that the

9

way they encode a certain symbol of the message depends not only upon this one symbol but also upon previous symbols of the message and the way they have been encoded.

We are now in a position to state the fundamental theorem for a noiseless channel transmitting discrete symbols. This theorem relates to a communication channel which has a capacity of C units per second, accepting signals from an information source of H units per second. The theorem states that by devising proper coding procedures for the transmitter it is possible to transmit symbols over the channel at an average rate which is nearly C/H, but which, no matter how clever the coding, can never be made to exceed C/H.

Viewed superficially, say in rough analogy to the use of transformers to match impedances in electrical circuits, it seems very natural, although certainly pretty neat, to have this theorem which says that efficient coding is that which matches the statistical characteristics of information source and channel. But when it is examined in detail for any one of the vast array of situations to which this result applies, one realizes how deep and powerful this theory is.

How does noise affect information? Information, we must steadily remember, is a measure of one's freedom of choice in

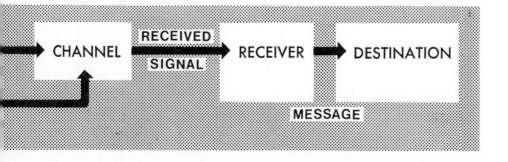

selecting a message. The greater this freedom of choice, the greater is the uncertainty that the message actually selected is some particular one. *Thus greater freedom of choice, greater uncertainty and greater information all go hand in hand.*

If noise is introduced, then the received message contains certain distortions, certain errors, certain extraneous material, that would certainly lead to increased uncertainty. But if the uncertainty is increased, the information is increased, and this sounds as though the noise were beneficial!

It is true that when there is noise, the received signal is selected out of a more varied set of signals than was intended by the sender. This situation beautifully illustrates the semantic trap into which one can fall if he does not remember that *"information" is used here with a special meaning that measures freedom of choice and hence uncertainty as to what choice has been made. Uncertainty that arises by virtue of freedom of choice on the part of the sender is desirable uncertainty. Uncertainty that arises because of errors or because of the influence of noise is undesirable uncertainty.* To get the useful information in the received signal we must subtract the spurious portion. This is accomplished, in the theory, by establishing a quantity known as the "equivocation," meaning the amount of ambiguity introduced by noise. One then refines or extends the previous definition of the capacity of a noiseless channel, and states that the capacity of a noisy channel is defined to be equal to the maximum rate at which useful information (*i.e.,* total uncertainty minus noise uncertainty) can be transmitted over the channel.

Now, finally, we can state the great central theorem of this whole communication theory. Suppose a noisy channel of capacity C is accepting in-

formation from a source of entropy H, *entropy corresponding to the number of possible messages from the source.* If the channel capacity C is equal to or larger than H, then by devising appropriate coding systems the output of the source can be transmitted over the channel with as little error as one pleases. But if the channel capacity C is less than H, the entropy of the source, then it is impossible to devise codes which reduce the error frequency as low as one may please.

However clever one is with the coding process, it will always be true that after the signal is received there remains some undesirable uncertainty about what the message was; and this undesirable uncertainty—this noise or equivocation—will always be equal to or greater than H minus C. But there is always at least one code capable of reducing this undesirable uncertainty down to a value that exceeds H minus C by a small amount.

This powerful theorem gives a precise and almost startlingly simple description of the utmost dependability one can ever obtain from a communication channel which operates in the presence of noise. One must think a long time, and consider many applications, before he fully realizes how powerful and general this amazingly compact theorem really is. One single application can be indicated here, but in order to do so, we must go back for a moment to the idea of the information of a source.

Having calculated the *entropy (or the information, or the freedom of choice)* of a certain information source, one can compare it to the maximum value this entropy could have, subject only to the condition that the source continue to employ the same symbols. *The ratio of the actual to the maximum entropy is called the relative entropy of the source.* If the relative entropy of a certain source is, say, eight-tenths, this means roughly

10

11

that this source is, in its choice of symbols to form a message, about 80 per cent as free as it could possible be with these same symbols. *One minus the relative entropy is called the "redundancy."* That is to say, this fraction of the message is unnecessary in the sense that if it were missing the message would still be essentially complete, or at least could be completed.

It is most interesting to note that the redundancy of English is just about 50 per cent. In other words, about half of the letters or words we choose in writing or speaking are under our free choice, and about half are really controlled by the statistical structure of the language, although we are not ordinarily aware of it. Incidentally, this is just about the minimum of freedom (or relative entropy) in the choice of letters that one must have to be able to construct satisfactory crossword puzzles. In a language that had only 20 per cent of freedom, or 80 per cent redundancy, it would be impossible to construct crossword puzzles in sufficient complexity and number to make the game popular.

Now since English is about 50 per cent redundant, it would be possible to save about one-half the time of ordinary telegraphy by a proper encoding process, provided one transmitted over a noiseless channel. When there is noise on a channel, however, there is some real advantage in not using a coding process that eliminates all of the redundancy. For the remaining redundancy helps combat the noise. It is the high redundancy of English, for example, that makes it easy to correct errors in spelling that have arisen during transmission.

The communication systems dealt with so far involve the use of a discrete set of symbols—say letters—only moderately numerous. One might well expect that the theory would become almost indefinitely more complicated when it

seeks to deal with continuous messages such as those of the speaking voice, with its continuous variation of pitch and energy. As is often the case, however, a very interesting mathematical theorem comes to the rescue. As a practical matter, one is always interested in a continuous signal which is built up of simple harmonic constituents, not of all frequencies but only of those that lie wholly within a band from zero to, say, W cycles per second. Thus very satisfactory communication can be achieved over a telephone channel that handles frequencies up to about 4,000, although the human voice does contain higher frequencies. With frequencies up to 10,000 or 12,000, high-fidelity radio transmission of symphonic music is possible.

The theorem that helps us is one which states that a continuous signal, T seconds in duration and band-limited in frequency to the range from zero to W, can be completely specified by stating 2TW numbers. This is really a remarkable theorem. Ordinarily a continuous curve can be defined only approximately by a finite number of points. But if the curve is built up out of simple harmonic constituents of a limited number of frequencies, as a complex sound is built up out of a limited number of pure tones, then a finite number of quantities is all that is necessary to define the curve completely.

Thanks partly to this theorem, and partly to the essential nature of the situation, it turns out that the extended theory of continuous communication is somewhat more difficult and complicated mathematically, but not essentially different from the theory for discrete symbols. Many of the statements for the discrete case require no modification for the continuous case, and others require only minor change.

The mathematical theory of communication is so general that one does not need to say what kinds of symbols are being considered—whether written letters or words, or musical notes, or spoken words, or symphonic music, or pictures. The relationships it reveals apply to all these and to other forms of communication. The theory is so imaginatively motivated that it deals with the real inner core of the communication problem.

One evidence of its generality is that the theory contributes importantly to, and in fact is really the basic theory of, cryptography, which is of course a form of coding. In a similar way, the theory contributes to the problem of translation from one language to another, although the complete story here clearly requires consideration of meaning, as well as of information. Similarly, the ideas developed in this work connect so closely with the problem of the logical design of computing machines that it is no surprise that Shannon has written a paper on the design of a computer that would be capable of playing a skillful game of chess. And it is of further pertinence to the present contention that his paper closes with the remark that either one must say that such a computer "thinks," or one must substantially modify the conventional implication of the verb "to think."

The theory goes further. Though ostensibly applicable only to problems at the technical level, it is helpful and suggestive at the levels of semantics and effectiveness as well. The formal diagram of a communication system on pages 60 and 61 can, in all likelihood, be extended to include the central issues of meaning and effectiveness.

Thus when one moves to those levels it may prove to be essential to take account of the statistical characteristics of the destination. One can imagine, as an addition to the diagram, another box labeled *"Semantic Receiver"* interposed between the engineering receiver (which changes signals to messages) and the destination. *This semantic receiver subjects the message to a second decoding, the demand on this one being that it must match the statistical semantic characteristics of the message to the statistical semantic capacities of the totality of receivers, or of that subset of receivers which constitutes the audience one wishes to affect.* [13]

Similarly one can imagine another box in the diagram which, inserted between the information source and transmitter, would be labeled *"Semantic Noise"* (not to be confused with "engineering noise"). *This would represent distortions of meaning introduced by the information source, such as a speaker, which are not intentional but nevertheless affect the destination, or listener. And the problem of semantic decoding must take this semantic noise into account.* It is also possible to think of a treatment or adjustment of the original message that would make the sum of message meaning plus semantic noise equal to the desired total message meaning at the destination. [14]

Another way in which the theory can be helpful in improving communication is suggested by the fact that error and confusion arise and fidelity decreases when, no matter how good the coding, one tries to crowd too much over a channel. *A general theory at all levels will surely have to take into account not only the capacity of the channel but also (even the words are right!) the capacity of the audience. If you overcrowd the capacity of the audience, it is probably true, by direct analogy, that you do not fill the audience up and then waste only the remainder by spilling. More likely, and again by direct analogy, you force a general error and confusion.*

The concept of information developed in this theory at first seems disappointing and bizarre—disappointing because it has nothing to do with meaning, and bizarre because it deals not with a single message but rather with the statistical character of a whole ensemble of messages, bizarre also because in these statistical terms the words information and uncertainty find themselves partners.

But we have seen upon further examination of the theory that this analysis has so penetratingly cleared the air that one is now perhaps for the first time ready for a real theory of meaning. An engineering communication theory is just like a very proper and discreet girl at the telegraph office accepting your telegram. She pays no attention to the meaning, whether it be sad or joyous or embarrassing. But she must be prepared to deal intelligently with all messages that come to her desk. This idea that a communication system ought to try to deal with all possible messages, and that the intelligent way to try is to base design on the statistical character of the source, is surely not without significance for communication in general. Language must be designed, or developed, with a view to the totality of things that man may wish to say; but not being able to accomplish everything, it should do as well as possible as often as possible. That is to say, it too should deal with its task statistically.

This study reveals facts about the statistical structure of the English language, as an example, which must seem significant to students of every phase of language and communication. It suggests, as a particularly promising lead, the application of probability theory to semantic studies. Especially pertinent is the powerful body of probability theory dealing with what mathematicians call the Markoff processes, whereby past events influence present probabilities, since this theory is specifically adapted to handle one of the most significant but difficult aspects of meaning, namely the influence of context. One has the vague feeling that information and meaning may prove to be something like a pair of canonically conjugate variables in quantum theory, that is, that information and meaning may be subject to some joint restriction that compels the sacrifice of one if you insist on having much of the other.

Or perhaps meaning may be shown to be analogous to one of the quantities on which the entropy of a thermodynamic ensemble depends. Here Eddington has another apt comment:

"Suppose that we were asked to arrange the following in two categories—*distance, mass, electric force, entropy, beauty, melody.*

"I think there are the strongest grounds for placing entropy alongside beauty and melody, and not with the first three. *Entropy is only found when the parts are viewed in association, and it is by viewing or hearing the parts in association that beauty and melody are discerned.* All three are features of arrangement. It is a pregnant thought that one of these three associates should be able to figure as a commonplace quantity of science. The reason why this stranger can pass itself off among the aborigines of the physical world is that it is able to speak their language, *viz.,* the language of arithmetic."

One feels sure that Eddington would have been willing to include the word meaning along with beauty and melody; and one suspects he would have been thrilled to see, in this theory, that entropy not only speaks the language of arithmetic; it also speaks the language of language.

1. Zero-order approximation

XFOML RXKHRJFFJUJ ZLPWCFWKCYJ
FFJEYVKCQSGXYD QPAAMKBZAACIBZLHJQD

2. First-order approximation

OCRO HLI RGWR NMIELWIS EU LL NBNESEBYA TH EEI
ALHENHTTPA OOBTTVA NAH BRL

3. Second-order approximation

ON IE ANTSOUTINYS ARE T INCTORE ST BE S DEAMY
ACHIN D ILONASIVE TUCOOWE AT TEASONARE FUSO
TIZIN ANDY TOBE SEACE CTISBE

4. Third-order approximation

IN NO IST LAT WHEY CRATICT FROURE BIRS GROCID
PONDENOME OF DEMONSTURES OF THE REPTAGIN IS
REGOACTIONA OF CRE

5. First-Order Word Approximation

REPRESENTING AND SPEEDILY IS AN GOOD APT OR
COME CAN DIFFERENT NATURAL HERE HE THE A IN
CAME THE TO OF TO EXPERT GRAY COME TO FUR-
NISHES THE LINE MESSAGE HAD BE THESE.

6. Second-Order Word Approximation

THE HEAD AND IN FRONTAL ATTACK ON AN ENGLISH
WRITER THAT THE CHARACTER OF THIS POINT IS
THEREFORE ANOTHER METHOD FOR THE LETTERS
THAT THE TIME OF WHO EVER TOLD THE PROBLEM
FOR AN UNEXPECTED

Artificial language results when letters or words are set down statistically. 1. Twenty-six letters and one space are chosen at random. 2. Letters are chosen according to their frequency in English. 3. Letters are chosen according to the frequency with which they follow other letters. 4. Letters are chosen according to frequency with which they follow two other letters. Remaining examples do the same with words instead of letters.

We would like to draw particular attention to the definition of communication put forth here: that communication includes *"all of the procedures by which one mind can affect another"* (1). Immediately we see that it has a behavioristic orientation— a stimulus is acting upon an organism. The model does give this organism a mind; at least the sender may choose into what signal the message is encoded. But it doesn't allow the "mind" of the receiver much freedom for creating its own stimulation or modifying the stimuli that it receives. It is a rather mechanistic model and assumes a series of computerlike steps through which the information passes and by which it is added to the bank of information already there. Let's not be too hasty to rid ourselves of a behavioristic model, however, for we may be throwing out the baby with the bath.

This type of model works very well for studying information flow between two stations, or even between two people, if we add to it the ability to flip-flop so that sender becomes receiver and vice versa. It works very well if you can *objectify* the people in the communication event. But perhaps there are concepts presented here that can be applied in a more "human" way. Certainly when we try to understand the problems presented on the semantic and influential levels (2) we must consider the humanist's whole-person model. Weaver's suggestion that the message is inside the speaker or listener (3) indicates a need for a consideration of mental processes. This is more clearly emphasized when he discusses encoding and decoding (9), the semantic receiver (13), and semantic noise (14). If the message is in the mind, then it must become a coded message in the form of a signal that can be transmitted (4).

This is a very important concept, for we have long been calling that which we speak or write the message. In reality, it is a *signal* with all kinds of information coded into it from which the recipient must decode a message. The form this coded message takes is a conscious or unconscious choice of the sender. If we could ascertain how many choices a person had in any given communication situation, we could then compute the information in any given signal (6). The one thing we can be sure of is that since a signal is inherently organized it is decreasing entropy, or degree of randomness (7). (Effective communication would decrease it even more. Why?) However, the presence of noise (5) interferes with this process and increases entropy. It should be noted that *noise may be defined as anything that interferes with effective communication,* and, therefore, it may occur at any juncture in the communication process (Borden 1963). We'll have more to say about this later.

The concept of desirable uncertainty (10) is definitely a humanistic concept. If we are free to choose, then our art of choosing decreases entropy because it organizes and structures a piece of reality. If it were a random process, we would be trying to communicate using signals such as those in Weaver's zero-order approximations of artificial language (see p. 66). The very act of communicating is a structuring of behavior and decreases entropy because it organizes our thoughts and, if effective, organizes the thoughts of our listeners. This counteracts the second law of thermodynamics (8) and "builds up" order in the universe. It is consistent with the laws of physical science in that energy must be expended to counteract this natural propensity to randomness, and we expend energy (both physical and mental) when we communicate.

When Weaver talks about relative entropy (11) and redundancy (12), it should be noted that he is talking about the word or letter level of the signal (i.e., for us to understand written English some letters are not needed, nor are some words). If he were to speculate on the message level, he would find the relative entropy to be much lower, for in any given situation we find that the expected (socially required?) messages are *only a small subset of the total number of choices we have.* At first you may disagree with that statement, but think back to any communication event you have been in recently and let your mind begin to list the *sayables* and *do-ables* in that event. Most of us are so locked into our environment that we lose the ability to communicate creatively in most situations (more on this in Part 5 of this book).

The suggestion that the message resides inside the person and that the signal is the external, coded, transmitted form of it has many implications for human communication. Signals are often subdivided into the categories of vocal-nonvocal and verbal-nonverbal. Though these categories are often confused and used interchangeably, it should be clear that "vocal" *refers only to sounds created by the vocalization mechanisms* and "verbal" *refers only to that part of the signal composed of words and their syntactic structures.* We can see that one can make a clear distinction between the categories and their interactions (see Figure 2). It is up to the speaker to choose the appropriate code by which he or she can evoke the desired message in the mind of the listener.

Using the Shannon-Weaver model, we may be able to pinpoint some of the sources of real or potential problems in the communication process. A

	VERBAL	NONVERBAL
VOCAL	speaking	stress, pitch, volume, etc.
NONVOCAL	writing	body language, dance, art, etc.

Figure 2 A four-way categorization of communication codes.

more humanistic representation of this model can be seen in Figure 3 (see p. 70). This depicts the seven stages through which information passes from the time it is conceived in the mind of the communicator as Message$_1$ until it evokes Message$_2$ in the mind of the communicatee. The return cycle shows the response of the communicatee, which is in reality a message conceived by this person, transforming him or her into a communicator and the original communicator into a communicatee.

The linearity of the figure makes it appear as though these processes occur in sequence, but in reality they may occur simultaneously, with several of the senses taking part in the reception of the signals and many facets of human behavior transmitting the signals. For example, depending on how close you are to a person and how intimate you are with him or her, you may be receiving signals of sight, sound, touch, heat, smell, and taste—all simultaneously. It's enough to make your head spin!

An interesting aspect of this communicative behavior is that neither person may be aware of sending or receiving most of the signals. We say that effective communication has occurred when Message$_1$ is similar to Message$_2$ (or Message$_3$ to Message$_4$). *The degree of effectiveness is equal to the degree of similarity of meaning created by the speaker and the listener:*

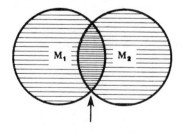

Similarity of meaning.

Using this model to explain human communication brings one to ask why Message$_1$ may differ from Message$_2$. A partial answer lies in the concept called "noise." There are five places where "noise" may occur in the communication process, identified as Noise$_1$ through Noise$_5$ in Figure 3. In human communication there are at least five distinct types of noise also. What we commonly call noise — that which drowns out another person's voice, or interferes with the signal while on its way from speaker to listener — is labeled Noise$_3$, and we call it *physical noise*. Within a person's mind, where encoding and decoding occur, there are three other types of noise: *neurological noise* — interference in the neurological processes that allow nerve impulses to pass from cell to cell, resulting in aphasia, mental retardation, or brain damage; *psychological noise* — thought, memories, repressed fears, etc., that interfere with the transformation of the message into a signal or a signal into a message and result in such things as stage fright, boredom, or stress; and *cultural noise* — that which stems from our acculturated beliefs (e.g., nonconscious ideologies, prejudices, and sensitivities). These three types of interference occur at Noise$_1$ and Noise$_5$ phases. In the transmitter and receiver phases, both neurological and psychological noise may occur, as well as *physiological noise* — interference from faulty muscle action or from physical structure, such as stuttering, lisps, a beautiful body, or a disfigured face. These three types of interference occur at Noise$_2$ and Noise$_4$ phases of the communication process.

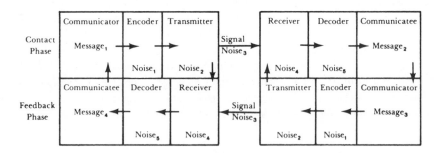

Figure 3 A somewhat humanized diagram of the Shannon-Weaver model of communication.

To aid you in understanding the Shannon-Weaver model of the communication process, the following activities are suggested.

INFORMATION-FLOW ACTIVITIES

1. Join a group of no more than four other class members and apply the definition of communication given by Weaver to several communication situations. Consider the effect of the following variables:

Source	Signal
Message	Entropy
Channel	Redundancy
Receiver	Noise
Feedback	

2. Using Figure 2 as a guide, where would you put (a) screams, (b) moans, (c) whistles, (d) traffic lights, (e) mathematics? Explain your answers.

3. Using the Shannon-Weaver model, discuss the noise from the following conditions (when might it occur? what might its effect be?): (a) psychological noise (paranoia, schizophrenia, etc.), (b) physiological noise (cleft palate, damaged eardrum, etc.), (c) neurological noise (optic and auditory nerve, etc.), (d) cultural noise (male-female communication, etc.), (e) physical noise (high winds, loud stereo, etc.).

4. List several situations in which you have perceived various types of noise. What factors might have caused this noise? How could this noise have been overcome? Did this noise cause communication problems or failures to communicate?

5. With the cooperation of other members of your class, attempt to determine ways we might discover what goes on in another person's mind. Might this be done through an analysis of behavior, psychoanalysis, self-disclosure, ESP, etc.?

6. There are other types of noise that may occur in the process of communication, including linguistic, conceptual, and symbolic. In a group, define these three types of noise and see how many more you can generate. Report your efforts to the class.

According to the Shannon-Weaver model, information flows through various phases and is acted upon by various processes. Although it is an extremely simplified model of human communication, it allows us to locate some of the problem areas in this process. Nevertheless, it suffers because of its simplicity. One of its shortcomings becomes apparent when we realize that *information is not additive*. If we tell you that you look cute and sexy, this does not add up to "We like you," for in reality we may have other feelings about "cute and sexy" boys. (And what does the last sentence add up to?!) The process is further complicated by the fact that *information acquisition is not sequential*. We have at least five senses that are all receiving stimuli simultaneously, all with the ability to process several dimensions of this information at the same time (volume, pitch, rate), and all processed with varying degrees of internal noise (past experiences, present emotions, and future expectations). Since we do not know the internal structures of the mind, it is difficult for us to use the Shannon-Weaver model for studying anything other than the information-flow definition of communication it presents. To our way of thinking this is not sufficient for an adequate understanding of human communication, even though it is helpful.

You may feel the same way, so we have included an inventory of communicative behaviors (Scale E) in which you can describe your communicative behavior. As you fill it out, think deeply about each activity so you can give an *honest* appraisal of *yourself.* Put a 1 for almost never, a 2 for sometimes, and a 3 for usually. *Remember, this is how you see yourself.*

SCALE E

A Communicative Behavior Inventory

I FEEL THAT I:

_____ 1. trust others as important human beings.

_____ 2. do not say things I don't mean.

_____ 3. assert myself when necessary.

_____ 4. like to get into deep intellectual discussions.

_____ 5. am open in my communication with others.

_____ 6. am able to express my feelings whenever I need to.

_____ 7. can talk about sex without being embarrassed.

_____ 8. am too intense in my communicative behavior.

_____ 9. can talk about personal things with close friends.

_____ 10. spend too much time talking about people.

_____ 11. am too concerned with people's appearance to really communicate with them.

_____ 12. am too structured to allow myself the freedom to "know" other people.

_____ 13. form my opinions of others very quickly.

_____ 14. allow my opinions about people to change.

_____ 15. encourage my friends to give me honest feedback.

_____ 16. commit too quickly to friendships.

_____ 17. understand why my friends behave as they do.

_____ 18. become attached too quickly to people of the opposite sex.

_____ 19. infer too much from other people's behavior.

_____ 20. give more than I get from my communicative experiences.

If you care to see how closely your feelings agree with someone else's perceptions of you, ask a friend to fill out this table for you (I FEEL THAT YOU). Then compare and discuss the results. If there are differences, see if you can find out why. This should help you begin to change in the direction you would like to go.

A Humanistic Approach to Communication

There is another definition of communication that presents a different view of this process. Gail Myers and Michele Myers (1973, p. 12) define communica-tion as *"a generally predictable, multilevel, continuous, and always-present process of the sharing of meaning through symbol interaction."* The words that bear the most significance for us in this definition are "sharing of mean-ing." What is implicit to sharing meaning? What is necessary for such sharing to take place? What can be expected to result from this sharing? Hopefully you have already answered these questions and are actively engaged in this type of communication. It is an orientation to communication that is advo-cated by nearly everyone involved in facilitating the development of healthy human beings, but few of us practice it. So let's see what it entails.

SHARING MEANING

To share is to let someone else have a part of or use something that belongs to you. In the material sense, it results in a loss to you of part of your possessions or some of the life expectancy of the item. Part of it is used up, and although this may bring you pleasure in other areas, it results in a depletion of your resources. For example, I loan you my car and you put 100 miles on it. That means I cannot put that 100 miles on it and have lost some of its usefulness. This aspect of sharing assumes that there are limitations in quantity or usefulness of the shared item. When sharing is applied to communication, however, the assumption of limitedness needs to be revised. There are instances when the above principles hold (sharing time, energy, emotions), but there are other instances when sharing enhances or prolongs the life of the shared item (experiences, ideas, love). In those cases, sharing itself becomes a part of the experience shared.

There are two things necessary for sharing to take place: involvement and commitment. These are the same two things that must be present for meaning to occur. We may be part of, or an observer of, an experience, a communication event, but that event does not tell us what it means. George Kelly (1970, p. 3) says that "events do not tell us what to do, nor do they carry their meanings engraved on their backs for us to discover. For better or worse we ourselves create the only meanings they will ever convey during our lifetime." It is only if we become involved in the experiencing of the event (and this necessitates some commitment to its outcome) that the event becomes meaningful. Thus, through involvement and commitment, sharing precipitates a meaningful relationship. The depth of my involvement with a friend is directly proportional to the commitment I have to that friendship; together they regulate the amount of sharing (of myself and my experiences) I participate in with that friend.

The reverse of the above situation may also occur. We meet someone and begin to share, perhaps just talk, with him or her. It may have been only a chance meeting, or perhaps we have something in common, like a class or apartment building or a friend. As we begin to share talk, we also begin to share ourselves (our time, our ideas, our opinions); we become more involved. We may not realize we are becoming committed to this person (that a relationship is developing) until we miss him or her at the usual sharing place (classroom, cafeteria, laundromat, bar). Of course there are all kinds of people—some get involved immediately, others take longer; some commit quickly, others hold back to see how the relationship will develop. But regardless of how it turns out in the long run, when one shares experiences with another, a relationship ensues. To communicate is to relate, and vice versa.

But how do we relate? What do we talk about? Does it matter? George Simmel (Wolff 1950, p. 53) says that "among all sociological phenomena whatever, with the possible exception of looking at one another, talk is the purest and most sublimated form of two-way-ness. It thus is the fulfillment of a relation that wants to be nothing but relation—in which, that is, what usually is the mere form of interaction becomes its self-sufficient content." Just the fact that we make contact with another is a form of sharing, telling the other that he or she exists. His or her feedback (response) tells us the same thing. This contact may be positive or negative. Though positive contact would seem to be the most welcomed, it is not always the most fruitful in terms of human growth and self-awareness.

Systems theory tells us that negative feedback is necessary, else the system will blow up. If your thermostat does not tell the furnace to shut off, it will keep getting hotter and hotter until it explodes or burns up. People may be this way too. If they are never given the limits of their activity through negative feedback (saying no), they may carry on until they destroy the relationship. It should be apparent, then, how crucial communication is in any relationship, for we must share our feelings about that relationship, whether they be positive or negative.

Many people have internal regulators that turn their system off before it blows up, but why is it so difficult for us to give negative feedback? Herbert Fensterheim and Jean Baer (1975, p. 114) say that "wearing a 'public face' proves effective in certain jobs or uncomplicated social situations (like cocktail parties); it cannot work in the close relationship. If you adopt a mask you will be unable to communicate intimately." If we are afraid to share negative feelings, we usually adopt a mask. We agree with everything everyone says, even when they disagree with us. Sometimes we carry this type of behavior into our intimate relationships, hoping (or thinking) that our friends will never see beneath our mask. We can rarely win at this game, for sooner or later we have to open up. This is particularly true in marriage-type relationships. Fensterheim and Baer (1975, p. 114) go on to say that

> good communication exists as the core of a successful marriage. *If you don't express your feelings openly, the intimacy of sharing decreases.* Misunderstandings develop. When things don't work out, good communication provides a corrective factor. Without this, small irritating situations grow into giant problems. Your dissatisfactions continue without abatement, and may come out in the most destructive ways. Eventually, the lack of openness makes strangers of two people who once promised at the altar to "love, honor, and cherish" each other until death. The relationship ceases to grow. The couple then has a choice: dead marriage or divorce. (emphasis ours)

What does it mean to open up? Are there certain subjects we must talk about—share? In a recent study we asked college students to rank ten areas of human involvement in their order of importance to long-term male-female relationships. The results are given in Table 2 and may say something about what we should be able to talk about, or take part in, in such a relationship. Essentially, the table shows that communication between two people in a long-term arrangement is affected by their feelings and needs in these areas. (It is interesting to note that all of these dimensions show up in many of the computer dating-information forms.) It also tells us what types of sharing are considered important in such a relationship.

TABLE 2
Dimensions of Communicative Involvement

Dimension	Definition
1. Personal	Degree to which one is able, comfortable, and/or needs to reveal oneself to another (e.g., to talk about fears, weaknesses, desires, feelings).
2. Emotional	Degree to which one is able, comfortable, and/or needs to be in control of or is controlled by one's emotions (e.g., ability to laugh, cry, feel, empathize).
3. Cognitive	Level of abstraction on which one is able, comfortable, and/or needs to communicate (e.g., accepts the way things are or asks why).
4. Sexual	Degree to which one is able, comfortable, and/or needs to partake of human sexual behavior (e.g., kissing, petting, intercourse, deviations).
5. Intensity	Degree to which one is able to cope with, is comfortable with, and/or needs a certain level of personal drive or motivation (e.g., psychological, physical, professional).
6. Domestic	Degree to which one is able to cope with, be comfortable with, and/or needs a specific type of home environment (e.g., children, structure, tidiness).
7. Physical	Degree to which another fits one's ideal image in terms of physical attractiveness, personal hygiene, physical behavior (e.g., body language, dress, comeliness).
8. Social	Degree to which one is able, comfortable, and/or needs to participate in social activities (e.g., parties, public entertainment, outings).
9. Environmental	Degree of desire, acceptance, and/or need for a specific environment in which to live (e.g., city, country, suburb, geographical location).
10. Spiritual	Degree to which one is able to cope with, be comfortable with, and/or needs some form of spiritual guidance in one's lifestyle (e.g., religion, mysticism, humanism).

We found it interesting that the ranking of these areas did not fit the publicized image of normal males and females in our culture. For example, some sources would like you to believe that sex is the most important form of sharing—it came out fourth. Others say that spiritual dimensions are the most important — it was ranked tenth. The fact that the personal dimension came out first is not too surprising, but discussions with the students revealed that this was the desired situation and not necessarily the way things were. It is also interesting to us that the first three dimensions are very humanistic ones. Since males and females did not differ significantly in their ranking of these dimensions, we must assume that they both see these as primary areas of concern in marriage-type relationships.

Communication may be described as a contact sport. It is the only way we have of contacting others, and although we may not be aware of our reliance on it, it is the hub of our existence. Our senses pick up the signals transmitted by others and we create meaning from them. The meaning we generate is contingent upon many facets of the communication events in which we are engaged — for example, the types of noise present. We should be very aware of the fact, however, that the climate of a relationship is affected significantly by the initial contact. If the first time you met a person he or she was cold and indifferent, it was probably hard to change this image (Zunin and Zunin 1972). These authors go so far as to say that when lovers (even husbands and wives!) wake up in the morning it would be beneficial for them to role-play a warm relationship for the first three or four minutes, whether they feel that way or not. Share something positive and the whole day may seem positive.

We cannot get away from the fact that our environment has a great deal to do with our communicative behavior. Immediate presence is a major factor in facilitating communication. (The Bell Telephone ads make this point very well.) You don't say good morning to someone who isn't there. (If you do, you are liable to be ferreted away to a "safe" place.) We all know how difficult it is to maintain a relationship across great distances. To the phrase "absence makes the heart grow fonder" we often hear added such phrases as "of someone else," "but *presents* do it better," or "of food and drink." There is just something about being together that facilitates a relationship!

We should not mistake this environmental variable as the source for or cause of the development of a good, lasting relationship, however, for the sharing of space, time, and one's physical world may also aid in the deterioration of a relationship. Too much togetherness may smother the participants. This is the focus of several books on freedom in marriage, such as *Open Marriage* by Nena and George O'Neill (1972), and is expressed very well by Kahlil Gibran in *The Prophet* (1971, pp. 16-17):

> Then Almitra spoke again and said, And what of Marriage, master?
> And he answered saying:
> You were born together, and together you shall be forevermore.
> You shall be together when the white wings of death scatter your days.
> Ay, you shall be together even in the silent memory of God.
> But let there be spaces in your togetherness,
> And let the winds of the heavens dance between you.

Love one another, but make not a bond of love :
Let it rather be a moving sea between the shores of your souls.
Fill each other's cup but drink not from one cup.
Give one another of your bread but eat not from the same loaf.
Sing and dance together and be joyous, but let each one of you be alone,
Even as the strings of a lute are alone though they quiver with the
     same music.

Give your hearts, but not into each other's keeping.
For only the hand of life can contain your hearts.
And stand together, yet not too near together :
For the pillars of the temple stand apart,
And the oak tree and the cypress grow not in each other's shadow.

We cannot say it better. Where, then, is the place of communication in a relationship, and how does this sharing of meaning fit into the development of a relationship? Perhaps the answer can be given in the form of a description of the stages of a developing relationship.

We may use the concept of "intensity of involvement" to indicate how a relationship develops (see Figure 4). The first stage, that of RECOGNITION, occurs many times each day. We pass someone on the street, our eyes meet, we nod or say hello — we have recognized that person as another living being. This does not differ much from the interaction we might have with a dog or some other animal. We have this type of interaction almost continuously in our social lifestyle. It is most noticeable when it is absent. If you do not recognize another living being as such (by pretending he or she is not there), you are communicating the fact that you do not want any part of even the beginning of a relationship.

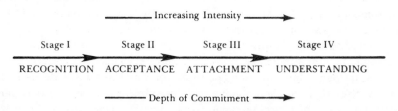

Figure 4   Intensity-of-involvement scale.

It goes without saying that you must recognize another person as a living being before you can accept that person as a human being. At the ACCEPTANCE stage the involvement becomes a little more intense. Two people may never go further than recognition, but if they have recognized each other, they are now able to do something about it. The old-fashioned ploy of a woman's dropping her handkerchief indicated her desire to move to the second stage. (Males are not immune to this behavior. They may borrow books, notes, or pencils to move to stage two.) ACCEPTANCE means that you are willing to get acquainted. The need to get acquainted is quite different for each person, and it is based on many different kinds of likes and dislikes. Physical attraction has been propagated as the major variable in bringing about this stage in a relationship, but since we are sharing very little at this stage, this type of beginning is pretty much an egocentric trip.

As the ACCEPTANCE stage develops, we must find more and more of ourselves and our experiences that we can and are willing to share with others. Mutual sharing, or, should we say, equal sharing (since sharing demands mutuality), increases the involvement we feel in the relationship. We may first only share (communicate) on an *environmental dimension* (e.g., where are you from, where do you live, or where are you going?). We may then move to the *social dimension* and talk about activities and people we know, and get friendly enough to say something about the attractiveness of the other person, the *physical dimension*. In all of these phases we are accumulating knowledge about the other person, who is doing the same with us. This leads to the stage of a relationship we call ATTACHMENT.

During the ACCEPTANCE period we are also picking up information about the other's *domesticity* and *intensity*. These dimensions appear to be very crucial in the move into the ATTACHMENT stage of relationships. The structure you exhibit in your life and the intensity with which you pursue it may make all the difference in the world whether a relationship develops or not. Strangely enough, you may be able to say all you want to about these two dimensions but not be able to override the meaning picked up by others from your behavior patterns. (Actions speak louder than words?) We have all lost one or two potential friends or lovers because we came on too fast ("Hello, my name is Harry, I'm from Pittsburgh, let's go to bed.") or too slow ("Aren't you going to call Bill tonight?" "No. I saw him three weeks ago. I really wish he would ask me out, though."). Have you noticed that the dimensions we have been talking about are progressing up the scale of importance as shown in Table 2?

Perhaps this is the place to say some more about the *intensity dimension*. This variable is often difficult to perceive and deal with in communication situations. We more often go away from such events feeling that something was wrong but not knowing what it was. It is very much involved with what we *expect* to happen. We are continually being made aware of expectations by the emergence of passive groups into active groups. Women's liberation is a case in point. When a woman displays active, aggressive, self-confident behavior, she is often described as a "bitch." When men do a similar thing, they are showing their leadership ability. Active, self-confident women are too intense for many men because they aren't expected to be that way. When women become as aggressive as men, particularly in sexual relations, maybe we can all relax a little and enjoy it more. At this time, such behavior is expected only of prostitutes.

As we pass from the ACCEPTANCE to the ATTACHMENT stage of a relationship, our communication becomes much more involved with "meaningful" experiences—with those events in which we have a more personal commitment. We become more involved with each other and more committed to this involvement. The ATTACHMENT stage may last for some time, and as we become more committed to the relationship, we may explore each other's feeling about sex, probe each other's minds to see how we think, experience each other's emotions to see how strong they are, and dig into each other's lives to see how open we care to be. We are now in the UNDER-STANDING stage of a relationship, and the depth of our commitment to this relationship depends very much on what we find out about each other in this stage. The hierarchy of dimensions given in Table 2 is indicative of the entire relating process (with the exception of the spiritual dimension, and that may be an artifact of college students).

We do not usully make a firm commitment to a long-term or marriage relationship until we have investigated each other's feelings or behaviors on each of these dimensions. Once we have, we can make a decision on whether we want to commit to this relationship or not. A frightening possibility (too often a reality) is that we may move into UNDERSTANDING and back into ATTACHMENT without ever knowing it. In that case we find out just enough about the other person to satisfy our immediate desires and generalize this knowledge to make the person fit our ideal. We may wake up sometime and wonder how we got hooked into this relationship. We can then, almost always, look back and see where and when we stopped communicating (sharing). Even when both parties consciously make a decision to commit to each other, they may find that the very fact that they have reached this level of their relationship seems to engender a lack of communication.

Why is this? What happens to communication when relationships become old? The second definition we gave, that of sharing meaning, is a key to this phenomenon. In a sense, we did not define communication as the sharing of meaning because that is what happens, but because *that is what should happen*. It takes energy and effort to maintain a relationship. Part of our satisfaction and sense of fulfillment in a developing relationship comes from the newness of it all. Since our minds are quick to generalize, we may soon feel that we know all there is to know about the other person and cease to inquire into the structure of the other's reality. We are apt to become as mechanical and unfeeling in our communication as the mechanical model. On the other hand, if we place our emphasis on sharing meaning, then our communication must become personal. To be sure, this places greater responsibility on the person, but it also has greater possibilities for continuing success.

What happens when we get used to someone? Some would say that the communication effectiveness increases because we know more about the other person. Let's look at that for a moment. In getting to know someone, we often ignore the negative aspects and concentrate on the positive ones. In doing so we fail to understand a good proportion of the whole person we are relating to. If we insisted on facing the negative aspects of one's behavior immediately in an open, communicative way (sharing our fears, biases, and longings), we might find that in understanding the other person's approach to life we are not compatible and thus should not commit to as intense a relationship as we had been heading for; we might find that through this openness we both grew in our understanding of each other and were able to modify our respective expectations and behaviors to make us more compatible and thus allow us to commit to the intensity level that we wanted; or we might find one of us could not be open and able to reveal oneself sufficiently to make the relationship fulfilling, thus necessitating an end to the relationship before we became more involved.

A relationship that becomes static and closed is mechanical, and at best we are communicating with stereotypes. This is very little different from the one-way communication of the mass media. They write and perform for a normative audience without immediate feedback. Their awareness of their audience is superficial in the sense of personal involvement. What about the audience? They receive the signal but are powerless to help create a climate of personal involvement. Even though they may be glued to the TV, they can only receive the signal. This feeling of powerlessness becomes apparent when a husband, wife, or friend becomes the "TV set" who just transmits signals but does not hear our feedback. This type of situation is often referred to as *one-way communication.*

We would like to take issue with the concept of *one-way communication and say that it is not communication at all.* By our second definition, communication is the sharing of meaning. We are using this in the sense of having meaning in common with others rather than the sense of partaking of a share of the meaning. To have "in common" implies that the meaning being shared is understood to be the same by both parties. This is an impossible situation if there is no feedback. One-way communication, then, becomes merely perception — the reception and interpretation of a signal. All the meanings generated by it can only be those in the mind of the recipient. This type of behavior makes an ongoing relationship precarious at best.

One way to illustrate the concept of one-way communication is to use the Shannon-Weaver model in its dehumanized form. In that case, we do not care who or what the sender is. If we are the recipient of a signal, we need only decode the meaning from it. The signal could be a beautiful sunset, a couple on the beach that we are "looking in on," a lecturer in the classroom, or John Denver on a record. Decoding information from a signal and generating meaning from it is perception, and we are wholly responsible for the message we generate from it. This messge may or may not be common to both parties. Certainly it lacks a great deal of the understanding of an ongoing relationship.

We mentioned above the idea that a communicator might not hear the feedback of a communicatee. It might also be the case that the communicatee does not provide any feedback. In this case, the sender never knows whether the message was even received, or, if it was, if there was understanding on the part of the recipient. Where is the commonality of the message, then? If both the communicator and the communicatee are closed, then feedback has little meaning, and it is as though they go about leaving signals here and there, with little or no possibility for sharing.

We have described some common communication situations, and they probably sound pretty bad. The real problem, however, is the fact that most of us do not know when we are contributing to such a situation. We may *think* we know when we are open but probably won't even entertain the idea that we may be closed. To help us see these situations more clearly and understand the behavior of the participants better, we would like to give you a quick introduction to one aspect of Eric Berne's world of transactional analysis (Berne 1961, 1964, 1972). The aspect in which we are most interested is his concept of the "stroke."

STROKING

A stroke is defined as "a unit of recognition" (1972, p. 448). Berne elaborates on this definition in his earlier work (1964, p. 15).

> Stroking may be used as a general term for intimate physical contact; in practice it may take various forms. Some people literally stroke an infant; others hug or pat it, while some people pinch it playfully or flip it with a fingertip. These all have their analogues in conversations, so that it seems one might predict how an individual would handle a baby by listening to him talk. By an extension of meaning, "stroking" may be employed colloquially to denote any act implying recognition of another's presence. Hence a *stroke* may be used as the fundamental unit of social action. An exchange of strokes constitutes a *transaction,* which is the unit of social intercourse.

We are not interested in social intercourse, at the moment, but we would like to emphasize the definition of stroking. Since we have settled on "sharing meaning" as the definition of communication, we would like to show that stroking is the basic unit of this process.

Berne makes a very strong point for the human condition called "stimulus-hunger." Studies of sensory deprivation make the same point. If we are cut off from all outside stimuli, our brain, requiring some type of stimulation, stimulates itself, and we begin to hallucinate. If this condition persists, we regress more and more within ourselves until eventually we die. This phenomenon is very much analogous to death through malnutrition. The conclusion that must be drawn is that *sensory stimulation is an absolute requirement of life.* Thus, stimulus-hunger is a fact of life, and one who is deprived of sensory stimulation will be deformed mentally in a way analogous to physical deformation caused by malnutrition. This basic fact of life makes it imperative that we understand the nature of our néed for sensory stimulation and, consequently, our need for human communicaiton.

We maintain that sensory stimulation is not enough. Even with the stimulation of an outside world a person would soon die — perhaps not physically, but certainly psychologically — if part of that stimulation is not contained in human communication. Why do we say this? There is abundant evidence to show that we need others in order to develop our own sense of self (see Part 4 of this book). Without this feedback (sharing of the other's point of view, experience, meaning), we would have no way of knowing what was real. All of our mental activity would be the result of perception, in which case we would be generating our own meaning from those experiences without checking it with others to see if we were still "in the ballpark." As a result, our view of reality would be completely egocentric and we would lose our ability to communicate with others. *Without sharing there is no human growth.*

There are very few real hermits in this world. All of us might like to be one some of the time, but very few, if any, would like to be one all the time. We need to be stroked — to have someone recognize us as human. We will do almost anything to get this attention. Some require more than others, but we all need it sometime. In terms of our intensity-of-involvement scale, it constitutes the first stage of a relationship and is the basic ingredient of all the remaining stages. If our stroke is returned, we have shared the recognition of "being" and have taken the first step into ACCEPTANCE (e.g., you pass someone on the mall and say "hello" [a stroke] and they smile back [a positive stroke] or say "get lost" [a negative stroke]). You may question the validity of the last remark as being a step toward ACCEPTANCE, but *we did not equate acceptance with approval.* I may accept you as a human being and hate your guts.

The nature of the stroke should be explained somewhat so you know where we are coming from. As Berne said, stroking is first thought of as intimate touching. This is no more true for the infant than it is for the adult. Stroking is much more than this. We have shown that stroking may be either positive or negtive. It may also be verbal (the words "I love you") or nonverbal (a kiss), vocal (a spoken endearment) or nonvocal (a written note). If you check back to Figure 2, you will find that strokes may fit into any one of the four categories. If you begin to count the strokes you give and receive, you may find that they fall into one or two of these categories fairly often. A deeper investigation will show that *most stroking is done nonverbally,* and that we trust the nonverbal strokes more than the verbal ones. It's easy to say "I love you" because it is a conscious behavior, but the way you say it (the vocal-nonverbal part) is usually unconscious and thus more to be trusted.

The eyes, rather than the voice, are the most active strokers we have. RECOGNITION is shown there first. (That is why we have the term "poker face.") If you show no emotions in your eyes, people do not know where you are in relation to them. This can be very disconcerting. The reverse is also true. If you are able to control the expressiveness of your eyes so you can stroke without meaning it, then you set up all kinds of false perceptions in others. If you were to smile at us with your eyes, we might think you were recognizing us approvingly when really you were faking it and hate us both (which may be the case if you don't like what you are reading). The only way we can find out is to have a session of strokes to see if our first perceptions were correct. This constitutes communication, or as Berne states it, "social intercourse."

We have written considerably about overt communicative behavior but have said little about the internal processes that characterize this behavior. If we engage someone in conversation, the very fact that we are talking to him or her is a positive stroke. What we say, as well as the way we say it, may add some more strokes. Sometimes these two types of strokes cancel each other out, but we are always left with the initial stroke, that of contact. Even this may be negated if we come into the event with negative expectations—if, for example, we feel the only reason you are talking to us is because you feel sorry for us. The psychological set with which we approach a communication situation affects the whole event. We have all experienced this both positively (thinking we were being accepted when we were not) and negatively (thinking we were not being accepted when we were).

In defining communication as the sharing of meaning and presenting the dimensions of communicative involvement, the stages of involvement, and the concepts of perception and stroking, we have left many aspects of human relationships unexplored. We are sure that you can explore these areas and glean many rewarding experiences from these activities. To aid you in these explorations, we make the following suggestions.

SHARING-OF-MEANING ACTIVITIES

1. What happens if one member of a male-female relationship becomes too intense (dimension no. 5) at any one of the stages of involvement?
    a. Form a group and role-play several situations of your own creation with varying degrees of intensity. After each one, have the players try to relate to the group how they felt during this experience.
    b. After group discussion, write a position paper on the effects of intensity on male-female relationships.
2. Find some couples who have lived together for at least six months and interview each person separately, to see who does what of the domestic chores.
    a. What are the problems, if any, in their relationship?
    b. Where do these problems fit in the dimensions of communicative involvement?

    c.   Where does the relationship fit on the intensity-of-involvement scale? Do this for at least one each of a male-female, male-male, and female-female couple.

    d.   Can you draw any conclusions?

    e.   Present your report to the class.

3.   Try to keep track of the strokes you give and receive in a two-hour period (say over lunch or dinner).

    a.   How many positive and negative strokes did you give?

    b.   Receive?

    c.   Did they stimulate like kinds of strokes?

    d.   Draw some conclusion about your behavior.

    e.   Draw some conclusion about the behavior of your acquaintances.

4.   It has been suggested that in order to effectively communicate we must *share* meaning—establish some degree of cognitive commonality. How would you respond to such a statement? Give three examples of effective communication and see if your group agrees with your evaluation.

5.   Each of us is involved in a number of relationships. How could we differentiate between the relationships we have with the following persons on the intensity-of-involvement scale? Which of the dimensions of communicative involvement do you feel free to partake of in each relationship: (a) parents, (b) teachers, (c) loved ones, (d) casual acquaintances?

6.   Identify instances in your relationships with others in which you have experienced different forms of stroking. Try to determine the means you employ in stroking others and the results of such activities.

A Model for Humanistic Communication

Our anticipations of how people (including ourselves) will behave in a communication situation is dependent upon (among other things) what model of human nature we hold. (You should go back and work through Scale C, p. 47, at this time.) If we are *behavioristic* and believe in a personality conditioned by the environment, we may feel as though we are responding to external stiumli (if we are aware of it at all). Further, if we do have this sense of awareness, we may very well feel that we are being manipulated by others. In turn, we may also feel that we must manipulate them (i.e., create an environment that will stimulate them to do what we want). There are too many examples of this to need much illustrating here. In keeping with our use of male-female-relationship examples, however, we need mention only one.

Why the dim lights, soft music, good wine, light cologne, and comfortable surroundings for that special evening? Atmosphere?

If you hold the *Freudian view,* you may have the same feelings about the external environment but also realize that you must be aware of the internal forces trying to get out. In the example above you may engage in conversation or visual imagery that will excite or inhibit the inner drives of the communicants, or even in some form of drugs (alcohol) in large enough doses to liberate or annihilate the urges, depending on what you want. In this case, you may see the whole affair as a game, where what you do and say has no direct relationship to what you are or think; it is only a means to an end. Thus, you will view others' behaviors as having ulterior motives and continually look for the hidden meaning. You may also wonder what *your* true motives are, if you stop to think that deeply.

One who holds the *humanistic view* might enter the above situation with the feeling that both parties are free to behave in any way they choose, but that whatever they do it will be an open, true picture of who they are. They will facilitate this behavior by letting each other know what they want to do. That doesn't rule out any of the situational variables stated in the behavioristic example, nor does it say that these conditions (soft music, etc.) will not help to instill the proper mood for the evening. It only says that these are not done to manipulate but rather because *both* parties want them that way.

In Part 1 we saw that a humanistic communicator is a person who is unique and autonomous, with mental processes that are actively seeking information, who is aware of the self and its embeddedness in society, has freedom of choice, and is responsible for the resulting behavior. In this section we took the humanistic definition of communication—sharing meaning—and showed how the humanistic communicator accomplished this through the development of interpersonal relationships. This involves the process known as stroking and may move through four stages, depending on the intensity of involvement and depth of commitment.

Now we would like to give a more detailed acount of what a humanistic communicator looks like. First we must give an overview of the structure within which the communicator moves. We see the human being as a system of systems (neurological, respiratory, muscular) operating in a hierarchy of systems (groups, organizations, societies, cultures) (Borden, Gregg, and Grove 1969). Human communication is the process through which this hierarchy of systems is created and maintained. To understand the function of communication in these systems, one must consider the basic entities of which the human communication process is composed. In doing this, some of the differences among the behavioristic, psychoanalytic, and humanistic approaches will become apparent.

From a humanistic point of view, the basic component of the human communication process is the human being—the whole person. This is in contrast to the behavioristic and psychoanalytic emphasis on messages (Weaver's signals). The basic function of human communication is to develop relationships as opposed to exchanging information. Since by definition human communication is the sharing of meaning, then we can expect meaningful communicative events to cluster around the ten dimensions of involvement and relationships to develop according to the intensity-of-involvement scale. The basic unit of the human communication process is the stroke, and it is around this unit that the rest of the model is organized.

The humanistic approach to human communication emphasizes the self-regulatory capacity of the person (as opposed to regulation by internal urges or motivation by external stimuli). This characteristic brings along with it freedom of choice and self-assertion. These too are very basic assumptions about the human communication process. We are not saying that a person has unencumbered freedom to do whatever he or she wants to do at any given time. Rather, we are saying that whatever a person does at any given time is his or her choice at that time. Our communicative behavior is our way of asserting the self. True, it may not be assertive in the aggressive sense, but it is assertive in the sense that it is the manifestation of our choices at that moment. We may choose to play games or to be open. In either case, that is how we choose to behave, and, therefore, that is our manifestation of our self. *No one can choose our behavior for us.*

Why do we make the choices we do? Another characteristic of the humanistic communication model is the emphasis on the fact that all communication takes place in a context; it cannot be objectified and isolated. That is why we emphasize the whole-person model. To help understand this model, we can delineate three aspects of the context of human communication: cultural, situational, and urgency aspects.

The *cultural* aspect of the context within which human communication takes place in concerned with the attitudinal frame of reference we develop throughout our lifetime. That is, it takes into consideration all of the beliefs, fears, desires, and expectations we have developed as a result of our exposure to the culture in which we live. Most of our attitudinal frame of reference is nonconscious; that is, we are not consciously aware of these feelings. Daryl Bem (1970, p. 89) calls them nonconscious ideologies, and explains them this way:

> As we noted earlier, only a very unparochial and intellectual fish is aware that his environment is wet. After all, what else could it be? Such is the nature of a nonconscious ideology.
>
> A society's ability to inculcate this kind of ideology into its citizens is the most subtle and most profound form of social influence. It is also the most difficult kind of social influence to challenge because it remains invisible. Even those who consider themselves sufficiently radical or intellectual to have rejected the basic premises of a particular societal ideology often find their belief systems unexpectedly cluttered with its remnants.

In our view, there is no ideology which better exemplifies these points than the beliefs and attitudes which most Americans hold about women. Not only do most men and women in our society hold hidden prejudices about the woman's "natural" role, but these nonconscious beliefs motivate a host of subtle practices that are dramatically effective at keeping her "in her place." Even many liberal Americans, who insist that a black skin should not uniquely qualify its owner for janitorial and domestic service, continue to assume that the possession of a uterus uniquely qualifies its owner for precisely that.

Male supremacy is a very good example of a nonconscious ideology. We aren't aware of it and most men (and women) will say, "How else should it be?"

How do these nonconscious ideologies develop? As we mentioned in Part 1, humanistic psychology posits that the person grows through many complex stages of cognitive development. We don't have to be motivated to do this because, once it is turned on (when we are born), it is a continuing process (unless we are conditioned out of it by a behavioristic world) (Greene and Lepper 1974). Through our own innate pattern recognition, assimilation, accommodation, and memory processes (see Furth 1969), we construct a mental (cognitive) model of reality. Thus, we carry around in our heads a model or view of reality that is developed from all the experiences we have had with the outside world in conjunction with the internal focus we apply to them. What's more, the pursuit of this cognitive structure must come from within:

> In our present undertaking the psychological initiative always remains a property of the person — never the property of anything else. What is more, neither past nor future events are themselves ever regarded as basic determinants of the course of human action — not even the events of childhood. But one's way of anticipating them, whether in the short range or in the long view — this is the basic theme in the human process of living. Moreover, it is that events are anticipated, not merely that man gravitates toward more and more comfortably organic states. Confirmation and disconfirmation of one's predictions are accorded greater psychological significance than rewards, punishments, or the drive reduction that reinforcements produce. . . .
>
> Thus we envision the nature of life in its outreach for the future, and not in its perpetuation of its prior conditions or in its incessant reverberation of past events. (Kelly 1970, pp. 10–11)

Those events which are meaningful to us shape our expectations about future events. Essentially, what our attitudinal frame of reference is, is a structure against which we can make predictions about future events. Thus, the human mind approaches each situation with an assumption about what the event will be like. It then compares its perception of the event with its anticipation, to see if they agree. If they don't, then it has to do something about the dissonance that occurs. A closed mind may alter its perception of the event or even reject the perception altogether, while an open mind would be more apt to accept its failure to anticipate correctly and revise its anticipation of future events. This is the core activity for a growing mind. The more mature a person is, the more consistent the agreement between anticipation and perception will be. With a little thought, it should be clear that one must be involved in an event before it can have much meaning. To be involved means that we are actively seeking congruence between our anticipations and perceptions by consciously updating our internal structure to enable it to make more precise anticipations of communicative events.

George Kelly (1970, pp. 18-19) gives some particularly good insights into this process:

> It begins to be clear that the succession we call experience is based on the constructions we place on what goes on. If those constructions are never altered, all that happens during a man's years is a sequence of parallel events having no psychological impact on his life. But if he invests himself—the most intimate event of all—in the enterprise, the outcome, to the extent that it differs from his expectation or enlarges upon it, dislodges the man's construction of himself. In recognizing the inconsistency between his anticipation and the outcome, he concedes a discrepancy between what he was and what he is. A succession of such investments and dislodgments constitutes the human experience. . . .
>
> The unit of experience is, therefore, a cycle embracing five phases: anticipation, investment, encounter, confirmation or disconfirmation, and constructive revision. . . .
>
> Stated simply, the amount of a man's experience is not measured by the number of events with which he collides, but by the investments he has made in his anticipations and the revisions of his constructions that have followed upon his facing up to consequences.

It appears that there is little learning without experience, little experience without involvement, and little involvement without commitment to our own understanding and growth. Investing yourself in a communication event means risking your self-image, for essentially you are projecting your anticipations of the outcome of the encounter, and if the outcome doesn't match your anticipations, then you must do something about it. The most obvious event by which this process may be illustrated is that of asking a person for a date. You males know how many different strategies you have used to keep from losing face if she says no. A refusal means that you have to revise some attitudes about that person or maybe about yourself. It is through experiences such as these that we build up our attitudinal frame of reference—our long-range approach to life, which we call the *cultural* aspect of the context of human communication.

The *situational* aspects of the context of human communication are those external aspects of the communication event that are immediately perceivable. That is, they are all the psychological, sociological, and physical variables that affect the choices we make in our communicative behavior (for example, the weather, our deadlines, the time, the place, the tension you perceive in the other person, and his or her sex, age, and status). All of these have a profound effect on what we feel we can do and say in a given encounter. Situational aspects of the communication process are most often recognized when they are not heeded. This is why we have what we call inappropriate behaviors, although in many instances appropriateness is in the mind of the beholder.

The third aspect of the context of human communication is that of *urgency*. This is best illustrated by seeing how long you can be in a room with another person without talking. You soon become very concerned with the silence and feel you need to say something. We can raise this feeling of urgency a level higher by changing the scene to a situation where you not only feel the urgency to talk but also to make a specific statement, as when your roommate gets on your nerves and you want to tell him or her to bug off. An urgency, then, has to do with the need to communicate or the need for a specific kind of communication. It includes all of the *internal* pressures, constraints, and needs that we feel in any communication event.

Because of the urgency of a communication situation, we often do not give sufficient consideration to what the do-ables and sayables may be. Too often we do not stop to think what alternatives we have, what our choices are. The humanistic model of human communication emphasizes the urgency aspect, with particular attention to the fact that we make the choices of what and how we communicate in any given situation. Therefore, we should be aware of our options and use the test of whether it facilitates growth in the other person as the criterion for what and how we communicate. This criterion puts demands on the other person as well as on you, for it may very well force that person to become aware of his or her own communicative behavior. We can conclude, with Rogers, that our primary communication urgency is an unconditional positive regard for the other *person-as-a-whole-person*. Thus, we can say that the primary goal in a humanistic model of the human communication process is the facilitation of growth in all participants.

In summary, we can enumerate some of the characteristics of a humanistic communication model.

1. Communication is defined as the sharing of meaning.
2. The human being is considered a system operating within a hierarchy of other systems.
3. The basic component of the human communication process is the person.
4. The basic function of the human communication process is to develop relationships.
5. The basic unit of the human communication process is the stroke.
6. The emphasis on the whole person necessitates awareness of one's self-regulatory capacity, with the related aspects of choice and self-assertion.

7. There are three aspects of the context of human communication: cultural, situational, and urgency.

All of these characteristics focus on the facilitation of growth in oneself and in the other person.

In this section we have exposed you to some of the characteristics of a humanistic communicator. The following activities should help you to crystallize these characteristics and reveal some of your own identity.

HUMANISTIC COMMUNICATOR ACTIVITIES

1. Form a group and create several role-playing situations in which you highlight the differences among the behaviorist, the Freudian, and the humanistic communicator. Present these to the class and discuss their respective behaviors.
2. Write down a list of characteristics that indicate how you feel about yourself (e.g., slow, intense, conservative, immediate, etc.). Can you think of specific events that point to these characteristics? Now compare these with those of the rest of your group. Are there any others with like characteristics? Do you feel a kinship with these people?
3. In a group, list six organizations (structures, systems) of which you are all members. Rank these hierarchically and indicate some behaviors that would be appropriate in some of these structures but not in others.
4. Where did the nonconscious ideology of male supremacy come from? Divide your group into two sections and discuss this question. Make sure you give examples to clarify and validate your positions.
5. Use the example of a male-female encounter (dinner at her place). In a group, list as many cultural norms, situational variables, and urgency considerations as you can that may affect the outcome of the evening. Now role-play some of these outcomes, showing what happens if: (a) you are aware of your anticipations and can modify them if your perceptions do not match them; (b) you are closed-minded and cannot modify your anticipations; (c) you are not aware of them.

THOUGHT QUESTIONS

After reading the foregoing section, you should be able to answer these questions.

1. Define the following concepts and relate them to the human communication process: noise, stroking, meaning, message, signal, feedback, intensity, communication event, information, entropy, sharing, redundancy,

commitment, encoding, relationship, decoding, contact, verbal-nonverbal, vocal-nonvocal, one-way communication, self-assertion.
2. Describe a self-regulating system and compare this to the human being.
3. Differentiate between cultural variables and urgency variables, giving an example of how these might conflict in a communication event.
4. Discuss the difficulties of applying the Shannon-Weaver model of communication to the human communication process.
5. Describe the human being as a system, giving three subsystems and showing their interdependence in the communication process.

RESEARCH QUESTIONS

To answer these questions, you should use sources other than this book, such as:

Buckley, Walter, ed. *Modern Systems Research for the Behavioral Scientist.* Chicago: Aldine Publishing Co., 1968 (especially pp. 143–182).
Howard, Jane. *Please Touch.* New York: Dell Publishing Co., 1970.
Lewis, Howard, and Streitfeld, Harold. *Growth Games.* New York: Bantam Books, 1970.
Pierce, J.R. *Symbols, Signals, and Noise.* New York: Harper & Row, Publishers, 1961.

1. Investigate the second law of thermodynamics and write a paper showing that communication counteracts it.
2. Investigate the truth of the statement that nonverbal stroking is more trusted than verbal stroking.
3. Investigate the dimensions of communicative involvement to see if students at your institution rank them in the same order as we did. If there are differences, can you explain them?

REFERENCES

Bem, Daryl. *Beliefs, Attitudes, and Human Affairs.* Monterey, Calif.: Brooks/Cole Publishing Co., 1970.
Berne, Eric. *Games People Play.* New York: Grove Press, 1964.
———. *Transactional Analysis in Psychotherapy.* New York: Grove Press, 1961.
———. *What Do You Say After You Say Hello?* New York: Grove Press, 1972.
Borden, George A. "Mathematical Transformations and Communication Theory." *Journal of Communication,* June 1963.
Borden, George A.; Gregg, Richard; and Grove, Theodore. *Speech Behavior and Human Interaction.* Englewood Cliffs, N.J.: Prentice-Hall, 1969, pp. 87–93.

Brown, Charles T., and Van Riper, Charles. *Communication in Human Relationships.* Skokie, Ill.: National Textbook Co., 1973.

Fensterheim, Herbert, and Baer, Jean. *Don't Say Yes When You Want to Say No.* New York: David McKay Co., 1975.

Furth, Hans. *Piaget and Knowledge.* Englewood Cliffs, N.J.: Prentice-Hall, 1969.

Gibran, Kahlil. *The Prophet.* New York: Alfred A. Knopf, 1971.

Greene, David, and Lepper, Mark R. "How to Turn Play into Work." *Psychology Today,* September 1974, pp. 49–54.

Kelly, George A. "A Brief Introduction to Personal Construct Theory," in *Perspectives in Personal Construct Theory,* edited by D. Bannister. New York: Academic Press, 1970.

———. *A Theory of Personality.* New York: W.W. Norton & Co., 1963.

Miller, George A., ed., *Communication Language and Meaning: Psychological Perspectives.* New York: Basic Books, 1973.

Myers, Gail E., and Myers, Michele Tolela. *Communicating When We Speak.* New York: McGraw-Hill Book Co., 1975.

———. *The Dynamics of Human Communication.* New York: McGraw-Hill Book Co., 1973.

O'Neill, Nena, and O'Neill, George. *Open Marriage.* New York: Avon Books, 1972.

Pace, R. Wayne, and Boren, Robert R. *The Human Transaction.* Glenview, Ill.: Scott, Foresman & Co., 1973.

Shannon, Claude, and Weaver, Warren. *A Mathematical Theory of Communication.* Urbana, Ill.: University of Illinois Press, 1962.

Stewart, John, and D'Angelo, Gary. *Together: Communicating Interpersonally.* Reading, Mass.: Addison-Wesley Publishing Co., 1975.

Watzlawick, Paul; Beavin, Janet Helmick; and Jackson, Don D. *Pragmatics of Human Communication: A Study of Interactional Patterns, Pathologies, and Paradoxes.* New York: W.W. Norton & Co., 1967.

Weaver, Warren. "The Mathematics of Communication." *Scientific American,* July 1949, pp. 11–15.

Wolff, Kurt H. *The Sociology of George Simmel.* New York: Free Press, 1950.

Zunin, Leonard, and Zunin, Natalie. *Contact — The First Four Minutes.* Plainview, N.Y.: Nash Publishing Corporation, 1972.

If psychologists aim to predict and control human behavior and experience, as in their textbooks they claim, they are assigning man to the same ontological status as weather, stars, minerals, or lower forms of animal life. We do not question anyone's right to seek understanding in order the better to control his physical environment and adapt it to his purposes. We properly challenge any man's right to control the behavior and experience of his fellows. To the extent that psychologists illumine human existence to bring it under the deliberate control of someone other than the person himself, to that extent they are helping to undermine some person's freedom in order to enlarge the freedom of someone else. . . . Thus, advertiser, businessmen, military leaders, politicians, and salesmen all seek to learn more about the determiners of human conduct, in order to gain power and advantage. If they can sway human behavior by manipulating the conditions which mediate it, they can get large numbers of people to forfeit their own interests and serve the interests of the manipulator. Such secret manipulation of the masses or of an individual by some other person is possible only if the ones being manipulated are kept mystified as to what is going on, and if their experience of their own freedom is blunted.

Sidney Jourard, Disclosing Man to Himself

Part 3

The Context for Humanistic Communication

Upon completion of this section you should be able to:

1. List five instances in which our society exerts an influence upon our behaviors.
2. Enumerate several norms of society which demand behavioral allegiance.
3. Define the idea of a relationship between people, and list at least five things involved in a relationship.
4. Define dehumanization and list at least five ways in which such dehumanizing takes place.
5. Understand the value of an open relationship with other people. Describe some drawbacks of such a relationship.
6. Develop a concern for others which *allows* an individual to become open in relationships with us. (What kinds of behaviors on our part allow others to feel secure in opening up?)
7. Write an "ethic" by which a humanistically oriented person should operate.
8. Understand why the responsibility for relationships and their consequences should properly be placed upon the individual.

Do you believe what Jourard is saying in the quote on page 94? What are your views of society in general and other people in particular? We are including the following inventory to let you see what some of your feelings are. Place a 1 in the blank for strongly agree, a 2 for disagree, a 3 for agree, and a 4 for strongly agree.

SCALE F
Social Conditions Inventory

I FEEL THAT MOST PEOPLE:

_____ 1. are actively creating their own world.

_____ 2. are eager to help people in trouble.

_____ 3. have strong feelings about most things.

_____ 4. are fully aware of who they are.

_____ 5. have more than enough good relationships.

_____ 6. look forward to an exciting future.

_____ 7. communicate as well as they would like.

_____ 8. do not feel that they have been dehumanized.

_____ 9. have very few moments of emptiness and loneliness.

_____ 10. feel they are in control of their destiny.

After filling out this inventory, you might want to discuss these items with others to see if you have similar opinions. It would be even more revealing to go back now and fill it out as you see yourself (I FEEL THAT I). Are there differences between how you feel and how you think most people feel? Why or why not? What does this tell you about yourself?

The Human Condition

Jourard speaks very forcefully about the present conditions. If what he says is true (and you can look around and get a pretty good indication that it is), then we are living in a behavioristic world. We outlined the guidelines of such a world in Part 1 of this book (i.e., human beings are passive in their relationships with society, control is vested in the environment, and normative behavior is obtained by operant conditioning). There are two other aspects of this behavioristic model that need to be mentioned to establish an insight into our present human condition. The first is the place of *responsibility*. The logical extension of the behaviorist's model says that society is responsible for our behavior, since it conditions us and controls us. The second is *manipulation,* the feeling that we have no choice in the way we behave in specific instances, that someone else is controlling our behavior.

If we look about us, we will probably see a society populated by passive people. Even if we look inside ourselves, we will find someone who is probably more often passive than active or assertive. For example, how many people do you know who voted in the last election—federal, state, or local? How many people do you know who have written a letter to their congressperson (state or federal), to an editor, or even to a friend expressing strong feelings about a specific issue? Or, more personally, when was the last time you asserted yourself in a situation where you were being taken advantage of, and how do you feel about someone who does this? Do you caution people to avoid rocking the boat? Do you suffer personal loss from the encroachment of others and pass it off as being self-transcendent—enduring such suffering "for the good of society," or feeling that "everyone has to suffer," while you live with a martyr complex?

Many of us were taught from youth onward to be giving and respectful of others' rights to the point that we often put their rights ahead of our own. We are not condemning this behavior, only the resultant condition of passivity and the feeling of being manipulated. Of course all people do not feel manipulated. Some have been so well conditioned that they accept the status quo as inevitable and unchangeable and close their minds to any suggestion that it might be otherwise. This becomes a nonconscious ideology. The feelings of manipulation come only with the view of self as an active, decision-making, autonomous being, capable of self-direction. We then realize that we might do something about external or internal pressures that are controlling our behavior. We also begin to see the paradox that society proceeds under. Namely, that we are constantly being pleaded with to let our thoughts and ideas be known, but when we do (unless they are in agreement with the controlling force), they are cast aside as irrelevant, ridiculous, or too avant-garde for the present situation.

If you think about this condition for a while, you may begin to ask yourself how we got caught in this paradox. Jourard (1968, p. 38) gives one explanation:

> The entire institutional structure of society is devoted to training people to con-form to those ways that will keep the economic and political system in its present form. The family begins a socialization process, shaping children to the habits, values, and beliefs that will make the child "fit." The school system, far from educating, is actually an additional training institution, directing people to the ways in which they must go, else they will not reach minimally privileged status. The organized churches, instead of liberating men from the sometimes crushing grip of social conformity, actually collude with "Caesar," admonishing people to live in ways that prevent constructive social and political change.

Such a statement sounds almost paranoid, yet this is how the cultural context of the communication process is developed. Who has control over our behavior? We have seen that the humanistic approach is to grant control and responsibililty to the person. Yet if we look at our socialization process, we see just the opposite. On every hand we are giving control of our lives to someone else, hoping that they will also assume the responsibility for its fulfillment.

Consider, for example, the labor unions. Management used to say to the workers, "I'll take care of you if you do as I say." But the workers found this not to be true, so they formed the unions. Now the unions say the same thing, but many of the workers are still dissatisfied. Why the dissatisfaction? It seems to stem from the realization (unconscious at times) that when push comes to shove (like the "depression" of 1975) the individual has the final responsibil-ity for his or her welfare, behavior, and dreams. The conscious realization of this fact is conditioned out of many of us by parents, teachers, preachers, and friends, all trying to convince us that they know what is best for us. Conse-quently, we begin to doubt our own abilities to make realistic, meaningful, appropriate decisions. Yet we never quite lose that sense of uneasiness over someone else's making our decisions for us. Our usual pattern seems to be to procrastinate until the decision is made for us. We grant others the control because we don't want to take the responsibility for our own actions, at the same time knowing that we are ultimately responsible.

The subtle manipulation demonstrated in the above examples should make you aware that we are not browbeaten into submission (usually) by any of the forces seeking to control us. A carrot is always held out in front of us, so we might say we are seduced into giving up our individuality for "the better-ment of the world," "the good of the order," "a piece of the action," or some material "goodie" (sounds like rape to me). If we try to do our own thing, we may be looked on as selfish, antisocial, or just plain weird. If you are dif-ferent, there must be something wrong with *you.* Perhaps one of the most striking paradoxes in the culture of the United States is our *strong emphasis on the rights of the individual* and the *equally strong pressures to get everyone to conform.* The pressures are seen in our school systems, our labor unions, our civil and criminal laws, and our families. In the excerpts you have read from Jourard, it is clear he feels that conformity comes from the manipulation and control these organizations hold over us. The way to break through this control is to understand how we are being manipulated so we can exert our individual freedom. But that is not so easy, for we first have to break out of our passive acceptance of other people's infringing on our freedom.

One of the primary objectives of behavioral research is the development of normative behaviors. We then see these norms reflected on television and appealed to by advertisers. The fact that advertisers have made a business out of telling us what we need to maintain our normative behavior speaks for their subtlety. (Perhaps the best example is clothing styles.) Just feeling that we might be deviating from the norm brings enormous pressure on us to conform. The power of appealing to norms cannot be overemphasized. In a recent study it was shown that, when students found out they were too far removed from the norm, either above or below, on some sociability tests which they chose to administer to themselves and for which they constituted the entire population (they set their own norms), they were devastated (Borden and Puhl 1973). It took us several weeks to reestablish their self-concepts. What is the effect of knowing you deviate from the norms in real-life situations? What is the condition of the human being that allows us to accept the rule of the norm—to have our behavior governed by it? From a humanistic point of view, why are we so sensitive to the norms of society and yet so insensitive to other human beings?

Rollo May, one of the leading humanistic psychologists of the day, has done some extensive research on the state of the human being in the present world. Rather than try to duplicate his efforts, we present his views in the excerpt from *Love and Will* that follows. As you read this paper, please pay particular attention to the numbered points. We have also italicized some important passages.

Our Schizoid World*

Rollo May

> *Cassandra: Apollo was the seer who set me this work. . . .*
> *Chorus: Were you already ecstatic in the skills of God?*
> *Cassandra: Yes; even then I read my city's destinies.*
> > —*from Agamemnon, by Aeschylus*

The striking thing about love and will in our day is that, whereas in the past they were always held up to us as the *answer* to life's predicaments, they have now themselves become the *problem*. It is always true that love and will become more difficult in a transitional age; and ours is an era of radical transition. The old myths and symbols by which we oriented ourselves are gone, anxiety is rampant, we cling to each other and try to persuade ourselves that what we feel is love; *we do not will because we are afraid that if we choose one thing or one person we'll lose the other, and we are too insecure to take that chance.* The bottom then drops out of the conjunctive emotions and processes — of which love and will are the two foremost examples. The individual is forced to turn inward; he becomes obsessed with the new form of the problem of identity, namely, *Even-if-I-know-who-I-am, I-have-no-significance.* I am unable to influence others. The next step is apathy. And the step following that is violence. For no human being can stand the perpetually numbing experience of his own powerlessness.

So great was the emphasis on love as the resolution to life's predicament that people's self-esteem ascended or fell depending on whether or not they had achieved it. Those who believed they had found it indulged in self-righteousness, confident in their visible proof of salvation as the Calvinist's wealth used to be tangible evidence of his being numbered among the elect. Those who failed to find it felt not simply bereft to a greater or lesser extent, but, on a deeper and more damaging inner level, their self-esteem was undermined. They felt marked as a new species of pariah, and would confess in psychotherapy that they awoke in the small hours of the morning not necessarily especially lonely or unhappy but plagued with the gnawing conviction that they had somehow missed the great secret of life. And all the while, with rising divorce rates, the increasing banalization of love in literature and art, and the fact that sex for many people has become more meaningless as it is more available, this "love" has seemed tremendously elusive if not an outright illusion.

Some members of the new political left came to the conclusion that love is destroyed by the very nature of our bourgeois society, and the reforms they proposed had the specific purpose of making "a world in which love is more possible."[1]

In such a contradictory situation, the sexual form of love — the lowest common denominator on the ladder of salvation — understandably became our preoccupation; for sex, as rooted in man's inescapable biology, seems always dependable to give at least a facsimile of love. But sex, too, has become Western man's test and burden more than his salvation. The books which roll off the presses on technique in love and sex, while still best-sellers for a few weeks, have a hollow ring: for most people seem to be aware on some scarcely articulated level that the frantic quality with which we pursue technique as our way to salvation is in direct proportion to the degree to which we have lost sight of the salvation we are seeking. It is an old and ironic habit of human beings to run faster when we have lost our way; and we grasp more fiercely at research, statistics, and technical aids in sex when we have lost the values and meaning of love. Whatever merits or failings the Kinsey studies and the Masters-Johnson research have in their own right, they are symptomatic of a culture in which the personal meaning of love has been progressively lost. Love had been assumed to be a motivating force, a power which could be relied upon to push us onward in life. But the great shift in our day indicates that the motivating force itself is now called into question. Love has become a problem to itself.

So self-contradictory, indeed, has love become that some of those studying family life have concluded that "love" is simply the name for the way more powerful members of the family control other members. Love, Ronald Laing maintains, is a cover for violence.

The same can be said about will. We inherited from our Victorian forefathers the belief that the only real problem in life was to decide rationally *what* to do — and then *will* would stand ready as the "faculty" for making us do it. Now it is no longer a matter of deciding what to do, but of *deciding how to decide. The very basis of will itself is thrown into question.*

Is will an illusion? Many psychologists and psychotherapists, from Freud down, have argued that it is. The terms "will power" and "free will," so necessary in the vocabulary of our fathers, have all but dropped completely out of any contemporary, sophisticated discussion; or the words are used in derision. *People go to therapists to find substitutes for their lost will: to learn how to get the "unconscious" to direct their lives, or to learn the latest conditioning technique to enable them to behave, or to use new drugs to release some motive for living.* Or to learn the latest method of "releasing affect," unaware that affect is not something you strive for in itself but a by-product of the way you give yourself to a life situation. And the question is, What are they going to use the situation *for?* In his study of will, Leslie Farber asserts that in this failure of will lies the central pathology of our day, and that our time should be called the "age of the disordered will."[2]

³

In such an age of radical transition, the individual is driven back into his own consciousness. When the foundations of love and will have been shaken and all but destroyed, we cannot escape the necessity of pushing below the surface and searching within our own consciousness and within the "collective unarticulated consciousness" of our society for the sources of love and will. I use the term "source" as the French speak of the

"source" of a river — the springs from which the water originally comes. If we can find the sources from which love and will spring, we may be able to discover the new forms which these essential experiences need in order to become viable in the new age into which we are moving. In this sense, our quest, like every such exploration, is a moral quest, for we are seeking the bases on which a morality for a new age can be founded. Every sensitive person finds himself in Stephen Dedalus' position: "I go forth . . . to forge in the smithy of my soul the uncreated conscience of my race."

My term "schizoid," in the title of this chapter, means out of touch; avoiding close relationships; the inability to feel. I do not use the term as a reference to psychopathology, but rather as a general condition of our culture and the tendencies of people which make it up. Anthony Storr, describing it more from the point of view of individual psychopathology, holds that the schizoid person is *cold, aloof, superior, detached.* This may erupt in violent aggression. All of which, says Storr, is a complex mask for a repressed longing for love. The detachment of the schizoid is a defense against hostility and has its source in a distortion of love and trust in infancy which renders him forever fearing actual love "because it threatens his very existence."[3]

⁴

I agree with Storr as far as he goes, but I am contending that the schizoid condition is a general tendency in our transitional age, and that the "helplessness and disregard" in infancy to which Storr refers comes not just from parents but from almost every aspect of our culture. The parents are themselves helpless and unwitting expressions of their culture. *The schizoid man is the natural product of the technological man.* It is one way to live and is increasingly utilized — and it may explode into violence. In its "normal" sense, the schizoid does not require repression. Whether the schizoid character state later breaks down into a schizophrenic-like state in any given case, only the future can decide. But this is much less apt to happen, as in the case with many patients, if the individual can frankly admit and confront the schizoid characteristic of his present state. Anthony Storr goes on to indicate that the schizoid character has a "conviction of being unlovable, and a feeling of being attacked and humilated by criticism."[4]

While I value Storr's description, there is one point where it breaks down. This is in his citing Freud, Descartes, Schopenhauer, and Beethoven as examples of schizoid. "In the case of Descartes and Schopenhauer, it is their very alienation from love which has given birth to their philosophies." And with Beethoven,

> In compensation for his disappointment with, and resentment of, actual human beings, Beethoven imagined an ideal world of love and friendship. . . . His music, perhaps more obviously than that of any other composer, displays considerable aggression in the sense of power, forcefulness and strength. It is easy to imagine that, had he not been able to sublimate his hostility in his music, he might well have succumbed to a paranoid psychosis.[5]

Storr's dilemma is that if these men are seen as psychopathological and then had assumedly been "cured," we would not have had their creations. Thus, I believe it must be admitted that the schizoid state can be a constructive way of dealing with profoundly difficult situations. Whereas other cultures pushed schizoid persons toward being creative, our culture pushes people toward becoming more detached and mechanical.

In centering upon the problems of love and will, I do not forget the positive characteristics of our time and the potentialities for individual fulfillment. It is an obvious fact that when an age is torn loose from its moorings and everyone is to some degree thrown on his own, more people can take steps to find and realize themselves. *It is also true that we hear most hue and cry about the power of the individual when the individual has least.* But I write about the problems; they are what clamor for our attention.

The problems have a curious characteristic not yet adequately appreciated: *they predict the future.* The problems of a period are the existential crises of what can be, but hasn't been, resolved; and regardless of how seriously we take that word "resolved," if there were not some new possibility, there would be no crisis — there would be only despair. Our psychological enigmas express our unconscious desires. Problems arise where we meet our world and find it inadequate to ourselves or ourselves inadequate to it; something hurts, clashes, and, as Yeats puts it,

> We . . . feel
> The pain of wounds,
> The labour of the spear. . . .

PROBLEMS AS PROPHETIC

I write this book on the basis of my experience of twenty-five years of working intensively as a psychoanalytic therapist with persons trying to meet and work through their conflicts. Particularly in the last decade or so, these conflicts have generally been based upon some aspect of love or will gone wrong. In one sense, every therapist is, or ought to be, engaged in *research* all the time — research, as the word itself states, as a "search" for the sources.

At this point, I hear my experimental-psychologist colleagues challenging me with the argument that the data we get in therapy are impossible to formulate mathematically and that they come from persons who represent the psychological "misfits" of the culture. At the same time, I hear philosopher friends insisting to me that no model of man can be based centrally on data from neuroses or character disorders. With both of these cautions I agree.

But neither these psychologists in their laboratories nor those philosophers in their studies can ignore the fact that we do get tremendously significant and often unique data from persons in therapy—data which are revealed only when the human being can break down the customary pretenses, hypocrisies, and defenses behind which we all hide in "normal" social discourse. It is only in the critical situation of emotional and spiritual suffering—which is the situation that leads them to seek therapeutic help—that people will endure the pain and anxiety of uncovering the profound roots of their problems. *There is also the curious situation that unless we are oriented toward helping the person, he won't, indeed in some ways cannot, reveal the significant data. Harry Stack Sullivan's remark on research in therapy is still as cogent as when he first made it: "Unless the interviews are designed to help the person, you'll get artifacts, not real data."* [6]

True, the information we get from our patients may be hard or even impossible to codify more than superficially. But this information speaks so directly out of the human being's immediate conflicts and his living experience that its richness of meaning more than makes up for its difficulty in interpretation. It is one thing to discuss the hypothesis of aggression as resulting from frustration, but quite another to see the tenseness of a patient, his eyes flashing in anger or hatred, his posture clenched into paralysis, and to hear his half-stifled gasps of pain from reliving the time a

score of years ago when his father whipped him because, through no fault of his own, his bicycle was stolen—an event giving rise to a hatred which for that moment encompasses every parental figure in his whole world, including me in the room with him. Such data are empirical in the deepest meaning of the term.

With respect to the question of basing a theory of man on data from "misfits" I would, in turn, challenge my colleagues: *Does not every human conflict reveal universal characteristics of man as well as the idiosyncratic problems of the individual?* Sophocles was not writing merely about one individual's pathology when he showed us, step by step, through the drama of King Oedipus, the agonizing struggle of a man to find out "who I am and where I came from." Psychotherapy seeks the most specific characteristics and events of the given individual's life—and any therapy will become weakened in vapid, unexistential, cloudy generalities which forgets this. But psychotherapy also seeks the elements of the human conflict of this individual which are basic to the perdurable, persistent qualities of every man's experience as man—and any therapy will tend to shrink the patient's consciousness and make life more banal for him if it forgets that.

Psychotherapy reveals *both* the immediate situation of the individual's "sickness" *and* the archetypal qualities and characteristics which constitute the human being as human. It is the latter characteristics which have gone awry in specific ways in a given patient and have resulted in the former, his psychological problems. The interpretation of a patient's problems in psychotherapy is also a partial revelation of man's self-interpretation of himself through history in the archetypal forms in literature. Aeschylus' *Orestes* and Goethe's *Faust*, to take two diverse examples, are not simply portrayals of two given characters, one back in Greece in the fifth-century B.C. and the other in eighteenth-century Germany, but presentations of the struggles we all, of whatever century or race, go through in growing up, trying to find identity as individual beings, striving to affirm our being with whatever power we have, trying to love and create, and doing our best to meet all the other events of life up to and including our own death. One of the values of living in a transitional age — an "age of therapy" — is that it forces upon us this opportunity, even as we try to resolve our individual problems, to uncover new meaning in perennial man and to see more deeply into those qualities which constitute the human being as human.

Our patients are the ones who express and live out the subconscious and unconscious tendencies in the culture. The neurotic, or person suffering from what we now call character disorder, is characterized by the fact that the usual defenses of the culture do not work for him — a generally painful situation of which he is more or less aware.[7] The "neurotic" or the person "suffering from character disorders" is one whose problems are so severe that he cannot solve them by living them out in the normal agencies of the culture, such as work, education, and religion. Our patient cannot or will not adjust to the society. This, in turn, may be due to one or both of the two following interrelated elements. First, certain traumatic or unfortunate experiences have occurred in his life which make him more sensitive than the average person and less able to live with and manage his anxiety. Second, he may possess a greater than ordinary amount of originality and potential which push for expression and, when blocked off, make him ill.

THE ARTIST AND THE NEUROTIC

The relation between the artist and the neurotic, often considered mysterious, is entirely understandable from the viewpoint presented here. Both artist and neurotic speak and live from the subconscious and unconscious depths of their society. The artist does this positively, communicating what he experiences to his fellow men. The neurotic does this negatively. Experiencing the same underlying meanings and contradictions of his culture, he is unable to form his experiences into communicable meaning for himself and his fellows.

Art and neurosis both have a *predictive* function. Since art is communication springing from unconscious levels, it presents to us an image of man which is as yet present only in those members of the society who, by virtue of their own sensitized consciousness, live on the frontier of their society — live, as it were, with one foot in the future. Sir Herbert Read has made the case that the artist anticipates the later scientific and intellectual experience of the race.[8] The water reeds and ibis legs painted in triangular designs on neolithic vases in ancient Egypt were the prediction of the later development of geometry and mathematics by which the Egyptian read the stars and measured the Nile. In the magnificent Greek sense of proportion of the Parthenon, in the powerful dome of Roman architecture, and in the medieval cathedral, Read traces how, in a given period of history, art expresses the meanings and trends which are as yet unconscious, but which will later be formulated by the philosophers, religious leaders, and scientists of the society. The arts anticipate the future social and technological development by a generation when the change is more superficial,

7

or by centuries when the change, as the discovery of mathematics, is profound.

By the same token, we find the artists expressing the conflicts in the society before these conflicts emerge consciously in the society as a whole. The artist — who is the "antennae of the race," to use Ezra Pound's phrase — is living out, in forms that only he can create, the depths of consciousness which he experiences in his own being as he struggles with and molds his world.

Here we are plunged immediately into the center of the issues raised in this book. For the world presented by our contemporary painters and dramatists and other artists is a *schizoid world*. They present the condition of our world which makes the tasks of loving and willing peculiarly difficult. *It is a world in which, amid all the vastly developed means of communication that bombard us on all sides, actual personal communication is exceedingly difficult and rare. The most significant dramatists of our time, as Richard Gilman reminds us, are those who take as their subject matter precisely this loss of communication — who show, as do Ionesco and Genet and Beckett and Pinter, that our present fate as man is to exist in a world where communication between persons is all but destroyed.* We live out our lives talking to a tape recorder, as in Beckett's *Krapp's Last Tape;* our existence becomes more lonely as the radios and TV's and telephone extensions in our houses become more numerous. Ionesco has a scene in his play, *The Bald Soprano,* in which a man and woman happen to meet and engage in polite, if mannered, conversation. As they talk they discover that they both came down to New York on the ten o'clock train that morning from New Haven, and suprisingly, the address of both is the same building on Fifth Avenue. Lo and behold, they also both

live in the same apartment and both have a daughter seven years old. They finally discover to their astonishment that they are man and wife.

We find the same situation among the painters. Cézanne, the acknowledged father of the modern art movement, a man who in his own life was as undramatic and bourgeois as only a middle-class Frenchman can be, paints this schizoid world of spaces and stones and trees and faces. He speaks to us out of the old world of mechanics but forces us to live in the new world of free-floating spaces. "Here we are beyond causes and effects," writes Merleau-Ponty of Cézanne; "both come together in the simultaneity of an eternal Cézanne who is at the same time the formula of what he wanted to be and what he wanted to do. There is a rapport between Cézanne's schizoid temperament and his work because the work reveals a metaphysical sense of the disease. . . . In this sense to be schizoid and to be Cézanne come to the same thing."[9] Only a schizoid man could paint a schizoid world; which is to say, only a man sensitive enough to penetrate to the underlying psychic conflicts could present our world as it is in its deeper forms.

But in the very grasping of our world by art there is also *our protection from the dehumanizing effects of technology. The schizoid character lies in both the confronting of the depersonalizing world and the refusing to be depersonalized by it.* For the artist finds deeper planes of consciousness where we can participate in human experience and nature below superficial appearances. The case may be clearer in van Gogh, whose psychosis was not unconnected with his volcanic struggle to paint what he perceived. Or in Picasso, flamboyant as he may seem to be, whose insight into the schizoid character of our modern world is seen in the fragmented bulls and torn villagers in *Guernica,* or in the distorted portraits with mislocated eyes and ears—paintings not named but numbered. It is no wonder that Robert Motherwell remarks that this is the first age in which the artist does not have a community; he must now, like all of us, make his own.

The artist presents the broken image of man but transcends it in the very act of transmuting it into art. It is his creative act which gives meaning to the nihilism, alienation, and other elements of modern man's condition. To quote Merleau-Ponty again when he writes of Cézanne's schizoid temperament, "Thus the illness ceases to be an absurd fact and a fate, and becomes a general possibility of human existence."[10]

The neurotic and the artist—since both live out the unconscious of the race—reveal to us what is going to emerge endemically in the society later on. The neurotic feels the same conflicts arising from his experience of nihilism, alienation, and so on, but he is unable to give them meaningful form; he is caught between his incapacity to mold these conflicts into creative works on one hand and his inability to deny them on the other. As Otto Rank remarked, the neurotic is the "artiste manqué," the artist who cannot transmute his conflicts into art.

To admit this as a reality not only gives us our liberty as creative persons but also the basis of our freedom as human beings. By the same token, confronting at the outset the fact of the schizoid state of our world may give us a basis for discovering love and will for our own age.

THE NEUROTIC AS PREDICTIVE

Our patients predict the culture by living out *consciously* what the masses of people are able to keep *unconscious* for the time

being. The neurotic is cast by destiny into a Cassandra role. In vain does Cassandra, sitting on the steps of the palace at Mycenae when Agamemnon brings her back from Troy, cry, "Oh for the nightingale's pure song and a fate like hers!"[11] She knows, in her ill-starred life, that "the pain flooding the song of sorrow is [hers] alone,"[12] and that she must predict the doom she sees will occur there. The Mycenaeans speak of her as mad, but they also believe she does speak the truth, and that she has a special power to anticipate events. Today, the person with psychological problems bears the burdens of the conflicts of the times in his blood, and is fated to predict in his actions and struggles the issues which will later erupt on all sides in the society.

The first and clearest demonstration of this thesis is seen in the sexual problems which Freud found in his Victorian patients in the two decades before World War I. These sexual topics—even down to the words—were entirely denied and repressed by the accepted society at the time.[13] But the problems burst violently forth into endemic form two decades later after World War II. In the 1920's, everybody was preoccupied with sex and its functions. Not by the furthest stretch of the imagination can anyone argue that Freud "caused" this emergence. He rather reflected and interpreted, through the data revealed by his patients, the underlying conflicts of the society, which the "normal" members could and did succeed in repressing for the time being. Neurotic problems are the language of the unconscious emerging into social awareness.

A second, more minor example is seen in the great amount of hostility which was found in patients in the 1930's. This was written about by Horney, among others, and it emerged more broadly and openly as a conscious phenomenon in our society a decade later.

A third major example may be seen in the problem of anxiety. In the late 1930's and early 1940's, some therapists, including myself, were impressed by the fact that in many of our patients anxiety was appearing *not merely as a symptom of repression or pathology, but as a generalized character state.* My research on anxiety,[14] and that of Hobart Mowrer and others, began in the early 1940's. In those days very little concern had been shown in this country for anxiety other than as a symptom of pathology. I recall arguing in the late 1940's, in my doctoral orals, for the concept of normal anxiety, and my professors heard me with respectful silence but with considerable frowning.

Predictive as the artists are, the poet W. H. Auden published his *Age of Anxiety* in 1947, and just after that Bernstein wrote his symphony on that theme. Camus was then writing (1947) about this "century of fear," and Kafka already had created powerful vignettes of the coming age of anxiety in his novels, most of them as yet untranslated.[15] The formulations of the scientific establishment, as is normal, lagged behind what our patients were trying to tell us. Thus, at the annual convention of the American Psychopathological Association in 1949 on the theme "Anxiety," the concept of normal anxiety, presented in a paper by me, was still denied by most of the psychiatrists and psychologists present.

But in the 1950's a radical change became evident; everyone was talking about anxiety and there were conferences on the problem on every hand. Now the concept of "normal" anxiety gradually became accepted in the psychiatric literature. Everybody, normal as well as neurotic, seemed aware that he was living in the "age of anxiety." What had been presented by the artists and had appeared in our patients in the late 30's and 40's was now endemic in the land.

Our fourth point brings us to contemporary issues — the problem of identity. This was first a concern of therapists with their patients in the late 40's and early 50's. It was described on the basis of data from psychological studies by Erikson in *Childhood and Society* in 1950, by myself in *Man's Search for Himself* in 1953, by Allen Wheelis in *The Quest for Identity* in 1958, and by other interpreters in psychotherapy and psychoanalysis. We find the problem of identity becoming a concern on every sophisticated person's lips in the last of that decade and the early 60's; it has taken its place as a "steady" in *New Yorker* cartoons, and the spate of books dealing with it became best-sellers in their fields. The cultural values by which people had gotten their sense of identity had been wiped away.[16] Our patients were aware of this *before* society at large was, and they did not have the defenses to protect themselves from its disturbing and traumatic consequences.

All of these problems, to be sure, carry a certian momentum related to the ups and downs of fashion. But it would fail entirely to do justice to the dynamic historical emergence of psychological problems and of social change to dismiss them as *mere* fashions. Indeed, van den Berg, in a stimulating and provocative book, argues that *all* psychological problems are a product of the sociohistorical changes in culture. He believes that there is no "human nature" but only a changing nature of man depending on the changes in the society, and that we should call the conflicts of our patients not "neurosis" but "sociosis."[17] We need not go all the way with van den Berg: I, for one, believe psychological problems are produced by a three-cornered dialectical interplay of biological *and* individual *and* historical-social factors. Nevertheless, he makes clear what a gross and destructive oversimplification it is to assume that psychological problems emerge "out of the blue" or simply because society is now aware of the problem, or to assume that the problems exist merely because we have found new words to diagnose them. We *find* new words because something of importance is happening on unconscious, unarticulated levels and is pushing for expression; and our task is to do our best to understand and express these emergent developments.

Freud's patients were mostly hysterics who, by definition, carried repressed energy which could be released by the therapist's naming of the unconscious. Today, however, when practically all our patients are compulsive-obsessional neurotics (or character problems, which is a more general and less intense form of the same thing), we find that the chief block to therapy is the incapacity of the patient to feel. *These patients are persons who can talk from now till doomsday about their problems, and are generally well-practiced intellectuals; but they cannot experience genuine feelings.* Wilhelm Reich described compulsive characters as "living machines," and in his book, David Shapiro refers to this as well as to the "restraint and evenness in living and thinking" of these compulsive-obsessives. Reich, here, was ahead of his time in insight into the problems of twentieth-century patients.[18]

THE EMERGENCE OF APATHY

Earlier, I quoted Leslie Farber's assertion that our period should be called the "age of disordered will." But what underlies this disordered will?

I shall take my own leap in proposing an answer. I believe it is *a state of feelinglessness, the despairing possibility that nothing matters, a condition very close to apathy.* Pamela H. Johnson, after reporting the murders on the moors

of England, found herself unable to shake loose her conviction that "We may be approaching the state which the psychologists call affectlessness."[19] If apathy or affectlessness is a dominant mood emerging in our day, we can understand on a deeper level why love and will have become so difficult.

What some of us were nonplussed to find in our patients in the 1950's has, in its predictive fashion, during the last few years, emerged as an overt issue gravely troubling our whole society. I wish to quote from my book, *Man's Search for Himself,* written in 1952 and published the following year:

> It may sound surprising when I say, on the basis of my own clinical practice as well as that of my psychological and psychiatric colleagues, that the chief problem of people in the middle decade of the twentieth century is *emptiness.*[20]

While one might laugh at the meaningless boredom of people a decade or two ago, the emptiness has for many now moved from the state of boredom to a state of futility and despair which holds promise of dangers.[21]

> . . . The human being cannot live in a condition of emptiness for very long: if he is not growing *toward* something, he does not merely stagnate; the pent-up potentialities turn into morbidity and despair, and eventually into destructive activities.[22]

The *feeling* of emptiness or vacuity . . . generally comes from people's feeling that they are *powerless* to do anything effective about their lives or the world they live in. Inner vacuousness is the long-term, accumulated result of a person's particular conviction about himself, namely his conviction that he cannot act as an entity in directing his own life, or change other people's attitudes toward him, or effectually influence the world around him.

10

11

Thus he gets the deep sense of despair and futility which so many people in our day have. And soon, since what he wants and what he feels can make no real difference, he gives up wanting and feeling.[23]

. . . Apathy and lack of feeling are also defenses against anxiety. When a person continually faces dangers he is powerless to overcome, his final line of defense is at last to avoid even feeling the dangers.[24]

It was not until the mid-60's that this problem erupted in the form of several incidents that shook us to the very foundations. Our "emptiness" had been turning into despair and destructiveness, violence and assassination; it is now undeniable that these go hand in hand with apathy. "For more than half an hour, 38 respectable, law-abiding citizens in Queens," reported *The New York Times* in March, 1964, "watched a killer stalk and stab a woman in three separate attacks in Kew Gardens."[25] In April of the same year, the *Times* said, in an impassioned editorial about another event in which a crowd urged a deranged youth who was clinging to a hotel ledge to jump, calling him "chicken" and "yellow": "Are they any different from the wild-eyed Romans watching and cheering as men and beasts tore each other apart in the Colosseum? . . . Does the attitude of that Albany mob bespeak a way of life for many Americans? . . . If so, the bell tolls for all of us."[26] In May of that year, a *Times* article was headed "Rape Victim's Screams Draw 40 But No One Acts."[27] A number of similar events occurred during the next months which awakened us from our apathy long enough to realize how apathetic we had become, and how much *modern city existence had developed in us the habit of uninvolvement and unfeeling detachment.*

I am aware how easy it is to exaggerate specific events, and I have no wish to overstate my case. Nevertheless, I do believe that there is in our society a definite trend toward a state of affectlessness as an attitude toward life, a character state. The anomie about which intellectuals had speculated earlier seemed now to emerge with a hideous reality on our very streets and in our very subways.

What shall we call this state reported by so many of our contemporaries — estrangement, playing it cool, alienation, withdrawal of feeling, indifference, anomie, depersonalization? Each one of these terms expresses a part of the condition to which I refer — a *condition in which men and women find themselves experiencing a distance between themselves and the objects which used to excite their affection and their will.*[28] *I wish to leave open for the moment what the sources of this are. When I use the term "apathy," despite its limiting connotations, it is because its literal meaning is the closest to what I am describing: "want of feeling; lack of passion, emotion or excitement, indifference." Apathy and the schizoid world go hand in hand as cause and effect of each other.*

Apathy is particularly important because of its close relation to love and will. Hate is not the opposite of love; apathy is. The opposite of will is not indecision — which actually may represent the struggle of the *effort* to decide, as in William James — but being uninvolved, detached, unrelated to the significant events. Then the issue of will never can arise. *The interrelation of love and will inheres in the fact that both terms describe a person in the process of reaching out, moving toward the world, seeking to affect others or the inanimate world, and opening himself to be affected; molding, forming, relating to the world or requiring that it relate to him.* This is why love and will are so difficult in an age of transition, when all the familiar mooring places are gone. The blocking of the ways in which we affect others and are affected by them is the essential disorder of both love and will. Apathy, or a-pathos, is a withdrawal of feeling; it may begin as playing it cool, a studied practice of being unconcerned and unaffected. "I did not want to get involved," was the consistent response of the thirty-eight citizens of Kew Gardens when they were questioned as to why they had not acted. Apathy, operating like Freud's "death instinct," is a gradual letting go of involvement until one finds that life itself has gone by.

Viewing the society freshly, students often have a clearer insight into this than older adults—though they tend, in oversimplified fashion, to blame it on the institutions. "We have just not been given any passionate sense of the excitement of intellectual life around here," said the editor of the Columbia *Spectator*.[29] A student columnist in *The Michigan Daily* wrote, "This institution has dismally failed to inculcate, in most of its undergraduates at least, anything approaching an intellectual appetite." He spoke of the drift "towards something worse than mediocrity—and that is absolute indifference. An indifference towards perhaps even life itself."[30] "We were all divided up into punches on an IBM card," a Berkeley student remarked. "We decided to punch back in the riots of 1964, but the *real* revolution around here will come when we decide to burn computer cards as well as draft cards."[31]

There is a dialectical relationship between apathy and violence. To live in apathy provokes violence; and, in incidents like those cited above, violence promotes apathy. *Violence is the ultimate destructive substitute which surges in to fill the vacuum where there is no relatedness.*[32] There are degrees of violence, from the relatively normal

15

shock effect of many forms of modern art, through pornography and obscenity—which achieve their desired reaction through violence to our forms of life—to the extreme pathology of assassinations and the murders on the moors. *When inward life dries up, when feeling decreases and apathy increases, when one cannot affect or even genuinely touch another person, violence flares up as a daimonic necessity for contact, a mad drive forcing touch in the most direct way possible.*[33] This is one aspect of the well-known relationship between sexual feelings and crimes of violence. *To inflict pain and torture at least proves that one can affect somebody.* In the alienated state of mass communication, the average citizen knows dozens of TV personalities who come smiling into his living room of an evening—but he *himself is never known.* In this state of alienation and anonymity, painful for anyone to bear, the average person may well have fantasies which hover on the edge of real pathology. The mood of the anonymous person is, If I cannot affect or touch anybody, I can at least shock you into some feeling, force you into some passion through wounds and pain; I shall at least make sure we both feel something, and I shall force you to see me and know that I also am here! Many a child or adolescent has forced the group to take cognizance of him by destructive behavior; and though he is condemned, at least the community notices him. *To be actively hated is almost as good as to be actively liked; it breaks down the utterly unbearable situation of anonymity and aloneness.*

But having seen the serious effects of apathy, we need now to turn to the fact of its necessity; and, in its "normal schizoid" form, how it can be turned into a constructive function. Our tragic paradox is that in contemporary history, we *have* to protect ourselves by some kind of apathy. "Apathy is a curious state," remarks Harry Stack Sullivan; "It is a way used to survive defeat without material damage, although if it endures too long one is damaged by the passage of time. Apathy seems to me to be a miracle of protection by which a personality in utter fiasco rests until it can do something else."[34] The longer the situation goes unmet, the more apathy is prolonged; and it sooner or later becomes a character state. This affectlessness is a shrinking-up in the winds of continuous demands, a freezing in the face of hyperstimuli, letting the current go by since one fears he would be overwhelmed if he responded to it. No one who has ever ridden the subway at rush hour, with its cacaphonous din and hordes of anonymous humanity, will be surprised at this.

It is not difficult to appreciate how people living in a schizoid age have to protect themselves from tremendous overstimulation—protect themselves from the barrage of words and noise over radio and TV, protect themselves from the assembly line demands of collectivized industry and gigantic factory-modeled multiversities. In a world where numbers inexorably take over as our means of identification, like flowing lava threatening to suffocate and fossilize all breathing life in its path; in a world where "normality" is defined as keeping your cool; where sex is so available that the only way to preserve any inner center is to learn to have intercourse without committing yourself—in such a schizoid world, which young people experience more directly since they have not had time to build up the defenses which dull the senses of their elders, it is not surprising that will and love have become increasingly problematic and even, as some people believe, impossible of achievement.

But what of the constructive use of this schizoid situation? We have seen how Cézanne could turn his schizoid personality into a way of expressing the most significant forms of modern life, and could stand against the debilitating tendencies in our society by means of his art. We have seen that the schizoid stand is necessary; now we shall inquire how, in its healthy dimensions, it can also be turned to good. The constructive schizoid person stands against the spiritual emptiness of encroaching technology and does not let himself be emptied by it. *He lives and works with the machine without becoming a machine. He finds it necessary to remain detached enough to get meaning from the experience, but in doing so to protect his own inner life from impoverishment.* 16

Dr. Bruno Bettelheim finds the same supremacy of the aloof person—whom I would call schizoid—in his experiences in the concentration camps during World War II.

According to psychoanalytic convictions then current . . . aloofness from other persons and emotional distance from the world were viewed as weakness of character. My comments . . . on the admirable way in which a group of what I call "annointed persons" behaved in the concentration camps suggest how struck I was with these very aloof persons. They were very much out of contact with their unconscious but nevertheless retained their old personality structure, stuck to their values in the face of extreme hardships, and as persons were hardly touched by the camp experience. . . . These very persons who, according to existing psychoanalytic theory, should have had weak personalities apt to readily disintegrate, turned out to be the heroic leaders, mainly because of the strength of their character.[35]

Indeed, studies have shown that the persons who survive most effectively in space ships, and who can adjust to the sensory deprivation necessary for such a life—our comrades of the twenty-first century—are those who can detach and withdraw into themselves. "There are reasons to believe," writes Arthur J. Brodbeck after summarizing the evidence, "that it may well be the schizoid personality that will be best able to endure the requirements of extended space travel."[36] They preserve the inner world which the very hyperstimuli of our age would take away. *These introverts can continue to exist despite the overpowering stimuli or lack of it, for they have learned to develop a "constructive" schizoid attitude toward life.* Since we must live in the world as we find it, this distinguishing of the constructively schizoid attitude is an important part of our problem.

Apathy is the withdrawal of will and love, a statement that they "don't matter," a suspension of commitment. It is necessary in times of stress and turmoil; and the present great quantity of stimuli is a form of stress. But apathy, now in contrast to the "normal" schizoid attitude, leads to emptiness and makes one less able to defend oneself, less able to survive. However understandable the state we are describing by the term apathy is, it is also essential that we seek to find a new basis for the love and will which have been its chief casualties.

NOTES

[1] Carl Oglesby, in *A Prophetic Minority,* by Jack Newfield (New York, New American Library, 1966), p. 19.

[2] Leslie Farber, *The Ways of the Will* (New York, Basic Books, 1965), p. 48.

[3] Anthony Storr, *Human Aggression* (New York, Atheneum, 1968), p. 85.

[4] *Ibid.*

[5] *Ibid.,* p. 88.

[6] Personal communication.

[7] Kenneth Keniston observes a parallel point, namely that the problems of our day bear down most heavily not upon the stupid and the bland, but upon the intelligent. "The sense of being inescapably locked in a psycho-

social vise is often most paralyzing to precisely those men and women who have the greatest understanding of the complexity of their society, and who therefore might be best able to plan intelligently for its future." *The Uncommitted: Alienated Youth in American Society* (New York, Harcourt, Brace & World, 1960).

[8] Sir Herbert Read, *Icon and Idea: The Function of Art in the Development of Human Consciousness* (Cambridge, Mass., Harvard University Press, 1955).

[9] Maurice Merleau-Ponty, *Sense and Non-Sense* (Evanston, Ill., Northwestern University Press, 1964), p. 21.

[10] *Ibid.*

[11] Aeschylus, *Agamemnon,* from *The Complete Greek Tragedies,* eds. David Grene and Richmond Lattimore (Chicago, University of Chicago Press, 1953), p. 71.

[12] *Ibid.,* p. 70.

[13] The fact that pornography and other aspects of sexuality were also present in the Victorian period, as shown by Steven Marcus in *The Other Victorians* (New York, Basic Books, 1964), does not invalidate my thesis. In such a compartmentalized society there would always be repression which would come out in the underground in proportion to the blocking off of vital drives.

[14] Published as *The Meaning of Anxiety* (New York, Ronald Press, 1950).

[15] See May, *The Meaning of Anxiety,* pp. 6–7.

[16] The drama that most clearly heralded the demise of the Horatio Alger values of work and success by which most of us had gotten our sense of individual identity and significance was *Death of a Salesman,* published by Arthur Miller in 1949. Willy Loman's basic trouble was, in Miller's words, that "he never knew who he was."

[17] H. van den Berg, "The Changing Nature of Man," intro. to *A Historical Psychology* (New York, W.W. Norton & Co., 1961).

[18] See David Shapiro, *Neurotic Styles* (New York, Basic Books, 1965), p. 23.

[19] P.H. Johnson, *On Iniquity: Reflections Arising out of the Moors Murder Trial* (New York, Scribners).

[20] Rollo May, *Man's Search for Himself* (New York, W.W. Norton & Co., 1953), p. 14. The problem which seemed to me to be emerging in a new and unique form I first called the patients' "emptiness," not an en-

tirely well-chosen phrase. I meant by it a state closely allied to apathy.

[21] *Ibid.,* p. 24.

[22] *Ibid.*

[23] *Ibid.,* pp. 24-25.

[24] *Ibid.,* p. 25.

[25] *The New York Times,* March 27, 1964.

[26] *Ibid.,* April 16, 1964.

[27] *Ibid.,* May 6, 1964.

[28] Keniston, in *The Uncommitted,* speaking of this anomie, writes: "Our age inspires scant enthusiasm. In the industrial West, and increasingly now in the uncommitted nations, ardor is lacking; instead men talk of their growing distance from each other, from their social order, from their work and play, and from the values and heroes which in a perhaps romanticized past seem to have given order, meaning, and coherence to their lives."

[29] James H. Billington, "The Humanistic Heartbeat Has Failed," *Life Magazine,* May 24, 1968, p. 32.

[30] *Ibid.*

[31] *Ibid.*

[32] "Public apathy," says Dr. Karl Menninger, "is itself a manifestation of aggression." Karl Menninger at a conference of the Medical Correctional Association on violence, covered by *The New York Times,* April 12, 1964.

[33] The vast need of our society for touch and the revolt against its prohibition are shown in the growth of all the forms of touch therapy, from Esalen on down to the group therapy in the next room. These rightly reflect the need, but they are in error in their anti-intellectual basis and in the grandiose aims which they assert for what is essentially a corrective measure. They are also in error in their failure to see that this is an aspect of the whole society which must be changed, and changed on a deeper level involving the whole man.

[34] Harry Stack Sullivan, *The Psychiatric Interview* (New York, W.W. Norton & Co., 1954), p. 184.

[35] Bruno Bettleheim, *The Informed Heart* (Glencoe, Ill., The Free Press, 1960), pp. 20-21.

[36] Arthur J. Brodbeck, "Placing Aesthetic Developments in Social Context: A Program of Value Analysis," *Journal of Social Issues,* January, 1964, p. 17.

Rollo May has just made some fascinating and revealing comments on the cultural context of human communication. Although the essay was written in the sixties, it is still a cogent view of today's society. It is not a very positive picture, yet we see that implicit in the statement of the condition are some possible ways of alleviating it. It is little wonder that, in a world of machines and norms, one of the main problems facing a person is "Who am I?" (1). Bound up in this question are many others, such as: Does it matter? Where am I going? What really matters? and Who cares? These questions relate very firmly to the self that is asking them. The person is saying let *me* answer these questions—don't tell me the answers. Naive persons search for the answers in what they think is love (2), though they only partake of the experience without getting involved (3).

The artificiality of our existence in a technical world without human involvement leads to the condition of being schizoid (4), and this condition seems to predict the future (5). Since machines cannot return our love, we become immune to feelings. We objectify our relationships, seek technique over openness, and develop into a superrace of robots. Even the attacks on humanistic research by "scientific" scholars are concerned with the theme of not getting involved with the subjects (people) you are studying (6). To become involved means that *you* might have some effect on these people. This means you would be sharing some of your experience with them. By doing this, you communicate with them, and you may be as influenced by what they are feeling as they are by your reaching out (7). Since the major symptom of the present human condition is the loss of communication (8), and since there is no lack of sensory stimuli (the basis of the Shannon-Weaver model) even from human sources (radio, television, print), we may conclude that *one-way communication* (perception) *is not a sufficient antidote for the condition.* A closer look makes us realize that these very man-made systems tend to dehumanize us even more (9) because they do not let us relate.

When this same type of depersonalized communication (sending and receiving signals) takes place in the supermarkets, the classrooms, the churches, and the family, we learn how to talk but not to feel (10). We become more concerned about information (the weather, the world, and the witches) than we do about feelings, our own and others. But cocktail chatter that lasts for days, weeks, and months isn't very meaningful and breeds a sense of emptiness (11). Why? Perhaps it is because there is nothing we can do about the things we are talking about. They are beyond our control, so we can *only talk* about them (12). This feeling of powerlessness leads to a state of apathy (13). Why get involved? You can't do anything anyway. And so we leave the world to be run by those few mortals who somehow see it differently.

What we have just described is a person withdrawing into a shell to protect against possible damage to self. The paradox is that, in protecting the self against damage, we damage it ourselves. The healthy person is one who reaches out (14). This is a communicator as the humanist sees one, not the passive responder that the behaviorist envisions. From May's description it would appear that communication — a reaching out — is a need of all of us. To shut it off increases the probability of an eruption into violence (15). This does not mean that we become exposed selves, for we must keep in mind our embeddedness in society. Learning to live in a feelingless world without adopting its ways is the goal of the humanistic communicator. May says "the constructive schizoid person" can operate a machine without becoming one. This person learns when and how to feel and not get hurt by a machinelike society (16).

We have tried to give you a view of the world "out there" and indicate how it affects each of us. We would now like to present you with some activities that may help you become more aware of what it is like out there, by calling on some of your past experiences, and by putting you in other situations where these awarenesses can be highlighted.

THE SCHIZOID-WORLD ACTIVITIES

1. Who is responsible? Form a group and discuss the responsibility and control aspects of some national incident, such as Watergate, the war in Southeast Asia, the Middle East problems, the energy crises.

  a. Who makes decisions?
  b. Who is affected?
  c. Who is responsible?
  d. Can one person make a difference?

2. Do people care? In a group format, determine what you think is a burning issue in some segment of your society (dorm, college, town). Formulate a few questions and use them to survey people you think should be concerned.
  a. What percent would even talk to you?
  b. How many were aware of the problem?
  c. How many had done something about it?
  d. How many voiced a concern about the problem?
  e. How does this make you feel?
  f. What can you do about this condition?

3. In a group, discuss whether there is a "sufficient danger" in a world where people are unwilling to become involved in the affairs of others. What might some of these problems of noninvolvement lead to? Might there be more problems if people do mind others' business too much? Who should draw a line or say, "That's far enough"?

4. With some of your classmates, try to find out if a major difference exists among different age groups in our society in their willingness to become involved. For example, do younger persons show greater willingness to experience involvement with their peers than do older people (i.e., parents with other adults)?

5. Using the following questions to structure your remarks, give a persuasive speech answering yes or no to: "Is it possible to conclude that communication plays a specific role in one's involvement with another?" What is crucial about the role that communication may play? How does this role differ in different relationships? How many different types of communication might accompany human involvement or relationships?

The Human Problem

The condition reviewed by Rollo May is frightening, to say the least. He mentions in several places that a lack of communication is apparent. He does not mean a lack of stimulation, for if anything we have too much stimulation. The deficiency is in the sharing aspect of communication. As we indicated in Part 2, there can be little if any sharing without involvement in the communication event. It is a paradox that in a world where we can send voice signals (as well as men) to the moon we probably cannot express our feelings to our closest friends. In a society where we are expert in clumping people together to determine normative behavoir, the very system we establish to affect these norms (television, advertising, education) drives the individuals deeper into their isolated selves.

Is there a solution to this problem? Do we even know the real problem? At a speech communication convention in 1971, I (George Borden) was asked to delineate what I saw as the major problem in human communication research. We feel that what I said then is still very much the problem now. Because it was a speech, the style differs somewhat from present writing, but we think the forcefulness of the language helps to put the point across. Therefore, we are including it, with only minor revisions, to help define the problem with which we are confronted today.

A Major Problem in Human Communication:
The Rehumanization of the Dehumanized Person

George A. Borden

The twentieth century has already seen many amazing accomplishments in the field of communication. Communication theorists as different as Warren Weaver, Marshall McLuhan, and Eric Berne have focused the study of communication on a myriad of different aspects of the human communicaiton process. In the last twenty years it seems that everyone from physicist to journalist to preacher has worked on the problem of man's increasing inability to get along with himself and others. Each has written his own book on the subject and overnight a new cure-all is born. The next morning man wakes up to find himself in the same mess he was in the night before, but he has different names for both the dependent and independent variables, new mathematical systems by which he can manipulate these variables, and a more complex computer to facilitate the manipulation. Unfortunately, all of the theoretical gym-

nastics one cares to perform will not make him an athlete.

The tragic part of the preceding fairy tale is that it is not a fairy tale. Scientists such as Galileo, Newton, and Einstein, in conjunction with creative geniuses like Gutenberg, Marconi, and Edison, have developed and disseminated an abstract structure called the scientific method, which many feel can save the world. Whatever this method is—and the fact that its referent is ambiguous is the major problem—man has been able to use it to build a society second to none. The amorphous magic of this term and the many images it evokes threaten to destroy all of mankind. This insidious congitive set pervades the very core of Western man's mental faculties. By the time a child can say his own name he has encountered a million miracles of science. It is looked to to solve problems in every facet of our society. It is little wonder that politicians turn to science to solve the world's problems, or that those disciplines whose primary concern is the human being are modeling their research methods after those that have gained such great success for the natural sciences.

Now, I have no fight with the scientific method per se, only with the naiveté with which so many of us use this tool without understanding the implications of its use. Let me give you a couple of examples to indicate the subtlety with which it captivates its user and defeats him in the process. One need only skim the documentation of the warfare between science and religion to see how religion, which purports to be the perfect model for human relationships, was duped into using the very methods it fought against to carry on its own fight. Science had won the war whether it could win its argument or not. For it wasn't the proving or disproving of the existence of God or the infallability of the Bible that was really at stake; it was the way in which man chose to construct his view of reality. When theologians began using scientific method to analyze their data (trying to find observable, measurable data from which they could infer desired conclusions in a cause-effect relation), they had already joined the enemy.

One more example might make it clearer. In a recent three-day conference on computers and the humanities held at Penn State University, the computer was castigated unmercifully for dehumanizing the humanities. It was said that, because everything had to be defined so precisely before the computer could be of any help in analyzing it, man's aesthetic works were being reduced to a series of mathematical equations. (And since most of the participants in the conference had a great fear of mathematics, they saw nothing aesthetic about it!!) What they failed to see was that this

dehumanizing process has been in existence since man could think. It is called *analysis,* and it is defined as the "breaking up of any whole into its parts so as to find out their nature, proportion, function, relationship, etc." The ability to do this may be one of the truly human characteristics of man, while at the same time leading him toward dehumanization. Analysis became the very essence of the scientific method and was nurtured and preached by the natural sciences, which were able to experiment at will and replicate with vigor, until it became the only accepted way to know, to understand, and to learn. Experimentation, then, became equated with the scientific method, and the only proper way to do analyses. It has been copied rigorously by the behavioral sciences, even though their problems and their experimental material differ greatly.

We hope everyone is aware that the data which are the subjects of analysis by the hard and the soft sciences have very little in common. The hard sciences can experiment and replicate using the same sample of material. They can tear it apart chemically, electronically, or physically; put it back together again; and end up with essentially the same sample. Did you ever try doing this with a college sophomore? The point here is that the data for the natural sciences are mere objects to be experimented with and cast away when we have found out all we can about them. They may be treated any we can think of, and though a scientist may fall in love with a cubic centimeter of moon dust, his attachment to it doesn't affect the properties of the moon dust. Try that with a college sophomore!

Scientific progress in the natural sciences has been built on the ability of their scientists to use objective measurements on quantifiable data and to extrapolate these results in a deterministic model. Behavioral scientists have tried to do the same thing. Stimulus-response psychology was conceived on a deterministic model. When S-R psychologists found that man didn't really behave deterministically they had the splendid insight to take larger samples and use probabalistic models. This too was copied from the physical sciences and with the same lack of concern for the differences in the basic characteristics of the data as they had shown before. A million electrons are easy to come by, and who cares if you lose 10 percent of them through faults in the experimental apparatus? Would you say the same for college sophomores?

The point we are trying to make is that the basic rules of the scientific method (i.e., objectify, quantify, and extrapolate) do not fit well in humanistic research. The reason being that *a basic characteristic of humanness is subjectivity.* Take this away from a person and you have dehumanized him. *The behavioral scientist analyzing his data objectively dehumanizes it.* He tries to build this dehumanizing factor into his experiments, though he knows he cannot succeed. For example, he tells his subjects not to give their name or any self-identifying data. Then he asks them such questions as: Do you hate your father? Did you have sexual relations before you were married? What is your goal in life? etc., etc. How can you answer these questions and not reveal yourself? The experimentalists say, "Oh, but we didn't ask you for your name, so we can't connect the data with any specific individual. We just put it all together and compute norms, so we can tell how the 'normal' person would behave in given situations." And that is precisely the point. *We have been dehumanized and made into a theoretical, statistical norm.* Technological advances such as the broadcast media and the computer only *allow* us to take large quantities of dehumanized man and predict what products he will buy and what politicians he will elect.

You have all heard the jokes about the married couples who have 2.7 children and 1.4 automobiles. That can be humorous until you realize that billions of dollars change hands every year because probabalistic mathematics has given the advertising executive the power to use us as a statistic and reap the profits. Perhaps we could even live with this knowledge if we had the proper reinforcement each day to make us realize that we were a human being and not a statistic. The difficulty arises when we realize that scarcely anyone will recognize us as a human being. We are a teacher, a student, a housewife, a secretary, a preacher, etc., etc. All of these entities have been analyzed, objectified, quantified, and extrapolated until we can scarcely recognize ourselves. There are so many norms published in popular magazines that we can no longer even enjoy orgasm for fear it may end up being deviant behavior because we reached our climax too soon, too late, or not at all. We can describe a college sophomore in almost any way you desire, but I doubt that we really know a single one.

Now, what does all of this have to do with problems in human communication? From our point of view it is the major problem facing the human communication theorist. In a world where the "scientific method" is a nonconscious ideology, with its precepts being applied naively to the investigation of human behavior, how can we recognize ourselves as human beings and give others the benefit of the doubt.?

There have been notable attempts to put humanizing theories of human behavior into practice on both large- and small-scale models. If we may be so bold as to suggest that the Judeo-Christian tradition is one such attempt, we can see immediately that the principles were good (i.e., love, joy, peace, long suffering, gentleness, meekness, patience), but the results have been disastrous. Man screwed it up, and some of the bloodiest wars in history were fought *over* the use of this model. On a smaller scale, we may look at the history of communes and see that the failure rate approximates 100 percent. On an even smaller scale, we see the short-term T-group, sensitivity group, or encounter group therapy having only limited success — perhaps the reason being that it is nearly impossible to make a person who has been an object most of his life change his perception of himself and others by giving him a two-week crash course in human sensuousness and then sending him back into the world to be perceived as an object again.

Perhaps the most obvious model of human behavior proposed to facilitate the recognition of one's humanness is that of the family: husband, wife, children. The latest statistics on this model are also depressing. Divorce rates are increasing, and psychologists estimate that only 5 to 10 percent of those marriages that remain intact are fullfilling to both partners, to say nothing of the kids. Our present wife-swapping fads are even less an answer to this problem, for they are based on the condition that you do not make your lovemaking personal. My God! How much more an object can one become? The very relationship which would seem to have the greatest potential for solving the problem is consciously being dehumanized. With *Playboy* and *Cosmopolitan* constantly preaching the gospel of the female as an object, and women's lib failing to support the female's obvious human points, how can one develop any thought but the fact that women are objects; as are black people, poor people, sick people — in fact everyone but you and me. Then, when we wake up in the morning, we discover that we too are only objects.

In my estimation, then, the major problem facing communication theorists is how to rehumanize the dehumanized person.

PSA Convention   Pittsburgh, Pa. 1971

If the major problem is that of rehumanization, what are the chances of this occurring? Do you feel that society can be changed to facilitate openness and caring? The inventory on page 120 will allow you to discover some of your feelings along this line. Again, put 1 for strongly disagree, a 2 for disagree, a 3 for agree, and a 4 for strongly agree.

After you have filled out the inventory, you should discuss the results with others to see if your views of people agree with most others'. If they don't, do you feel a tendency to change your views? Why? Do you think most people are like you? How can we find out if it is possible to rehumanize the dehumanized person?

One of the primary goals of humanistic psychology is to humanize the investigative process by which we learn the underlying reasons for human behavior. Very little of this information can be obtained in the traditional laboratory, where people are objectified and processed much like an inert

---

SCALE G

A Humanistic Ethic Inventory

I FEEL THAT:

_____ 1. people will change if given the opportunity.

_____ 2. there is a great potential for goodness in the world.

_____ 3. people will accept the responsibility for improving human conditions.

_____ 4. people are interested in more than immediate satisfaction.

_____ 5. basically, people are really good.

_____ 6. most people are seeking a real, deep, intimate relationship.

_____ 7. most people would like to be open and honest in their relationships.

_____ 8. most people are aware of their real feelings.

_____ 9. most people have firm commitments to their relationships.

_____ 10. most people genuinely desire to grow into more mature persons.

---

gas. As has been indicated before, the only way to understand another's behavior is to understand the whole person. This takes time and involvement with the person. The understanding gained by such involvement helps both you and the other person become more humanistically oriented and better able to know your true self. But this necessitates an awareness of the situational variables that are contributing to the dehumanizing process.

It is possible to look at the problem of the dehumanized person from a different perspective and say that the problem isn't that the person has been dehumanized, but rather the problem is how the person can be rehumanized. Can situational variables be changed to facilitate this rehumanization? This perspective takes the problem out of the static world of the status quo and brings it into the dynamic world of human involvement. It may be stated in a behavioristic mode: How can we rehumanize the person? Or a humanistic mode: How can a person become rehumanized? A researcher working with the first question might increase the dehumanization in the process of trying to construct an environment that would stimulate or motivate the organism to participate in more humanizing activities. A researcher working with the second question might explore the potentialities of persons in general until he found what humanizing potentials were inherent in a person and then attempt to facilitate the development of these potentials.

One humanistic psychologist, James Bugental, has done this by developing a concept he calls the humanistic ethic, which when understood might help to facilitate a person's rehumanization. Dr. Bugental's article explaining the humanistic ethic follows. Again, as you read, pay particular attention to the numbered points and italicized passages.

The Humanistic Ethic—The Individual in Psychotherapy as a Societal Change Agent*

James F. T. Bugental
Psychological Service
Associates of
Northern California
Palo Alto

In our usual perspective, we think of the individual who seeks psychotherapy for himself as one who desires to change his own life experience. In this paper I want to take a somewhat different perspective and to suggest that many who have had a growthful therapeutic course emerge from that experience as societal change agents themselves. *The person who has discovered he can change what he doesn't like in himself may well seek to change that which he doesn't like in his environment as well.*

It will be recognized at once that I am speaking of a kind of therapeutic experience that has as its goal something quite other than producing "adjustment" in the patient. Indeed, that to me abhorrent term is almost diametrically opposite to what I hope those who honor me by being my patients will attain. I say *"almost diametrically opposite"* because I do not feel that my patients become anti-adjusted.

I hope—as I suppose many therapists do—that a patient completing therapy

* This article was reprinted, with permission, from the Spring 1971 issue of *The Journal of Humanistic Psychology*.

with me will support those societal forms which seem authentic to him in his own life and will work to change those that seem anti-authentic. In other words, I believe that we are social beings and that the healthy person will, in greater or lesser degree, express the social aspect of his life through concernedly being pro or con various phases of his world. Of course, these individuals will vary widely in the extent to which they choose to be so involved and in the stands they will take on particular issues. But the points I want to emphasize here are two: first, *the patient is apt to emerge from his therapeutic experience with heightened concern about his society and second, people who have really come to grasp what I want to call here the humanistic ethic are apt to share an impatience—or indignation—with that which is anti-therapeutic in our culture.*

I must note also that when I refer to the bloc of growth-oriented persons, of people supporting a humanistic ethic, I am by no means only speaking of those who have had a formal psychotherapeutic experience. We must recognize that this evolution—for that is what it is—is being supported also by those who have come to share some or all of the ethic by reason of unusually fortunate childhoods, by participation in basic encounter or sensitivity training programs, by reading and contemplation, through exceptional churches, classes, or seminars in connection with their work, or through the growth centers (e.g. Esalen).

The bulk of my presentation will be devoted to setting forth a first survey of this growth orientation.[3] I do not presume to see this statement as an ultimate or definitive one. It is more in the nature of a progress report. As the humanistic ethic emerges more onto the cultural scene, it may evolve in ways I cannot now estimate (Bugental, 1967). That is, indeed, one of its characteristics: It is not to be captured and contained within any one formulation for it is constantly evolving and has many forms and facets (Bugental, 1970). After making this sketch of my perspective on the therapeutic ethic, I will speculate very briefly about the impending collision between the anti-therapeutic and mechanomorphic forces in our culture and the growing numbers of persons who subscribe in some degree to the humanistic ethic.

A HUMANISTIC ETHIC

Centered Responsibility for One's Own Life

A foundation postulation of the humanistic ethic is that each person is the most responsible agency in his own life. While certainly recognizing the influence of contingency, of social pressure, and of concern for others, the humanistic ethic insists that these do not displace the person from being *the one who mediates all such influences and in large part determines how they will influence his being.* This is an aspect of what Rollo May (1959) has called "centeredness."

This responsibility is not one that can be delegated or displaced. One is certain to find that at times it involves feelings of guilt, of great emotional pain, and of course, of remorse, but it also can lead to an awareness of one's own potency, dignity, and meaningfulness.

[3] I will use the terms "humanistic ethic," "therapeutic ethic," and "growth orientation" largely interchangeably. This is not only to relieve the repetitiousness which would otherwise result but to make evident that I am not describing a fixed creed so much as an evolving set of attitudes shared in widely varying degrees and with much variation in specifics by a growing number of persons.

To the person who has not grasped the humanistic ethic, this orientation often seems at first to be a counsel of isolation or of unreal self-centeredness. It is neither; indeed, it is in many ways the reverse of both. *Claiming and accepting subjecthood in one's own life is a necessary pre-step to any valid encounter with another person, and it means accepting responsibility for one's own actions and experience, rather than acting as though licensed for self-indulgence.*

There is in the humanistic ethic an insistence on the right and the necessity of each person to be the subject — and the only subject — of his own life. This tenet is set in opposition to so much in our culture that tends toward transforming persons into semi-human objects: the credibility gap, propaganda and news manipulation, mass-produced entertainment for passive viewers, depersonalized educational curricula and procedures, and so on — including a mechanomorphic psychology that seeks to reduce the human experience to the banalities of rats, pigeons, and robots (Jourard, 1967).

The growth orientation may be illustrated by the way basic encounter groups call on their members to assert their own autonomy. Such groups grow impatient when someone attempts to explain himself largely in terms of outside influences. The following kinds of statements typically are challenged in such groups:

"I can't do that because my husband doesn't like it."
"It wouldn't be right for me to tell her how I feel if it might hurt her."
"What would people think if my feelings just came out?"

These statements do not express an authentic, responsible concern for others, but are instead expressions of a robot-like subservience to rules originating outside the self.

It is a familiar observation in psychotherapy that many of us in our middle class culture find it difficult to recognize our own feelings or to accept them as valid data. Our language is replete with disclaimers of our centered responsibility: We speak in the second and third persons when meaning the first. We say, "It occurred to me . . . ." when meaning "I think . . . ." And probably we find it hardest of all to explain our actions or intentions in such simple terms as "I felt like it," or "I want it" (Bugental, 1962).

Some have seen dynamic psychology — especially when a certain use is made of the concept of psychic determinism — as excusing all because whatever the individual found objectionable in himself could be blamed on his "unconscious." This, to my mind, is a perversion of a valuable concept. *Responsibility does not reside only in what is conscious but is intrinsic in the nature of being.* "Blame" is, of course, quite distinct from "responsibility" as I am using these terms here (Bugental, 1965).

The humanistic tenet is a recognition that each individual is the chief determinant of his own behavior and experience. This, of course, includes both conscious and unconscious processes in the person and recognizes that one cannot be responsible for all outcomes of his actions. It insists, however, that while we cannot choose all that befalls us, *we can choose how we will respond to it* — in Frankl's language, "the attitude we take toward it" (1957).

It is a familiar observation that people react very differently to the same event — be it a concentration camp, a professional success, a love relationship, the death of a friend. While, certainly, differences of early history are influential, I don't believe that even these are completely determining. *Each person ultimately is the only* aware *influence in determining his own life* (Bugental, 1969b).

Mutuality in Relationship

5   *A second tenet of the humanistic ethic is that the ideal for relationships between people is one of mutuality between persons each of whom is the subject of his own life and each of whom values and recognizes the subjecthood of the other.* This is Buber's "I-thou" relation. It is also the Hippies' "You do your thing, and I'll do mine," although in that form it is too easily mistaken for a counsel of non-relationship, or isolation. Neither in the best of the Hippie movement nor in the humanistic ethic is there an implication of detachment from concern for the other. The intent is, on the contrary, a kind of genuineness of encounter in which the autonomy of each is not only respected but is a solid foundation for meaningful relationship. It is, in a paradoxical way, a foundation which makes possible deeper encounter, greater caring, and less selfishness in the limited and pejorative meaning of that word.

So much in our culture teaches a form of relationship which treats the other person as an object to be manipulated, reacted to, or owned. How to Win Friends and Influence People stands as an epitome of the subject-to-object kind of pseudo-relating in which "friends" are *won* by stratagems and maneuvered with tactics to serve one's purposes. Until fairly recently, such a philosophy was the almost universal guide in employer-employee relations, and in more intimate relations it has been advanced with notable popular success by many.

The humanistic ethic, growing out of the therapeutic relation, the encounter group, and the teachings of men like Buber, Rogers, and others, insists that one depersonalizes others only at cost to his own humanness. *Relationship is too rich in its potentialities to be reduced to the level of operating as a machine.* Moreover this is so whether the intent in doing so is exploitative or seemingly beneficent. To treat the other person as an object in order to gain advantage over him is easily recognized as reprehensible. But to so treat him in order to help him is often heralded as a good thing. The humanistic ethic decries both equally, recognizing that the "management" of news by a well-intentioned president, the paternalistic policies of a "benevolent dictator" type of employer, and the soft-hearted reluctance to set limits for his child on the part of a "liberal" parent are all instances of the failure of relationship and the loss of the humanness to both parties to such maneuvers.

Among other generally accepted patterns of relationship, which therapeutically-oriented people are calling into question, would be that of exclusivity in man-woman relations. This means the end to the double-standard, to the myth of the virgin marriage, to the extreme value placed on marital fidelity, to the folk-tale of the wolf with his string of "conquests," and to the pseudo-ideal of sex for its own sake.

Now since this is a paradoxical list of folkways to be lumped together and since this area of man-woman relations is so central to human concerns, let me enlarge on this point.

The relation between a man and a woman which a society considers the expected model provides, it seems to me, a significant index of what that culture views as desirable in human relations generally. In some, but by no means all, antique societies, *women were clearly regarded as things, as generally interchangeable, and as seldom capable of attaining subjecthood in their own right.* Thus a man might have a number of women among his possessions.

In our culture—especially the middle class segment—we have a hodge-podge of folkways describing ideals for man-woman relations. These are often conflicting, much ignored at the level of behavior, and frequently the causes of emotional and relationship distress. Many are survivals in changed forms of the women-as-chattel tradition.

The "official" morality is, of course, that of the virginal man and woman who first discover their own and each other's bodies on the wedding night. This model is in some ways laughable, it is so little descriptive of what is lived out. It would be laughable, that is, except for the truly tragic toll it takes in human misery as people blame themselves for falling short of achieving it.

A contrasting morality is that of the virgin woman and the experienced man. This is, in many ways, the more general expectancy in our culture. And it is truly shocking that this is so, for it demonstrates a societal repression of an obvious inequality, with its callous disregard for the girls inevitably branded "bad." A societal model that so clearly ignores the humanity of an appreciable number of its members is only quantitatively different from the Roman acceptance of butchery in the Coliseum.

A third morality is that of the playboy. This is essentially the view that sex is a good thing and that one does well to get as much as possible—at least until marriage. Then the playboy and his playmate are supposed to undergo a metamorphosis and accept the traditional morality thereafter. Sex—before marriage, be it noted—is seen as a relatively simple natural function with only incidental implications for relationship or self-maturing.

The therapeutic ethic does not, as I see it, specify patterns of sexual behavior as such. Rather it focuses on relationship, and it values authenticity in relationship as among the highest goods potential in the human experience. Yet this position has important implications for sexuality. *Probably the epitome of intimate encounter is sexual intercourse between a man and woman who deeply love each other, who are mutually self-and-other respecting, and who are free to invest themselves fully in their coming together—free, that is, of fear, guilt, and of the need to act out other motives than those intrinsic to their own being together.* In such an experience there is genuine transcendence possible. It can mean a transcending of the separateness which is usually part of being human, a transcending of the difference between giving and receiving, a transcending of the boundaries of time and daily concerns. Clearly, the fullest loving and sexual meeting is a psychedelic experience, the potential for which is in our very nature.

The wise lover knows, however, that there is a Gresham's law governing such experiences. One may accept the discipline of being selective in his relationships and thus preserving their transcendent potentials, or he may yield to the invitations of opportunity and content himself with the pale simulations of the fullness that is potential. Although the choice is certainly not completely either-or, it is not possible to be both an indiscriminate playboy and a fully authentic lover.

What is implied here is that realization of the fullest potentials of one's sexual nature calls for realization of one's fullest potentials as a human being. One must come to terms in some measure with his own internal conflicts and one must relate to the other person in a genuine, mutually respecting fashion if there is to be a sexual meeting of meaningfulness. "Sexual," of course, here means much more than "physical." It subsumes emotional, personal, and relational.

6

What has just been said should make it evident also that the humanistic ethic does not include the idea of exclusivity in relationships, for that would amount to a kind of ownership of the other. Rather it counsels a selectivity or discrimination such as one would exercise in the care of any precious talent. This means that promiscuity will be seen as sad wastefulness but that the same can be said of blind fidelity.

Moreover, this orientation may free the area of sexual relations from the inappropriate annexations which custom has given it. Thus nudity or semi-nudity is not in itself a matter crucial to sexuality. Our culture generally, is coming to realize this, and newspapers can report — as I read recently about a "Love-in" — that many of the girls were near-nude without a fearful outcry resulting. As some encounter groups are discovering and as current styles are demonstrating, exposure of some or all of the body can be pleasant, even stimulating, without engendering mass orgies. Similarly, moderate sensuality—as in touching, embracing, and some caressing—is increasingly being lifted out of the realm of the fearful and forbidden.

All of these developments will surely have their effects on the institution of marriage. Just what evolution in the nature of marriage will result is difficult to foresee at this point; however, I believe that marriage may be becoming more an individual—may I say, creative?—expression of the relationship of particular couples rather than a socially monolithic imposition. The basis for this view may be summarized as follows.

I think the range of possible growth and fulfillment that is potential in human relationship is truly infinite. This means that two people dedicated to exploring all that their relation can yield may well devote their life-times to that exploration without exhausting its possibilities. *At the same time it seems self-evident that our existential situation is such that one must choose some experiences and relinquish others. One cannot, accordingly, choose to explore to the full the potentialities of relationship with a number of partners. When a person selects one partner and commits himself with that person to a full exploration of their relation's possibilities, then a marriage has occurred, and it is fitting that it should be celebrated with ceremony.*

But note, it is essential to this meaning of marriage that both parties be aware of the commitment they are jointly making and of the meanings each is giving to that commitment. If there are hidden codicils about ownership of one by the other, of urgency for material gain, of attempts to change the other, then the real meaning of marriage as I am depicting it is undermined. Moreover, if the passage of time results in one or the other of the spouses becoming unwilling or unable to continue such a total commitment, then the marriage itself no longer exists and the formal contract needs re-examination.

Further, there is in this conception no implication of exclusivity beyond that intrinsic to the joint exploration to which both are committed. *Relations with others—sexual or not—would be evaluated by the extent to which they contributed to or detracted from the common goal.* And, I believe, such other relations may at times help and at other times hinder movement toward such a shared goal.

Now, of course, I have presented an extreme, an idealistic picture. Couples may well choose any degree of commitment to such an exploration. It requires dedication and discipline to seek the far reaches of relationship potential. What is called for by the humanistic ethic, it seems to me, *is mutuality and openness in the choice and recognition that any affirmative choice also means some relinquishment.*

7

Here-and-Now Perspective

A third tenet of the humanistic ethic may be designated in a shorthand way as the here-and-now perspective. This outlook reminds us that one always lives only at the present moment. It is not devaluing of the past, but it recognizes that in a very real sense the past is mute and only the interpretations we make of it today give it meaning. The here-and-now perspective, similarly, does not counsel that we be blind to the future, but *it does insist that we are in this moment doing much that will determine that future and that it is only in the ever-flowing present that we can realize our own potentials.*

That somewhat poetic phrase I just used, "the ever-flowing present," evokes an image, I hope, of the process nature of being— an image important to appreciation of the here-and-now perspective. We are accustomed in much of our thinking to regarding ourselves as relatively static entities, having fixed natures, and seeking a consistency and stability in our own lives. The dearly loved homeostasis of the behaviorists is but one instance. Consistency is so highly prized that you have only to show a man how he has said one thing at one time and a contrasting thing at another to evoke from him a flood of rhetoric designed to demonstrate that both statements are really the same or that one is the logical outgrowth of the other. It is rare to hear, "I've learned differently" or "I was mistaken" or "I've changed my view."

Moreover, we press each other to be constant. We say, "But John, you're always so optimistic, how can you be doubtful now?" We resist seeing ourselves or others change and accuse the one who changes of bad faith. Yet one clear outcome of successful psychotherapy—as of other growth experiences—is that *the authentic person is constantly flowing, evolving, becoming. Moreover he values his own and others' flowingness and sees greater possibility rather than threat in it.*

The here-and-now perspective is expressed when a person seeks to know as well as possible what it is he is experiencing at each moment and what is the genuine nature of the situation in which he finds himself. In familiar terms, such a person seeks to be free of transference or parataxic distortions of his self-and-world view. This means he is less concerned with what he *should* think, feel, or do than are most of us in our culture.

A concomitant result of this present-valuing perspective is *a reduced emphasis on striving, on deferred living, and competitive attainment.* This is not to say that the authentic person imitates the grasshopper in Aesop's fable and idles away all his hours, but neither does he pattern himself on the ant and forego all experiencing of his life as it is in a narrow focus on trying to make it something else. This is certainly not a counsel of irresponsibility but a realistic reminder that living truly today is among the most important opportunities we have and is, at the same time, the best preparation for tomorrow.

Probably one of the places where a collision between the here-and-now perspective and the contemporary culture is most desirable is in the realm of education. I think it no exaggeration to say that our educational philosophy when viewed in the perspective of human history is almost tragically wasteful and even destructive. Twelve to twenty or more years of each person's most formative years are given over to an experience implicit with learnings about deferred living, extrinsic and competitive values, highly authoritarian social accommodation, and devaluing of the individual, the creative, and the immediate. Surely if there are future social historians, they will wonder that we could have been so ruthless with the greatest of our natural resources: our youth.

But I have broadened my indictment beyond our perspective in this paper. Let me return to that by emphasizing that the schools for the most part are organized to treat pupils as interchangeable objects and to enforce uniformity on those who resist it. This means that learning is supposedly fostered in terms of some distant period at which it will be valued, while spontaneous curiosity, investigativeness, and immediate application are regarded as distractions, devalued as "play," or punished as disruptions of discipline. That is a harsh picture, but unfortunately a reasonably accurate one in thousands of classrooms.

In all fairness, I want to acknowledge that not a few educators are aware of this situation and are seeking against great odds to bring about changes. I am here chiefly indicting the culture at large and its complacency in assuming we have an outstanding educational system.

Also let's look at that word "play" for a minute. By and large it means activity engaged in for its own sake rather than as a means to some other end. This latter is termed "work." I commend to you to watch a pre-school child at the beach or in some other setting unfamiliar to him. He will, if undistrubed, quite confound the experts who tell us how short is his attention span as he spends hours in exploring his world and himself. Is he playing or working? Clearly, he is doing both and going to school at the same time as he learns about gravity, about what his body parts can and cannot do, about the properties of water and sand, about heat and cold, and so on through an extensive and vital curriculum. Watch a grammar school child in a sand lot ball game intently learning more about the physical world and broadening his studies to include social relations. Watch a teenager, if you can, in a setting relatively free of adult supervision, and you will see him taking advanced studies in a variety of essential subjects: language and communication, sexuality and intimacy, limits and lack of limits in society, individuality vs. conformity.

In brief, the most life-significant learnings occur outside the educational structure, on a random basis, with little meaningful guidance from the adult world. Is it surprising that an appreciable number of the brighter, more creative, and more independent of our young people are tempted to drop out of the stultifying schools?

Acceptance of
Non-hedonic Emotions

A fourth phase of the humanistic ethic is *the recognition that such emotions as pain, conflict, grief, anger, and guilt are parts of the human experience to be understood and even valued rather than to be suppressed and hidden.* In the culture at large there is a general outlook which tends to see these "negative emotions or experiences" as evidence of something wrong or even shameful. While, to be sure, they may signal the need for attention, they are not, in the view of the humanistic ethic, seen as unexpected or disgraceful.

We have had, in our culture, a general attitude toward all of our emotions that seemed to regard them as dangerous potentials which each person carried within him and which might go off without warning or reason. We have feared strong feelings of all kinds and counseled one another not to feel "too happy," "too miserable," "too hopeful," and so on. Concurrently, immense amounts of talent invention, money, and time have been devoted to evoking emotions in controlled and even artificial ways through the arts, literature, sports, news media, and countless other forms. It is obvious that the suppression of the immediate, personal experience of one's emotions is intimately linked to the great demand for vicarious emotion.

10

Now all that I have just said about emotions in general is even more true when one considers those experiences which may be grouped as non-hedonic: anger, fear, conflict, grief, guilt, pain, and so on. We have treated these as unfortunate defects in our constitution and often have railed at God or nature for including them in the human design.

Those who have come to terms with their own being through psychotherapy or some other means usually learn, however, that these seemingly unwanted parts of life are in fact essential to full human experience. Encounter group members, for example, come to reject premature reassurance to one of their fellows who is troubled and to object to those who seek to smooth over or evade differences and antagonisms. We have learned that emotion of any character is not simply "disorganized response" (as at least some mechanomorphic psychologists see it). It is, rather, *an expression of an experienced meaning in the person's life.*

Repeatedly the psychotherapist sees how full confrontation of intense, even excruciating, feelings is essential to his patient's (and his own) preservation of what is valid and significant in life (Bugental, 1969a). Moreover, since the non-hedonic emotions are often aroused at life junctures at which choices of lasting significance must be made, the suppression of such feelings — as many attempt — only results in incomplete and ill-founded decisions being made with the inevitable consequences of failing commitment and renewed distress.

An area in which this recognition of the importance of accepting all emotions is finding a new and very practical application is that of human relations training in industry. Where once business people sought conflict-free working environments and regarded personal emotions as intrusions on the supposedly reasonable workaday world, some better

informed companies are recognizing today that personal feelings are essential parts of human beings and must be included in the way the firm is administered. Thus work-family encounter groups are being developed in which a new candor between boss and subordinates is encouraged, and conflicts — with their attendant anger and hurt — are brought out into the open (Rogers, 1967).

Similarly, in friendships and marriages, *the humanistic ethic recognizes that such feelings — including guilt and grief, as well — are to be expected and that, expected, they may be disclosed and used as the basis for strenghtening the bonds between the people involved.*

It is difficult, in a way, to convey what a significant change this means for the human experience. It implies an outlook on one's own life and on relations with others in which the threat of catastrophe is materially lessened. It means, as well, that a man learns that he, his fellows, and the ties they have to each other are not as fragile or tenuous as he may have feared. In sum it increases our sense of our own durability and our dignity.

Growth-oriented Experiencing

A final aspect of the humanistic ethic with which I will deal here has to do with the *seeking for growth-facilitating experiences* which is characteristic of people who have incorporated the humanistic ethic. Of course, what I have already said depicts this valuing as much as it does the specifics with which I have dealt. However, since at root the humanistic ethic is more a value statement about how one experiences his life than anything else, it is important to render this statement as explicit as possible.

The centering of attention on the individual person, on his autonomy and dignity, on his seeking to be authentic and the subject of his own life is, of course, a value position of keystone importance. Correlatively, the kinds of life experiences which are sought will be those in which the relations among persons express the valuing of the individual in mutuality. Here it is important to recognize that the value orientation is not in terms of the traditional "good and bad" or "should and should not," but is cast in a perspective which respects each person's efforts to do what he can with his life and appreciates his gains in authenticity while regretting or even challenging his dropping back from what is potential.

This latter point is important to make more evident: If in a relationship one person does something that hurts the other, traditionally the hurt one had the social "right" to blame the doer of the hurt. Alternatively, he could be long-suffering and hide that he was hurt. The growth-orientation would insist that both of these courses are inauthentic and destructive to the relation and thus to the individuals involved. *Instead, the ideal would be for the hurt person and the other to face candidly what has occurred, for the anger and regret intrinsic to the situation itself to be expressed, and for the two to attempt then to forestall recurrences.* This last step would surely call for the one who was hurt to seek out those ways in which he himself cooperated — perhaps unconsciously — in bringing about the hurt, for it is very much in keeping with the concept of mutual subjecthood that no person in a relationship is seen as solely responsible for what happens.

Notably absent from this account are recriminations, allusions to other matters outside the point at issue, requirements of compensatory pain, or personal charges and countercharges. *It is recognized, instead, that people who risk being genuinely open and close to each other will inevitably hurt each other at times and that any attempt to keep score and balance out hurts ignores the omnipresent mutual responsibility and makes one or the other or both into objects rather than subjects.*

It may be protested that this is an ideal not humanly attainable, but I do not believe it is so extreme but what many people are working toward it with evident gains for themselves and their relationships. The long-term freeing of relationships and of the individuals involved is a benefit hard to overestimate.

The therapeutic ethic, thus, centers its values around a perception of each person as worthy in his own right and of genuine relationship as one of life's prime fulfillments. This centering is most evident in the communication that exists among people who share commitment to the humanistic ethic.

Among such people there is a sense of rapport which contrasts markedly with the banality of usual conversation. There is a quality of directness, meaningfulness, and self-disclosure that arises from involvement and willingness to risk. Much talk, as we all know, in ordinary situations is superficial, safe, and detached.

As a consequence of the personal feelings arising from this contrast in ways of relating, persons committed to the humanistic ethic frequently express a need and desire to develop social structures to provide more opportunities for such communication. In some cases, these take the form of leaderless encounter groups which meet regularly and provide an opportunity for more meaningful interaction than do the more usual social occasions. Another emerging medium for such encounters is typified by the pioneering of Esalen and other growth centers where people come together for more intense, emotional, and meaningful exchanges. These exchanges contrast radically with the "entertainment" through vicarious emotion described above. At these centers personal experiencing is valued and facilitated.

Similarly, unmarried people who have come to accept the growth ethic frequently find they do not want to marry someone who does not share this perspective, and married persons whose spouses do not have such an orientation are deeply troubled by the resulting discrepancy.

All of this, of course, smacks of cultism, and in our culture that tends to be a bad word. Yet I believe that there is much that is hopeful in the growing numbers of these people whom one social scientist has half-humorously called an "emotional aristocracy." Cultish they may be, in that they still are a minority bound together by values and attitudes that the surrounding majority does not understand or share. But cultish they are not in any invidious sense or with any intent to keep others out. Admission is simply a matter of a person's seeking to come to terms with himself and to deal with others on a basis of mutual dignity and responsibility. In other words, this is an aristocracy, if you like, that would gladly become a democracy and whose ranks are open to any who will accept the challenge and opportunity to live more genuinely and openly.

THE COLLISION BETWEEN THE HUMANISTIC ETHIC AND CONTEMPORARY SOCIETY

As the number and influence of persons committed to the humanistic ethic grow, there are certain to be points of collision with the environing culture (Bugental, 1968). Although a society must grow and change to survive, every society—ours most certainly—needs and has forces which resist change. These too are essential. However, when a society is affluent,

the conservative forces often tend to be disproportionately strong and then there is the danger that evolution will be stifled. Of course, then revolution becomes more likely. This, I think, is what is happening in our own society. There is clearly a Black revolution in process. Less often recognized is the youth revolution, of which the Hippies are one wing. I think a humanistic evolution may be in the offing.

Now the humanistic ethic, as I have tried to show, runs counter to much that has long been traditional in our culture. As it increases in its impact, a counter force is arising. Today psychotherapy, for example, is seen as a good thing by some, as a dangerous influence by others, and is largely outside the perceptual worlds of a majority of people. But as the variance between therapeutic values and traditional values increases, as the contrast between the popular image of the therapist as a wise man who tells people how to adjust to society and the actuality of therapists pioneering new orientations to human relations becomes more evident, then we may well see a backlash. It is likely that many psychotherapists today could be charged with malpractice, communism, atheism, immorality, and creating dissent, and the charges would be supported in many tradition-conserving settings. Tomorrow, when the traditions are more clearly endangered, we may experience just such prosecutions. Then issues of professional discretion, confidentiality, freedom of professional judgment, the right of an individual to choose his therapist, the public meaning of having been in therapy—all these and others may become points of conflict, hurt, and challenge to the well-being of therapists and others. Another Joe McCarthy could have a field day with psychotherapists and their patients, given the right combination of timing and ruthlessness.

For make no mistake about it, we who share this emerging ethic are a threat to the establishment. It is only that the size and pervasiveness of that threat is as yet unrecognized.

If an evolved humanistic ethic is to make its contribution to the evolutionary stream of man's development, it will require our courage, our dedication, and our persistence. The preliminary statement I have offered here of what I have chosen to call a humanistic ethic must be revised, expanded, and better articulated. This process will also call for us to find improved ways of helping more people to fuller realization of their human potentials. *But in the end it calls upon us as individuals to try to live as fully human lives as we can and to know that by doing so we are not only gaining a measure of our own living but adding our bits to the humanization of man.*

REFERENCES

Bugental, J.F.T. A phenomenological hypothesis of neurotic determinants and their therapy. *Psychological Reports*, 1962, *10*, 527–530.

————. *The search for . authenticity.* New York: Holt, Rinehart & Winston, 1965.

————. The challenge that is man. In J.F.T. Bugental (Ed.), *Challenges of humanistic psychology.* New York: McGraw-Hill, 1967, Ch. 1.

————. Psychotherapy as a source of the therapist's own authenticity and inauthenticity. *Voices*, 1968, *4*, 13–23.

————. Intentionality and ambivalence. In R. McLeod (Ed.) *The unfinished business of William James.* Washington: American Psychological Association, 1969, 93–98. (a)

————. Someone needs to worry: The existential anxiety of responsibility and decision. *Journal of Contemporary Psychotherapy*, 1969, *2* (1), 41–53. (b)

————. Changes in inner human experience and the future. In C.S. Wallia (Ed.), *Toward Century 21: Technology, society and human values.* New York: Basic Books, 1970, 283–295.

Frankl, V.W. *The doctor and the soul.* New York: Knopf, 1957.

Jourard, S.N. Experimenter-subject dialogue: A paradigm for a humanistic science of psychology. In J.F.T. Bugental (Ed.) *Challenges of humanistic psychology.* New York: McGraw-Hill, 1967, 109–116.

May, R. Toward the ontological basis of psychotherapy. *Existential Inquiries*, 1959, *1* (1), 5–7.

Rogers, C.R. The process of the basic encounter group. In J.F.T. Bugental (Ed.), *Challenges of humanistic psychology.* New York: McGraw-Hill, 1967, 261–276.

Leading up to this article, we had painted a pretty bleak picture. In considering the rehumanizing of the dehumanized person, we were concerned primarily with the individual, how the situational variables could be changed to facilitate humanistic trowth. Bugental gives evidence that rehumanization may be contagious, that the situational variables to be changed are the people themselves. The claim that "the person who has discovered he can change what he doesn't like in himself may well seek to change that which he doesn't like in his environment as well" is exciting to consider. The changed behavior in one person may facilitate a change in the behavior of another, thus changing society as a whole (1). The basis of the rehumanizing force is the realization that each person is responsible for his or her own life (2). This means that we must look at ourselves subjectively (3). We have been taught so thoroughly to look at things objectively that we treat ourselves in the same manner. Subjectifying ourselves means that we must recognize our own feelings (4) and not be afraid to express them.

The Dale Carnegie approach to human friendship and influence has so penetrated our culture that we feel we have to be pleasant, say what "should" be said, be interested in what our "potential friends" are interested in, and praise them for what they are doing whether we believe in it or not. This approach has led to an atmosphere of suspicion and mistrust in interpersonal communication. Bugental points out that we must reverse this procedure and approach relationships in an honest and open fashion (5). He uses the male-female relationship as an example and indicates that the more healthy the relationship, the more "self-and-other respecting" the participants are (6). This means that they each are able to look at themselves and the other subjectively and not as an object for which certain functions are specified (e.g., female as sexual object and male as provider object). This is not to say that each relationship is to be completely consuming. It does mean that relationships should be entered into with open realization and commitment to their individual potential (7)—some may only have a sexual, professional, or friendship potential, not an exclusive mating.

An overriding consideration in the humanistic ethic is that we must be conscious of living in the here and now to gain the most from each experience we have (8). This affects our communication in many ways because it requires us to find out the "genuine nature of the situation." To do this, we must be able to change our perspective on life from one of attainment to one of living (9)—working to live versus living to work. The ability to accept ourselves as we are and others as they are in situations that result in pain, fear, grief, or guilt helps us to develop the fullness of our human potential (10) by being able to express these emotions without fear of reprisal. Thus, we are able to explore these emotions in growth-producing experiences and to develop a firm self-concept (11). We should be aware, however, that *there is a risk involved in being open and honest in a relationship.* If the other is not able or willing to approach the relationship with the same feelings, there can be disastrous results. Though openness may at times hurt, if both members of a relationship are committed to the potential of that relationship, the growth produced by mutual understanding can only be good for both parties (12).

We have now considered the problem of rehumanizing the dehumanized person by facilitating personal growth through *self-actualization—the realization of one's potential through constructive assertion of one's individuality.* We include the following activities to help you understand the above principles better.

HUMANISTIC ETHIC ACTIVITIES

1. Keep a diary for a day or two noting each instance of dehumanization that occurs to you.
   a. Through group discussion see if you can determine what "causes" this behavior in others.
   b. Do you sometimes practice the same behavior?
   c. Is this type of behavior reflexive? (If you do it to someone, is he or she apt to respond in the same way?)
   d. How can we change this pattern of behavior?
2. Where does society's responsibility end and the individual's begin? Interview several administrators (company executives, college administrators), professional people (doctors, lawyers), and service people (mechanics, plumbers) to determine what precautions they take for mistakes they might make.
   a. Do they have insurance to cover such things?
   b. Do they take the responsibility for their decisions?
   c. What effects do these precautions have on the integrity of the individual?
   d. Can you rank the relative responsibleness of various occupations?
3. Consider the person as object and review various creeds to see how prevalent this concept is in (a) the Bible, (b) the U.S. Constitution, (c) the *Communist Manifesto,* (d) *Mein Kampf.* Report your findings to the class.
4. What are some of the difficulties in living a here-and-now existence? Form a group and discuss the problems of maintaining this attitude, considering one's (a) goal in life, (b) possibilities of employment, (c) intimate relationships, (d) personal development (growth).
5. Can you express your emotions? Keep a diary noting the times when you suppressed an emotion.
   a. Why did you do this?
   b. How do you feel when others express their emotions (cry, scream, laugh)?
   c. Why do you feel this way?
   d. Form a group and discuss the cultural taboos on the showing of emotions. Which emotions are socially acceptable? Which are not?
   e. What are the effects of emotion-expressing behavior? On you? On those around you?
6. What kinds of experiences would you like to have? Daydream for a while and jot down the experiences you see yourself having.
   a. Are there any patterns to them?
   b. What keeps you from doing these things?
   c. Would these experiences help you to develop a better knowledge of yourself?
   d. See if you can find others who have similar desires and feelings.

The Human Potential

We have seen that the humanistic view of the present situation is that our society has been allowed to develop persons without feelings. This has been done by a rather subtle form of dehumanization called operant conditioning, which is reinforcement for exhibiting desired normative behavior. The problem facing us is how to rehumanize the dehumanized person. The development of a humanistic ethic has been proposed as one solution to this problem. But such a solution has problems in itself. How does one develop this ethic? Can we just inform everyone that they are free and expect them to become responsible, expressive, loving people? What will it take to develop this type of behavior in our society?

Certainly Bugental's idea that humanistic behavior is reflexive (people will respond to behavior in like manner) is intriguing. Unfortunately, it works both ways. Our society has progressed so far into the crass, competitive, commercial world that it doesn't want to be bothered with human interaction. Its reflexiveness is seen in the statement "If you don't meddle in my affairs, then I won't meddle in yours." Under the guise of letting each individual be autonomous, we are really cutting each other off from human contact. This may lead to the situation in which the respondent takes advantage of Bugental's person. But are our feelings about the humanistic person really true, or do they reflect the image we have of someone who shows love by letting others have their way and running roughshod over him or her? This is not the image that Bugental presented, nor is it the image presented by other humanistic psychologists. Rather, they present the image of a "fully functioning" person as one who knows the self, the other, and is able to be open about their interrelationships.

It seems that the humanistic person has a different set of values from one who is not. In Scale H on page 136 we have given you ten values of the humanistic person. Fill in each blank as the value applies to you, putting a 1 for almost never, a 2 for sometimes, and a 3 for usually.

It would help you see yourself better if you could get a friend or two to fill out this scale as they see you (I THINK YOU). A discussion of the difference between your perceptions will facilitate your growth.

Openness and *integrity* are two key concepts here. If we are in tune with our own selves to the point that we know our values and how and why we feel about an event, then we should be able to stand by these values and not allow our integrity to be compromised. This means asserting the self, not as a manipulative device by which to gain control of another's behavior, but in open, honest, dialectic discussion to move toward a solution of problems that is agreeable to both parties. It means not having hidden agendas or role-

---

SCALE H

A Humanistic Values Inventory

I THINK THAT I:

_____ 1. am able to transcend myself and integrate others' needs with my own.

_____ 2. am open and real in my relationships.

_____ 3. will maintain my integrity even though I may lose face.

_____ 4. value the human experience above all else.

_____ 5. strive for deep, intimate relationships.

_____ 6. appreciate others for being just themselves.

_____ 7. am more interested in process than product.

_____ 8. am not controlled by the expectations of others.

_____ 9. am aware of, and value, my own feelings.

_____ 10. prefer to be myself rather than putting up a front.

---

playing to falsely influence another's behavior. It also means facilitating this type of behavior in others to the point of insisting that *other people be responsible for their behavior,* by helping them see when and where they are not. This type of behavior should encourage others to understand their own behavior and in doing so move toward self-actualization.

This view sees the person as one who is active, assertive of self, constructive, helpful, patient, and empathetic with others' problems. However, being empathetic does not mean excusing anyone's behavior. It means attempting to find out why the behavior occurred by getting to know the whole person and coincidentally helping that person to know him- or herself. It means encouraging people to express themselves openly so relationships can be built on solid understandings of each other. The key to this sequence of events is interpersonal communication — individuals relating in open discourse, revealing honest feelings about each other to see if they can find a potential for their relationship that will make it worth committing to. If not, they can go their separate ways knowing themselves better from having had the experience. If they find a potential, then they can commit to it and continue to work towards realizing it.

What we are talking about here is the development of the urgency variables to be active in *all* our communication events. When we communicate, the uppermost urgency should be unconditional positive regard for that person. This cannot, however, take complete precedence over our own value system. We must maintain our integrity. If we can develop our value system in conjunction with our concern for others, perhaps we will be able to transcend both the situational and cultural variables. To do so, we must know ourselves and be aware of our urgency to facilitate growth in other people.

How can we develop this kind of understanding of ourselves and commitment toward others? Carl Rogers has investigated this problem for many years and gives us some guidelines in the following article. He focuses his comments on the development of values, which he considers the crucial element in personal growth. As you read his article, pay particular attention to the numbered and the italicized passages.

Toward a Modern Approach to Values: The Valuing Process in the Mature Person*

Carl R. Rogers
Western Behavioral
Sciences Institute,
La Jolla, California

There is a great deal of concern today with the problem of values. Youth, in almost every country, is deeply uncertain of its value orientation; the values associated with various religions have lost much of their influence; sophisticated individuals in every culture seem unsure and troubled as to the goals they hold in esteem. The reasons are not far to seek. *The world culture, in all its aspects, seems increasingly scientific and relativistic, and the rigid, absolute views on values which come to us from the past appear anachronistic.* Even more important, perhaps, is the fact that the modern individual is assailed from every angle by divergent and contradictory value claims. It is no longer possible, as it was in the not too distant historical past, to settle comfortably into the value system of one's forebears or one's community and *live out one's life without ever examining the nature of the assumptions of that system.*

In this situation it is not surprising that value orientations from the past appear to be in a state of disintegration or collapse. Men question whether there are, or can be, any universal values. It is often felt that we may have lost, in our modern world, all possibility of any general or cross-cultural basis for values. One natural result of this uncertainty and confusion is that there is an increasing concern

* This article was originally published in Volume 68 of the *Journal of Abnormal and Social Psychology* (ii), pp. 160–167. Copyright 1964 by The American Psychological Association. Reprinted by permission.

about, interest in, and a searching for, a sound or meaningful value approach which can hold its own in today's world.

I share this general concern. As with other issues the general problem faced by the culture is painfully and specifically evident in the cultural microcosm which is called the therapeutic relationship, which is my sphere of experience.

As a consequence of this experience I should like to attempt a modest theoretical approach to this whole problem. I have observed changes in the approach to values as the individual grows from infancy to adulthood. I observe further changes when, if he is fortunate, he continues to grow toward true psychological maturity. Many of these observations grow out of my experience as therapist, where I have had the mind stretching opportunity of seeing the ways in which individuals move toward a richer life. From these observations I believe I see some directional threads emerging which might offer a new concept of the valuing process, more tenable in the modern world. I have made a beginning by presenting some of these ideas partially in previous writings (Rogers, 1951, 1959); I would like now to voice them more clearly and more fully.

Some Definitions

Charles Morris (1956, pp. 9–12) has made some useful distinctions in regard to values. There are "operative values," which are the behaviors of organisms in which they show preference for one object or objective rather than another. The lowly earthworm, selecting the smooth arm of a Y maze rather than the arm which is paved with sandpaper, is giving an indication of an operative value.

There are also "conceived values," the preference of an individual for a symbol-ized object. "Honesty is the best policy" is such a conceived value.

There is also the term "objective value," to refer to what is objectively preferable, whether or not it is sensed or conceived of as desirable. I will be concerned primarily with operative or conceptualized values.

Infant's Way of Valuing

Let me first speak about the infant. The living human being has, at the outset, a clear approach to values. *We can infer from studying his behavior that he prefers those experiences which maintain, enhance, or actualize his organism, and rejects those which do not serve this end.* Watch him for a bit:

Hunger is negatively valued. His expression of this often comes through loud and clear.

Food is positively valued. But when he is satisfied, food is negatively valued, and the same milk he responded to so eagerly is now spit out, or the breast which seemed so satisfying is now rejected as he turns his head away from the nipple with an amusing facial expression of disgust and revulsion.

He values security, and the holding and caressing which seem to communicate security.

He values new experience for its own sake, and we observe this in his obvious pleasure in discovering his toes, in his searching movements, in his endless curiosity.

He shows a clear negative valuing of pain, bitter tastes, sudden loud sounds.

All of this is commonplace, but let us look at these facts in terms of what they tell us about the infant's approach to values. It is first of all a flexible, changing, valuing *process,* not a fixed system. He likes food and dislikes the same food.

He values security and rest, and rejects it for new experience. What is going on seems best described as an organismic valuing process, in which each element, each moment of what he is experiencing is somehow weighed, and selected or rejected, depending on whether, at that moment, it tends to actualize the organism or not. This complicated weighing of experience is clearly an organismic, not a conscious or symbolic function. These are operative, not conceived values. But this process can nonetheless deal with complex value problems. I would remind you of the experiment in which young infants had spread in front of them a score or more of dishes of natural (that is, unflavored) foods. Over a period of time they clearly tended to value the food which enhanced their own survival, growth, and development. If for a time a child gorged himself on starches, this would soon be balanced by a protein "binge." If at times he chose a diet deficient in some vitamin, he would later seek out foods rich in this very vitamin. The physiological wisdom of his body guided his behavioral movements, resulting in what we might think of as objectively sound value choices.

Another aspect of the infant's approach to values is that the source or locus of the evaluating process is clearly within himself. Unlike many of us, he knows *what he likes and dislikes, and the origin of these value choices lies strictly within himself.* He is the center of the valuing process, the evidence for his choices being supplied by his own senses. He is not at this point influenced by what his parents think he should prefer, or by what the church says, or by the opinion of the latest "expert" in the field, or by the persuasive talents of an advertising firm. It is from within his own experiencing that his organism is saying in nonverbal terms, "This is good for me."

"That is bad for me." "I like this." "I strongly dislike that." He would laugh at our concern over values, if he could understand it.

Change in the Valuing Process

What happens to this efficient, soundly based valuing process? By what sequence of events do we exchange it for the more rigid, uncertain, inefficient approach to values which characterizes most of us as adults? Let me try to state briefly one of the major ways in which I think this happens.

The infant needs love, wants it, tends to behave in ways which will bring a repetition of this wanted experience. But this brings complications. He pulls baby sister's hair, and finds it satisfying to hear her wails and protests. He then hears that he is "a naughty, bad boy," and this may be reinforced by a slap on the hand. He is cut off from affection. As this experience is repeated, and many, many others like it, he gradually learns that what "feels good" is often "bad" in the eyes of significant others. Then the next step occurs, in which he comes to take the same attitude toward himself which these others have taken. Now, as he pulls his sister's hair, he solemnly intones, "Bad, bad boy." He is introjecting the value judgment of another, taking it in as his own. To that degree he loses touch with his own organismic valuing process. *He has deserted the wisdom of his organism, giving up the locus of evaluation, and is trying to behave in terms of values set by another, in order to hold love.*

Or take another example at an older level. A boy senses, though perhaps not consciously, that he is more loved and prized by his parents when he thinks of being a doctor than when he thinks of being an artist. Gradually he introjects the

as a guide to his behavior. Gendlin (1961, 1962) has elaborated the way in which this occurs. As his experiencing becomes more and more open to him, as he is able to live more freely in the process of his feelings, then significant changes begin to occur in his approach to values. It begins to assume many of the characteristics it had in infancy.

Introjected Values in Relation to Experiencing

Perhaps I can indicate this by reviewing a few of the brief examples of introjected values which I have given, and suggesting what happens to them as the individual comes closer to what is going on within him.

The individual in therapy looks back and realizes, "But I *enjoyed* pulling my sister's hair — and that doesn't make me a bad person."

The student failing chemistry realizes, as he gets close to his own experiencing, "I don't like chemistry; I don't value being a doctor, even though my parents do; and I am not a failure for having these feelings."

The adult recognizes that sexual desires and behavior may be richly satisfying and permanently enriching in their consequences, or shallow and temporary and less than satisfying. He goes by his own experiencing, which does not always coincide with social norms.

He recognizes freely that this communist book or person expresses attitudes and goals which he shares as well as ideas and values which he does not share.

He realizes that at times he experiences cooperation as meaningful and valuable to him, and that at other times he wishes to be alone and act alone.

Valuing in the Mature Person

The valuing process which seems to develop in this more mature person is in some ways very much like that in the infant, and in some ways quite different. It is fluid, flexible, based on this particular moment, and the degree to which this moment is experienced as enhancing and actualizing. Values are not held rigidly, but are continually changing. The painting which last year seemed meaningful now appears uninteresting, the way of working with individuals which was formerly experienced as good now seems inadequate, the belief which then seemed true is now experienced as only partly true, or perhaps false.

Another characteristic of the way this person values experience is that it is highly differentiated, or as the semanticists would say, extensional. The examples in the preceding section indicate what were previously rather solid monolithic introjected values now become differentiated, tied to a particular time and experience.

Another characteristic of the mature individual's approach is that the locus of evaluation is again established firmly within the person. It is his own experience which provides the value information or feedback. This does not mean that he is not open to all the evidence he can obtain from other sources. But it means that this is taken for what it is — outside evidence — and is not as significant as his own reactions. Thus he may be told by a friend that a new book is very disappointing. He reads two unfavorable reviews of the book. Thus his tentative hypothesis is that he will not value the book. Yet if he reads the book his valuing will be based upon the reactions it stirs in *him,* not on what he has been told by others.

There is also involved in this valuing process a letting oneself down into the immediacy of what one is experiencing, endeavoring to sense and to clarify all its complex meanings. I think of a client who, toward the close of therapy, when puzzled about an issue, would put his head in his hands and say, "Now what *is* it that I'm feeling? I want to get next to it. I want to learn what it is." Then he would wait, quietly and patiently, trying to listen to himself, until he could discern the exact flavor of the feelings he was experiencing. He, like others, was trying to get close to himself.

In getting close to what is going on within himself, the process is much more complex than it is in the infant. In the mature person it has much more scope and sweep. For there is involved in the present moment of experiencing the memory traces of all the relevant learnings from the past. This moment has not only its immediate sensory impact, but it has meaning growing out of similar experiences in the past (Gendlin, 1962). It has both the new and the old in it. So when I experience a painting or a person, my experiencing contains within it the learnings I have accumulated from past meetings with paintings or persons, as well as the new impact of this particular encounter. Likewise the moment of experiencing contains, for the mature adult, hypotheses about consequences. "It is not pleasant to express forthrightly my negative feelings to this person, but past experience indicates that in a continuing relationship it will be helpful in the long run." Past and future are both in this moment and enter into the valuing.

I find that in the person I am speaking of (and here again we see a similarity to the infant), the criterion of the valuing process is the degree to which the object of the experience actualizes the individual himself. Does it make him a richer, more complete, more fully developed person? This may sound as though it were a selfish or unsocial criterion, but it does not prove to be so, since deep and helpful relationships with others are experienced as actualizing.

Like the infant, too, the psychologically mature adult trusts and uses the wisdom of his organism, with the difference that he is able to do so knowingly. He realizes that if he can trust all of himself, his feelings and his intuitions may be wiser than his mind, that as a total person he can be more sensitive and accurate than his thoughts alone. Hence he is not afraid to say, "I feel that this experience [or this thing, or this direction] is good. Later I will probably know *why* I feel it is good." He trusts the totality of himself, having moved toward becoming what Lancelot Whyte (1950) regards as "the unitary man."

It should be evident from what I have been saying that this valuing process in the mature individual is not an easy or simple thing. The process is complex, the choices often very perplexing and difficult, and there is no guarantee that the choice which is made will in fact prove to be self-actualizing. But because whatever evidence exists is available to the individual, and because he is open to his experiencing, errors are correctable. If this chosen course of action is not self-enchancing this will be sensed and he can make an adjustment or revision. He thrives on a maximum feedback interchange, and thus, like the gyroscopic compass on a ship, can continually correct his course toward his true goal of self-fulfillment.

Some Propositions Regarding the Valuing Process

Let me sharpen the meaning of what I have been saying by stating two propositions which contain the essential elements of this viewpoint. While it may not be possible to devise empirical tests of each proposition in its entirety, yet each is to some degree capable of being tested through the methods of psychological science. I would also state that though the following propositions are stated firmly in order to give them clarity, I am actually advancing them as decidedly tentative hypotheses.

Hypothesis I. There is an organismic base for an organized valuing process within the human individual.

It is hypothesized that this base is something the human being shares with the rest of the animate world. It is part of the functioning life process of any healthy organism. It is the capacity for receiving feedback information which enables the organism continually to adjust its behavior and reactions so as to achieve the maximum possible self-enhancement.

Hypothesis II. This valuing process in the human being is effective in achieving self-enhancement to the degree that the individual is open to the experiencing which is going on within himself.

I have tried to give two examples of individuals who are close to their own experiencing: the tiny infant who has not yet learned to deny in his awareness the processes going on within; and the psychologically mature person who has relearned the advantages of this open state.

There is a corollary to this second proposition which might be put in the following terms. *One way of assisting the individual to move toward openness to experience is through a relationship in which he is prized as a separate person, in which the experiencing going on within him is empathically understood and valued, and in which he is given the freedom to experience his own feelings and those of others without being threatened in doing so.*

This corollary obviously grows out of therapeutic experience. It is a brief statement of the essential qualities in the therapeutic relationship. There are already some empirical studies, of which the one by Barrett-Lennard (1962) is a good example, which give support to such a statement.

Propositions Regarding the Outcomes of the Valuing Process

I come now to the nub of any theory of values or valuing. What are its consequences? I should like to move into this new ground by stating bluntly two propositions as to the qualities of behavior which emerge from this valuing process. I shall then give some of the evidence from my experience as a therapist in support of these propositions.

Hypothesis III. In persons who are moving toward greater openness to their experiencing, there is an organismic commonality of value directions.

Hypothesis IV. These common value directions are of such kinds as to enhance the development of the individual himself, of others in his community, and to make for the survival and evolution of his species.

It has been a striking fact of my experience that in therapy, where individuals are valued, where there is greater freedom to feel and to be, certain value directions seem to emerge. These are not chaotic directions but instead exhibit a surprising commonality. This commonality is not dependent on the personality of the therapist, for I have seen these trends emerge in the clients of the therapists sharply different in personality. This commonality does not seem to be due to the influences of any one culture, for I have found evidence of these directions in cultures as divergent as those of the United States, Holland, France, and Japan. I like to think that this commonality of value directions is due to the fact that we all belong to the same species—that just as a human infant

4

5

tends, individually, to select a diet similar to that selected by other human infants, so a client in therapy tends, individually, to choose value directions similar to those chosen by other clients. As a species there may be certain elements of experience which tend to make for inner development and which would be chosen by all individuals if they were genuinely free to choose.

Let me indicate a few of these value directions as I see them in my clients as they move in the direction of personal growth and maturity.

They tend to move away from facades. Pretense, defensiveness, putting up a front, tend to be negatively valued.

They tend to move away from "oughts." The compelling feeling of "I ought to do or be thus and so" is negatively valued. The client moves away from being what he "ought to be," no matter who has set that imperative.

They tend to move away from meeting the expectations of others. Pleasing others, as a goal in itself, is negatively valued.

Being real is positively valued. The client tends to move toward being himself, being his real feelings, being what he is. This seems to be a very deep preference.

Self-direction is positively valued. The client discovers an increasing pride and confidence in making his own choices, guiding his own life.

One's self, one's own feelings come to be positively valued. From a point where he looks upon himself with contempt and despair, the client comes to value himself and his reactions as being of worth.

Being a process is positively valued. From desiring some fixed goal, clients come to prefer the excitement of being a process of potentialities being born.

Sensitivity to others and acceptance of others is positively valued. The client comes to appreciate others for what they are, just as he has come to appreciate himself for what he is.

Deep relationships are positively valued. To achieve a close, intimate, real, full communicative relationship with another person seems to meet a deep need in every individual, and is very highly valued.

Perhaps more than all else, the client comes to value an openness to all of his inner and outer experience. To be open to and sensitive to his own *inner* reactions and feelings, the reactions and feelings of others, and the realities of the objective world—this is a direction which he clearly prefers. This openness becomes the client's most valued resource.

These then are some of the preferred directions which I have observed in individuals moving toward personal maturity. Though I am sure that the list I have given is inadequate and perhaps to some degree inaccurate, it holds for me exciting possibilities. Let me try to explain why.

I find it significant that when individuals are prized as persons, the values they select do not run the full gamut of possibilities. I do not find, in such a climate of freedom, that one person comes to value fraud and murder and thievery, while another values a life of self-sacrifice, and another values only money. Instead there seems to be a deep and underlying thread of commonality. I believe that when the human being is inwardly free to choose whatever he deeply values, he tends to value those objects, experiences, and goals which make for his own survival, growth, and development, and for the survival and development of others. I hypothesize that it is *characteristic* of the human organism to prefer such actualizing and socialized goals when he is exposed to a growth promoting climate.

A corollary of what I have been saying is that in any *culture, given a climate of respect and freedom in which he is* 7   *valued as a person, the mature individual would tend to choose and prefer these same value directions.* This is a significant hypothesis which could be tested. It means that though the individual of whom I am speaking would not have a consistent or even a stable system of conceived values, the valuing process within him would lead to emerging value directions which would be constant across cultures and across time.

Another implication I see is that individuals who exhibit the fluid valuing process I have tried to describe, whose value directions are generally those I have listed, would be highly effective in the ongoing process of human evolution. If the human species is to survive at all on this globe, the human being must become more readily adaptive to new problems and situations, must be able to select that which is valuable for development and survival out of new and complex situations, must be accurate in his appreciation of reality if he is to make such selections. The psychologically mature person as I have described him has, I believe, the qualities which would cause him to value those experiences which would make for the survival and enhancement of the human race. He would be a worthy participant and guide in the process of human evolution.

Finally, it appears that we have returned to the issue of universality of values, but by a different route. Instead of universal values "out there," or a universal value system imposed by some group—philosophers, rulers, priests, or psychologists—we have the possibility of universal human value directions *emerg-*

ing from the experiencing of the human organism. Evidence from therapy indicates that both personal and social values emerge as natural, and experienced, when the individual is close to his own organismic valuing process. The suggestion is that though modern man no longer trusts religion or science or philosophy nor any system of beliefs to *give* him values, he may find an organismic valuing base within himself which, if he can learn again to be in touch with it, will prove to be an organized, adaptive, and social approach to the perplexing value issues which face all of us.

REFERENCES

Barrett-Lennard, G.T. Dimensions of therapist response as causal factors in therapeutic change. *Psychol. Monogr.*, 1962, 76 (43, Whole No. 562).

Glendlin, E.T. Experiencing: A variable in the process of therapeutic change. *Amer. J. Psychother.*, 1961, 15, 233–245.

———. *Experiencing and the creation of meaning.* Glencoe, Ill.: Free Press, 1962.

Morris, C.W. *Varieties of human value.* Chicago: Univer. Chicago Press, 1956.

Rogers, C.R. *Client-centered therapy.* Boston: Houghton Mifflin, 1951.

———. A theory of therapy, personality and interpersonal relationships. In S. Koch (Ed.), *Psychology: A study of a science.* Vol. 3. *Formulations of the person and the social context.* New York: McGraw-Hill, 1959. Pp. 185–256.

Whyte, L.L. *The next development in man.* New York: Mentor Books, 1950.

Now that you have read Rogers's article, let us see what steps we may take in answering the question posed before: "How can we rehumanize the dehumanized person?" How can we develop the dominant urgency of facilitating growth in others and continue our own self-actualization? It appears that Rogers's approach would be one of education to understand the self, for when the self is sufficiently strong it can stand as an autonomous, self-actualizing, fully functioning person. Isn't it a coincidence that this is his approach? Developing the self is precisely what you do through open interpersonal communication, and that is what this book is all about. In communicating with others we extend ourselves, risk ourselves, and, with feedback, strengthen the self by understanding ourselves better. Only the rare person can do this in isolation.

Rogers points out that a major determinant in our ability to function as an autonomous, healthy individual is where we place our locus of evaluation (1). You should dwell at length on the examples he gives to be able to feel the locus of evaluation shift from inside to outside as you become socialized. We do not want to make it sound as though this is all bad, for it is how we become conscious of our social embeddedness. The difficulty arises when society's pressures are not recognized, understood, and dealt with in an open, communicative way. Surely the live-for-now shortsightedness of a child must be tempered by what we have learned from past experience and what we desire of future events. Yet we must agree with Rogers that most of our values seem to be inculcated with little if any reflection on their underlying assumptions (2). This puts us squarely in conflict with ourselves (3).

Few of us would argue with the statement that we have an internal valuing process that may enhance our self-concept if it is allowed to (4). The crux of our whole discussion rests on the answer to the question "How may this valuing process be encouraged to assert itself?" It is expedient to quote Rogers's answer here. "One way of assisting the individual to move toward openness to experience is through a relationship in which he is prized as a separate person, in which the experiencing going on within him is empathically understood and valued, and in which he is given the freedom to experience his own feelings and those of others without being threatened in doing so" (5). *Do we encourage others to experience this freedom?* Unfortunately, most of us are so governed by our internalization of society and our "games" for getting what we want from it that we cannot allow others the freedom to be open, for that may threaten our position. Thus, we continue to threaten them with the loss of friendship, love, or support to keep them bound to us for their locus of evaluation. They, then, are much more likely to behave the way we want them to than they are to behave the way they want to. Since we all have many loci of evaluation, it is no wonder we are confused about who we are. The only way to find out is by pulling the locus of evaluation back inside ourselves.

Rogers argues that if one is able to live in a facilitating atmosphere he will exhibit human characteristics that appear to be universal (7). If we are respected as persons and allowed to express our individual feelings, we will move towards (6): (a) more honest interactions; (b) doing what we feel we should rather than fulfilling others' expectations; (c) being open to change; (d) being sensitive to the feelings and freedoms of others; (e) deep, lasting relationships; and (f) a deeper openness to our own inner feelings and the realities of the world out there. The answer to our problem is clear: create a climate that will respect human freedom and autonomy (quite the opposite of what Skinner advocated, p. 5). Unfortunately, this atmosphere cannot be created by legislation or massive advertising campaigns. They might help, but *genuine human communication must come from a genuine human being.*

Humanistic psychologists believe that human beings have a natural predisposition toward self-actualization and that, given the proper teaching and experience, they will develop this tendency into an active way of life. In Part 4 of this book we will explain more about the development of self-concepts and the behavior of a fully functioning person. We include the following activities to help you understand the valuing process that Rogers presented.

VALUING-PROCESS ACTIVITIES

1. What are the basic assumptions of our culture on the value of human life? In a group project, discuss this question in terms of (a) the military, (b) medicine, (c) religion, (d) your own value system. Can you find a common thread running through all of these? If so, what is it?
2   Where is your locus of evaluation? Review the major decisions in your life and see if you can determine:
    a. Who you relied on for your decision.
    b. Was this reliance in the form of consultation or dependence?
    c. If the decision turned out to be a bad one, did you "blame" someone else?
    d. If it was a good one, did you thank the person who helped you?
    e. Can you discuss these matters with a close friend?
    f. If so, does he or she agree with your analysis?
3. Where did you get some of your specific values? In a group format, discuss your feelings about (a) smoking pot, (b) premarital intercourse, (c) legalizing drinking at age eighteen, (d) mercy killing, (e) abortion. Did you get these values from another source (parents, peers, politicians, etc.), or did you reason them through yourself? (Is there anything wrong with accepting someone else's values as long as you recognize where they came from and you can live with them?)
4. What value direction has highest priority for you? Rank the ten values given by Rogers on page 145 from highest to lowest priority as you see them. Now form a group and come to a consensus on the priority ranking for the group.

a. How closely does the group ranking agree with yours?

b. If you differed somewhat from the group, do you feel much pressure to change?

c. What does this say about your locus of evaluation?

d. If you are open about your feelings and genuine in your consideration of others' views, is a change in your priorities justified?

e. What does the group think about this?

5. In a simulation exercise, imagine you are a member of a board of directors that is in charge of constructing a program for the rehumanization of a group of people. How would you go about constructing such a program? What would be included in the program? What kinds of activities would be provided? What goals would you try to achieve with this program? (You may wish to go ahead and form a group for the purpose of developing this program of rehumanization.)

6. Society seems to have certain rules and regulations that prohibit behaviors that do *not* conform to the norms established by that society. What kind of rules exist? What means of enforcing these rules are available? What behaviors seem not to be acceptable to society? Are all the behaviors society will not accept bad? Try to differentiate between those you consider undesirable behaviors and those which are restricted but do not injure society at all.

THOUGHT QUESTIONS

1. Defend or refute the proposition that "no man is an island unto himself."

2. Defend or refute the idea that we should enjoy sex for sex's sake in terms of objective versus subjective relationships.

3. Defend or refute the slogan "If it feels good, do it!" Give examples of some of the problems one might get into by making this a way of life.

4. Compare the schizoid world of Rollo May with the humanistic world of Bugental and Rogers, in light of the need for a productive society.

5. Discuss five ways in which dehumanization takes place.

6. Discuss three problems that might arise in an "open" relationship.

RESEARCH QUESTIONS

Use sources other than this book to answer the following questions.

1. Defend or refute May's statement that art and neurosis both have a *predictive* function.

2. Defend or refute the proposition that the "scientific method" is the root of our dehumanizing problem.

3. What are the pressures that change a person's locus of evaluation from internal, as a child, to external, as an adult? When and how does this transfer take place?

REFERENCES

Borden, George A., and Puhl, Carol A. "Observations of the Effects of Population Norms on the Members of the Population." *The Pennsylvania Speech Communication Annual,* July 1973, pp. 71–77.

Bugental, James F.T. *Challenges of Humanistic Psychology.* New York: McGraw-Hill Book Co., 1967.

Erikson, Erik H. *Identity: Youth and Crisis.* New York: W.W. Norton & Co., 1968.

Fromm, Erich. *Escape from Freedom.* New York: Avon Books, 1941.

———. *Man for Himself: An Inquiry into the Psychology of Ethics.* New York: Holt, Rinehart & Winston, 1947.

Jourard, Sidney M. *Disclosing Man to Himself.* New York: Van Nostrand Reinhold Co., 1968.

———. *The Transparent Self.* New York: Van Nostrand Reinhold Co., 1971.

May, Rollo. *Love and Will.* New York: W.W. Norton & Co., 1969.

Montagu, Ashley. *The Direction of Human Development.* New York: Hawthorn Books, 1970.

Rogers, Carl R., and Stevens, Barry. *Person to Person: The Problem of Being Human.* New York: Pocket Books, 1971.

Skinner, B.F. *About Behaviorism.* New York: Alfred A. Knopf, 1974.

———. *Beyond Freedom and Dignity.* New York: Alfred A. Knopf, 1972.

———. *Walden Two.* New York: Macmillan, 1948.

Storr, Anthony. *Human Aggression.* New York: Atheneum Publishers, 1968.

*If I am transparent enough to myself, then I can become less
afraid of those hidden selves that my transparency may
reveal to others. If I reveal myself without worrying about
how others will respond, then some will care, though others
may not. But who can love me, if no one knows me? I must
risk it, or live alone. It is enough that I must die alone. I am
determined to let down, whatever the risks, if it means that
I may have whatever is there for me. . . .*
Before a man can be free, first he must choose freedom.
Then *the hard work begins. . . . disclosure of
myself to myself must precede disclosure to the other.*

Sheldon B. Kopp, If You Meet the Buddha
on the Road, Kill Him!

*If we define the now as the only authentic
human time, we are forced to conclude that man's true
home is in the Eden of childhood which is forever lost
and not in civilization. Human culture differs from the
associations formed by lower animals because it tempers
spontaneity with wisdom inherited from the past and by
hopes projected into the future. . . . We come home to
the fullness of our humanity only in owning and taking
responsibility for present awareness as well as for the
full measure of our memories and dreams. Graceful
existence integrates present, past, and future.*

Sam Keen, To a Dancing God

Part 4

The Development of the Humanistic Communicator

Upon completion of this section you should be able to:

1. Construct arguments for the importance of a good concept of self.
2. List the stages of development of self according to humanistic psychologists.
3. Compare and contrast the psychoanalytic stages of development with those suggested by the humanistic psychologist.
4. Define the concept of transcendence.
5. List ten characteristics of the healthy (mature) personality.
6. List the five dimensions of maturing as posited by Heath.
7. Differentiate among the conceptions of maturation as espoused by: (a) Freud, (b) Skinner, and (c) Maslow.
8. Identify the forces acting upon the development of the self.
9. Compare and contrast the implications of a favorable self-image with a negative self-image.
10. List at least ten areas of behavior in which a person's self-image exerts an influence.
11. Describe the interdependence of the concepts of relationship and communication.
12. Define each of the following concepts as they constitute the "core" of human relationships: (a) awareness, (b) honesty, (c) acceptance, and (d) freedom.

Concern for the self—its birth, its growth, its disclosure—that's where it's all at! As Kopp and Keen have stated above, it is only through the process of living in the present by integrating the memories of the past with dreams of the future that we can develop the mature self. Self-actualizers or fully functioning persons have a strong self-concept, are not afraid to risk being open, and happily take the responsibility for the resulting behavior. They have chosen to be free and are willing to accept the life this choice brings, knowing that they will be confronted with this same choice over and over again.

Because society would like to impose its norms on our behavior, we must develop a strong sense of self if we are to be free. In this section we will concentrate on the self-concept as the basic or "core" construct of humanistic psychology and relate its development to the general areas of education and personal relationships. In the discussion of these notions, we will first consider the development of a self-concept, then the mature person, and the relationships such a person may wish to enter. The person concerned with these applications of self-concept should pursue the diverse ideas discussed here and develop additional approaches and applications of his or her own.

Concern for the Person

Perhaps the single most distinguishing characteristic of humanistic psychology is its avowed concern for the *person*. As Willard Frick (1971, p. 10) observed:

> Humanistic psychology, however, also presents us with a more positive philosophical position and, in the final analysis, represents a psychology with certain characteristic commitments of its own as to the *nature of man* and the nature and scope of that science which is necessary to explore and acquire a broader, more profound *understanding of man*. This philosophical position of *humanistic psychology places man, the human person and his experiences at the center of its concern.* (emphasis ours)

Further studies of the thoughts and beliefs of this "new branch" of psychology are available from the organization responsible for many of these new ideas—the Association of Humanistic Psychology. While admitting a lack of unanimity in some areas, the association's members were able to subscribe to certain mutual concerns (Buhler and Allen 1972, pp. 1-2):

1. A centering of attention on the experiencing *person,* and thus a focus on experience as the primary phenomenon in the study of man. Both theoretical explanations and overt behavior are considered secondary to experience itself and to its meaning to the person.

2. An emphasis on such distinctively human qualities as choice, creativity, valuation, and self-realization, as opposed to thinking about human beings in mechanistic and reductionistic terms.

3. An allegiance to meaningfulness in the selection of problems for study and of research procedures, and an opposition to primary emphasis on objectivity at the expense of significance.

4. An ultimate concern with and valuing of the dignity and worth of man and an interest in the development of the potential inherent in every person. Central in this view is the person as he discovers his own being and relates to other persons and to social groups.

Here again, we see humanistic psychology's overwhelming concern for individuals as they experience life itself, as they develop, mature, and interact with other persons.

The following discussion deals with these three areas of concern for all people: their psychological and psychosocial development, maturation, and interaction with others. To some degree, at least, all of us "advance" through similar stages, although the manner in which we *experience* may differ considerably from individual to individual, depending on our involvement. In addition, the effect such experiences have upon each of us is unique and, in many cases, quite far-reaching.

As we stated in Part 2, it is through our experiences that we develop an *attitudinal frame of reference,* our view of reality. Part of this frame of reference is a view of ourself. What are our strengths and weaknesses and how do they fit into our anticipations of communicative events? There has been a great deal of research dealing with self-image and how it affects one's behavior. How do you feel about this? Have you ever taken time to think about this? *Not* how you feel about yourself, but *how your feelings about yourself affect your behavior.* If you feel you are incompetent, will you *be* incompetent?

We have included Scale I on page 156 so that you can see what effect you think your opinion of yourself might have on subsequent behavior. We could have included many more items, but these will get you started thinking about the effect your self-image has on you. Put a 1 for strongly disagree, a 2 for disagree, a 3 for agree, and a 4 for strongly agree.

Be sure to discuss these items with friends to get a general opinion about them. *Your* opinions must remain *your own,* however. As we continue through this part of the book, you will be able to see more of the importance of a good self-image.

Although humanistic psychology struggles in its infancy, interest in the self-concept is time-honored. Lengthy discussions concerning the self are to

---

SCALE I

The Effect of Your Self-Image

I FEEL THAT:

_____ 1. my self-image is the major factor in my ability to relate to others.

_____ 2. a well-adjusted person can put up a good front.

_____ 3. if I feel inferior, I usually act that way.

_____ 4. if I feel depressed, it is probably my fault.

_____ 5. when things don't go right, it is probably my fault.

_____ 6. I can psych myself up enough to do well in most experiences.

_____ 7. regardless of how hard I try, I can't change my fate.

_____ 8. if I don't like my appearance, nobody else will.

_____ 9. a good self-image goes a long way toward a successful life.

_____ 10. my attitudes toward sex will affect my ability to perform.

---

be found in the early writings of William James (1890), M.W. Calkins (1915), and G.H. Mead (1934), and the more recent publications of Carl Rogers (1951), Abraham Maslow (1962), Rollo May (1969), D.E. Hamachek (1971), and K.J. Gergen (1971).

Admittedly, notions concerning the concept of self have differed widely among and even within varied disciplines. For, while some authors have chosen to concentrate on the self-concept as the core of personality, others have steadfastly refused to even recognize such a concept (Hall and Lindzey 1970). The existence of such significant differences between usually closely related disciplines obviously introduces certain ambiguities.

In addition, there seems little doubt that such confusions are aided by the seemingly random substitution of related terms for "self." For instance, in talking about "ego" (Sherif and Cantril 1947), "proprium" (Allport 1955), and "identity" (Erikson 1956), theorists appear to be discussing a similar concept but in different and therefore confusing terminology. Concurrently, the terms "self" and "ego" refer to a number of different yet somewhat overlapping descriptions. For instance, such terms have been employed in referring

> to the "inner nature" or "essential nature" of man (Fromm, 1941, 1947; Maslow, 1954; Moustakas, 1956); to the experience and content of self-awareness (Chein, 1944); to the center of the psychophysical field (Koffka, 1935); to inner or subjective being, or psychological faculties or dispositions, taken concreately (James, 1950); to the individual as known to the individual (Hilgard, 1949; Murphy, 1947; Raimy, 1948; Rogers, 1951; Wiley, 1961); to a constellation of attitudes having reference to "I," "me," or "mine" experiences (James, 1950; Sherif and Cantril, 1947); to the individual identity and continuity of personal character (Erickson, 1956); to a set of mental processes operating in the interest of satisfying inner drives (Freud, 1933; Symonds, 1951); and, most simply, to the person. (Rosenberg 1967, p. 26)

To discount the conclusion that such concerns are the mere busywork of the pedant, we refer the reader to a most relevant discussion of this very problem by A.W. Combs and D.W. Soper (1957).

While one should remain aware of such inconsistencies and their potential for confusion, it seems necessary to supply certain definitional parameters within which one can consider the remainder of the material discussed on this subject. Quite simply, *the present discussion will consider the "self" to be "the individual as known to the individual"* (Murphy 1947), and as R. Fox and his colleagues have asserted, "man's search for an understanding of himself and his efforts to achieve a self that meets certain standards of desirability are probably as old as the human species" (Fox, Luszki, and Schmuck 1966).

THE DEVELOPMENT OF THE SELF

Two aspects of self-concept warrant special consideration and discussion. First, the development of a self-concept is a social process, and secondly, such a development does *not* take place over a period of a year, nor does it appear to have an overwhelmingly culminating "year." It is, instead, a lifelong process. Mead (1934, p. 140), more than any other single author, has gone to great length in his explanation of the former contention. He suggests that "the self, as that which can be an object to itself, is essentially a social structure, and it arises in social experience. After a self has arisen, it in a certain sense provides for itself its social experiences, and so we can conceive of an absolutely solitary self. But it is impossible to conceive of a self arising outside of social experience."

In a similar but more contemporary vein, G.A. Lundberg (1968, p. 271) adds further emphasis to such a belief when he reports that "the self is acquired by the individual as a result of his participation in social life. Skills and habits are learned through social contact, including the rewards and

punishments meted out by parents, peers, groups and organizations.
. . . Thus, the function of socialization is to transform the untrained
organism into an effective member of society."

To be sure, the development of one's self-image is a result of the social interactions experienced by that person with others, the major impact coming
from interactions with "significant" others—those that we hold in high
esteem.

Regarding the second fundamental aspect of the development of a self-
concept, Erikson (1956, p. 69) contends that "identity formation . . . is a
lifelong development largely unconscious to the individual and to his society.
Its roots go back all the way to the first self-recognition: In the baby's earliest
exchanges of smiles there is something of a self-realization coupled with
mutual recognition."

Most theorists concerned with the concept of self have devoted considerable time to discussions surrounding its development. Excellent summaries
of such developments are to be found in the works of G.W. Allport (1961),
F.L. Ruch (1958), M. Sherif and H. Cantril (1947), and G. Murphy (1947).
Several others have investigated the concept of self at varying stages in this
development. Such an interest is represented by the work of D. Felker and R.
Kay (1971) and R. J. Havighurst, M. Z. Robinson, and M. Dorr (1946).

Though there are marked differences among the aforementioned theories, perusal of them will lead to a general framework within which to consider the developing image of the self. (This may make a good term paper.)
Allport (1961), for instance, views the developing self in the following
chronological divisions:

Aspect 1:	Sense of bodily self	First three years
Aspect 2:	Sense of continuing self-identity	of life
Aspect 3:	Self-esteem, pride	
Aspect 4:	The extension of self	Ages 4–6
Aspect 5:	The self-image	
Aspect 6:	The self as rational coper	Ages 6–12
Aspect 7:	Propriate striving	Adolescence

Although he does not continue his specificity regarding the development
of the self, he does discuss the concept of the developed *proprium* (Allport's
term for self) as it experiences strivings in life.

The approach suggested by Ruch (1958, p. 62) is similar in context but somewhat more precise. Although not presented in its entirety, selected aspects of the theory are reported here:

> As the infant begins to find order in his environment, one of the most important things he learns is a *concept of self,* or a self-image. At first, he probably cannot distinguish between himself and the rest of the world, nor does he even seem to realize that parts of his body belong to him.
>
> The development of the self-concept involves a process of gradual *differentiation.* The child early begins to distinguish the sound of his own voice as being different from that of his mother's. As his sensory mechanisms and musculature become more mature, he explores his environment more attentively. During this process of exploration, he begins to discover himself—just as he learns to distinguish between his bottle and rattle, so does he accidentally discover his mouth, fingers, genitals, toes and other parts. Finally, as his background of experience increases, he begins to *integrate* the separate elements he has differentiated out of the blur that greeted him at his birth. He gradually realizes, for example, that his mother's voice and his mother's image are really only different aspects of the same object; later he will learn to call this object "Mother." In the same way, he learns to recognize all of his body parts and inner feelings as belonging to a single world.
>
> The *body image* may be defined as the composite of feelings and perceptions we have of our own body, its nature and its limits. Its growth starts in infancy, and throughout life it forms an important part of the self-concept. As the child grows physically and psychologically, however, his self-concept develops into an elaborate system which includes not only his body-image but all his thoughts, feelings, attitudes, values, and aspirations concerning himself.
>
> As the child learns to understand and use language, his concept of himself develops at an increasing rate. In fact, most of his most basic ideas about himself come from the comments of others. If he usually hears, "Johnny is a good boy," he will probably develop a more satisfying self-concept than if he usually hears, "Johnny is a bad boy." His ideas not only about himself but about the world in general will reflect the appraisal of those guiding his development.
>
> By the time the child is about two years old, he uses the word "mine" often and decisively. He begins to refer to himself as "I," and learns by the time he is three that "you" are a person with feelings and rights also. Little by little he has come to recognize differences between his own purposes and those of others around him, who may either help or oppose him. By the age of four, he can see himself in some perspective, as one of a group of children, all persons more or less equivalent of himself. Thus, the child gradually differentiates himself from the world about him and so doing becomes capable of relating himself to others.*

Most surely, the concept or image of self appears to be in a constant, although not often drastic, state of flux. It is the result of processes that last a veritable lifetime. According to Erikson (1956, p. 69), "while the end of adolescence thus is the end of an overt identity crisis, identity formation neither

---

begins nor ends with adolescence: it is a lifelong development largely uncon-scious to the individual and to his society."

At least two reasons loom as necessary considerations for such self-development. First, one attempts to actualize him- or herself over a period of time. C.E. Moustakas (1956, p. 17) suggests that "it is within the nature of the individual to actualize himself and become whatever he is meant to be, to explore his individual potential as fully as possible. He will resist all attempts to change him that threaten his perception of self, and will respond favorably to situations which permit him to express and explore his potentials."

The second and more obvious but closely related rationale for continued interest in self as lifelong development is the concern of the individual for maintenance. Again, Moustakas (1956, p. 17) supplies the rationale: "Maintenance of the real self is of primary significance for the individual. It is the most stable consistent value in his life. The real self is the central core within each individual which is the deep source of growth. To operate in terms of the persons we are is natural, comforting, and satisfying. It permits us to be creative, to utilize our capacities."

Clearly, then, two conclusions are warranted. First, the concept of self is a product of social interactions. Secondly, the development of one's self-concept continues through life—although it may "slow down" following the teens.

A DIFFERENCE THAT MAKES A DIFFERENCE

Wendell Johnson, the noted midwestern general semanticist, was often given to discussing only differences that made any real difference. Such a para-digm, it seems, might justifiably be applied to a discussion of the self-concept. Is there anything about such a concept that looms important enough to be taken into consideration? Is the concept of self "a difference that really makes a difference"?

There is evidence to indicate that the development of a healthy per-sonality necessitates a satisfactory concept of self. According to Rogers (1951, p. 513), there is little doubt that the so-called well-adjusted personality exists only "when the concept of the self is such that all the sensory and visceral ex-periences of the organism are, or may be, assimilated on a symbolic level into a consistent relationship with the concept of self." Thus, we may conclude that a well-adjusted personality comes about, at least partially, as a result of a fully functioning image of oneself.

Additionally, the subsequent development of an image of self is crucial to the eventual, full maturation of the general personality of an individual. As Victor Raimy (1948, p. 155), observed, "It is postulated that a person's Self-Concept is a significant factor in his behavior and personality organization. By measuring changes which occur in clients' attitudes toward themselves, it is believed that changes in Self-Concept and therefore in personality organiza-tion can be detected."

It is in this somewhat vague area of personality that Arthur Jersild (1952, p. 34) has suggested "we have the individual as seen by the individual himself, irrespective of how others see him." More specifically, it is in the area of personality that the individual subjectively "says of himself that he can make up his mind, or that he has a lot of self-confidence, or that he feels inferior, or that he has a cheerful outlook on life."

In two well-established works, authors E.C. Kelley and Carl Rogers offer an answer to the queries "Just what does the fully functioning personality resemble?" and "What are the noticeable and distinguishing characteristics of the personality that has experienced its development alongside the full development of a satisfactory self?"

Kelley (1962, pp. 18–29) writes that the fully functioning self is evidenced by:

1. Thinking well of him- or herself.
2. Thinking well of others.
3. Seeing his or her stake in others.
4. Seeing him- or herself as part of a world in movement.
5. Seeing the value of mistakes.
6. Developing and holding human values.
7. Knowing no other way to live except in keeping with such human values.

Although Rogers (1962) is much more general in his comments, his well-traveled essay echoes strikingly similar observations. To wit, he views the fully functioning person as one who practices creativity and trustworthiness of human nature, is sensitively open to all experiences, and is eminently change oriented. Such are those persons "who appear to have made important strides toward psychological health" (p. 31).

An even larger corpus of evidence, however, is accumulating with regard to the impact of one's concept of self upon that person's subsequent behaviors in a variety of situations—not the least important of which is the learning environment. Kelley (1962, p. 10) writes that, in a very general sense, "an inadequate concept of self, so common in our culture, is crippling to the individual. Our psychological selves may become crippled in much the same way as our physical selves may be crippled by disease or by an accident. They are the same, in effect, because each limits what we can do."

Similar beliefs are expressed by James Coleman (1960) and L. Carlton and R.H. Moore (1962), who say that one's self-concept determines whether a person sees the learning situation as threatening, challenging, or of any importance at all. This directly supports the notion that the way we perceive ourselves does have a significant impact upon our achievements. Perhaps even more important, such perceptions influence the actual goals we set for ourselves—they aid in determining what we think we will be able to achieve.

Good feelings about self usually lead to high goals, while low opinions of self point toward mediocre goals or failure.

For those directly concerned with learning, the implications are apparent. It seems, to use Johnson's phrase, the concept of self may well be "a difference that really makes a difference." Hamachek (1971, p. 219) summarizes such concerns:

> The role of the school in the development and change of self-concept is enormous. It dispenses praise and reproof, acceptance and rejection on a colossal scale. School provides not only the stage upon which much of the drama of a person's formative years is played, but it houses the most critical audience in the world — peers and teachers. And it is here, in the face of his severest critics, that a student, whether in kindergarten or graduate school, is likely to be reminded again and again of either his failings and shortcomings or of his strengths and possibilities.

At this juncture, the concept of the self becomes increasingly relevant to the classroom teacher for two major and closely related reasons:

1. One's self-image is crucial with regard to that person's subsequent behaviors or achievement.
2. As teachers, in contact with the student for a good portion of that student's day, we are in a strategic position to have some impact upon the formation and modification of his or her self-concept.

It has been suggested that a student's self-image will have a significant impact upon how well that student does in his or her studies. To be sure, "there is substantial evidence to link both a student's school behavior and achievement to his feelings about himself" (Hamachek 1971, p. 219).

In essence, the teacher becomes a significant other to the student and has a great deal to do with the student's picture of him- or herself. As H.H. Davidson and G. Lang (1960) put it: "The children's perception of their teacher's feelings toward them correlated positively and significantly with self-perception" (p. 116). Perhaps even more important, these authors conclude that "the more positive the children's perception of their teachers' feelings, the better was their academic achievement" (p. 116). Obviously, the teacher has an impact upon how a student views him- or herself; such a view, in turn, relates directly to the level at which that student is able to achieve.

The importance of the self-image to a student's achievement is further substantiated by B. Borislow (1962) in his examination of self-images and academic achievement:

> Using seventh-grade students in an urban school system, it was found that: (1) There is a significant and positive correlation between self-concept and performance in the academic role; this relationship is substantial even when measured I.Q. is controlled. (2) There are specific self-concepts of ability related to specific areas of academic role performance, which differs from the general self-concept of ability. These are, in some subjects, significantly better predictors of specific subject achievement than is the general self-concept of

ability. (3) Self-concept is significantly and positively correlated with the perceived evaluations that significant others hold of the student; however, it is the composite image rather than the images of specific others that appears to be most closely correlated with the student's self-concept in specific subjects. (Brookover, Thomas, and Paterson 1964, p. 275)

Not only does Borislow conclude that concepts of self have an important and significant impact upon subsequent achievements, he also advances evidence to further support the conclusion that significant others at least take part in the formation of such an image.

Although the previous research dealt exclusively with seventh-graders, W. W. Wattenberg and C. Clifford (1964, p.467) emphasize the importance of such concerns even *as the child starts school*. These researchers found that *"measures of self-concept and ego-strength made at the beginning of kindergarten were more predictive of reading achievement two and one-half years later than were measures of intelligence"* (emphasis ours).

In making ourselves aware of such "signs," we might well heed the summary Hamachek (1971, p. 177) offers. He suggests that "if a child starts with a negative self-image about his ability to do school work, we might expect that signs of low or poor academic achievement will be apparent during the early elementary years."

Support for such a conclusion is directly added by M. B. Fink (1962, p. 61), who concludes that *"results of this study appear to confirm the hypothesis that a relationship does in fact exist between adequacy perceived of self-concept and level of academic achivement"* (emphasis ours). He adds that this "appears to be unquestionable for boys, considerably less for girls." Such a conclusion has received verifiable support from Paul Campbell (1966).

Even though we have been able to determine certain relationships, it would be self-defeating to even suggest closure at this point. Tentatively, however, we are able to suggest:

1. The thing to which we refer as the "self," "self-concept," or "self-image" develops over a period of years.
2. The self is a social phenomenon. As such, it develops as a result of social interactions and relationships—the people around us have much to do with the image we subsequently develop. Human communication asserts itself as one of the major bases of such social interactions and relationships.
3. The image one has of oneself has considerable impact upon subsequent behaviors of that individual.
4. One of the most fundamental of those subsequent behaviors is learning. One's self-concept has a great deal to do with the manner in which and degree to which one can and does achieve.
5. An area in which one's self-concept exerts a significant force is that of personality development and modification.
6. The self-concept one has can be altered and modified.

7. The teacher stands as one of the most significant others in the life of the developing child. This provides opportunity for teachers to exercise changes in image, resulting in a modification of the subsequent behaviors of the child.

To be sure, such conclusions are cautious. If one is of the belief, however, that the concept of the self really constitutes "a difference that really makes a difference," we most surely have an obligation to deal with such a crucial determinant.

We have presented evidence showing that one's self-concept does make a difference. Although the self has been studied under a number of different terms, the conclusion is always the same — the way you feel about yourself is reflected in the way you behave. Your behavior, then, is the basis upon which others react to you, and if they are not facilitative, or if you are not assertive, a poor self-image may become poorer. This is true only because the self cannot be developed in isolation. The way people treat us has a great deal to do with how we feel about ourselves. This begins with our families and spreads to our peer groups and the institutions of which we are members. It is continuous over time and may be strengthened or shattered at any time in our lives.

The major variable affecting the development of the self seems to be the language one uses to evaluate us. Referring to Part 2 of this book, we might say that, if the stroking we get is primarily negative or noncomittal, it may be difficult for us to develop a strong positive view of ourself. On the other hand, if we constantly need positive stroking and are devastated by a single negative stroke, perhaps we are not looking at reality squarely and need professional help. We have spoken of the need for both positive and negative stroking to insure a realistic view of ourself and our embeddedness in society. Now we can see how this is related to the development of our self-concept and its implications for a healthy personality.

Evidence of a fully functioning self or an inadequate self is seen in the way one perceives communication events. Do you perceive them as threats, a challenge, or as routine? Do you play games because you are afraid to reveal your true self? Or are you threatened by most demands on you because you feel inadequate? How does this affect your work, and how does your work affect your feelings about yourself? Because so much of our early years is spent in a learning situation, it is only reasonable to look to this experience to help establish our concept of self. In doing so we see that teacher attitudes have been major factors in the development of healthy self-concepts. The awareness of this fact cannot be too great, for the shaping of healthy self-concepts should be the primary goal of our educational system.

Though we have made some strides in the definition of the concept of self and in specific applications of self-concept theory, we have not given an inclusive review of all the far-reaching implications and applications of this theory. In the research questions at the end of this section we will make suggestions on how and where one might look to dig deeper into the ramifications of the concept of self. The following activities are to allow you to get a better grasp of the concept of self and to look inside yourself to see what your own self-concept is.

ACTIVITIES FOR THE AWARENESS OF SELF

For Individuals: (When individuals are asked to turn in these answers as part of their grade, they should be allowed to remain anonymous.)

1. Can you think of instances or situations that may have affected the image you have of yourself (your self-concept) that occurred as you were growing up? *How* have these instances affected you? Try to develop alternative explanations for these events. What effect might those alternative explanations have on your self-concept?
2. Are you aware of situations confronting others that may have some impact upon the development of their self-concept? Are you personally involved in any of these situations? In what ways? How might you influence their self-concept?
3. Is it possible to determine something about an individual's self-concept by analyzing the ways in which he or she interacts (or refuses to interact) with others? What kinds of cues or keys do we tend to look for? Do we tend to base subsequent decisions on such judgments? Give examples.
4. How much time do we spend analyzing ourselves? How often do we ask ourselves why we are the way we are and why we tend to do the things we do? Do we tend to ignore such queries? If yes, do we avoid them because they are embarrassing or because we do not have any answers for them? Might it be because we are afraid of what such answers might involve and that we may open Pandora's box if we strive to answer such questions? Discuss the relevance of this behavior to your own feelings of the importance of a healthy self-concept.
5. Why does it seem so much easier to analyze someone else's problems rather than our own? Do we find ourselves concerned only with the problems of others when such problems affect us? Do we consider it butting in other people's business if we attempt to help others solve their problems? How do we feel if we fail in such attempts to help others—do we feel much differently about trying again if we succeed? Should we evaluate such attempts at helping others on the basis of success-failure only? What might some other criterion be?

For Groups:

1. Who are the significant others? Form a group and trace the development of an individual from birth to age twenty-five with the emphasis on the impact of others on that person's self-concept. Come to a consensus as to whom the ten most significant others might be. Compare with the rest of the class.

2. In a group, make a list of six activities you would deem harmful to an in-
    dividual's concept of self. Opposite that list, construct one that denotes
    those things you feel would have a positive impact on one's self-concept.
    Compare with the rest of the class.
3. Join a group of four other students and attempt to create an environment
    you feel would greatly enhance the chances for children to develop a
    positive concept of themselves. List the major items you would include in
    such an environment. Make special note of the people and their per-
    sonalities or attitudes. Submit this plan as a term paper.

Human Growth through
Human Involvement

We have given you evidence indicating that one's concept of self continues to
develop throughout life. The manifestations of this development are often
seen in how "mature" one is considered to be. However, the criteria for
maturity may change drastically from place to place and person to person. All
of us have a feeling of what it means to be mature and often use our own
criteria to condemn or excuse the behavior of others. We usually resent being
called immature, but have probably often been told to "act our age." The
way our self-concept fits into the structure of society is the crux of the problem
of immaturity.

As indicated above, our self-image is developed through interaction with
others. The importance or meaningfulness of our interactions (involvement
with others) has been shown to be dependent upon the commitment we have
to the relationship (Part 3). In light of our humanistic model, we might say
that the more we are committed to a relationship, the more significant the
other person in the relationship is to us, and the more meaningful the event
will be in the formation of our attitudinal frame of reference. The more significant relationships are, the more effect they might have on our self-concept.
So we can see that it is a continuous process, in which relating and growth go
hand in hand. If we look back to our intensity-of-involvement scale (p. 78),
we can see that the fourth stage, understanding, implies understanding of
ourself as well as the other.

As we have seen, expectations are often generated by norms, and so we
become acquainted with maturity as others see it. Using their perceptions as a

guide, we can create our own criteria for maturity and can evaluate our own need for growth. It is doubtful that these inner structures of our personal constructs could be accomplished without the aid of others. Their feelings about us, their evaluations of our behavior, and their facilitative or destructive behavior toward us help us develop our self-concept. Human growth would be severely limited without involvement with others.

But is it fair to evaluate people on the basis of maturity? Aren't our lifestyles sufficiently different to warrant totally different scales by which to measure maturity? We have included the following inventory so you can find out how *you feel* about the concept of maturity. Put a 1 for strongly disagree, a 2 for disagree, a 3 for agree, and a 4 for strongly agree.

SCALE J

Characteristics of Maturing

I AM MATURE IF I:

_____ 1. have a consistent perception of reality.

_____ 2. view reality the way the majority sees it.

_____ 3. do not try to change the way things are.

_____ 4. am able to be spontaneous in my involvements with others.

_____ 5. am concerned with problems other than my own personal ones.

_____ 6. can be detached from immediate surroundings so I can make my own choices.

_____ 7. do not have to depend on others for my fulfillment.

_____ 8. continually take a new and refreshing view of my life.

_____ 9. am able to have deep, meaningful experiences.

_____ 10. identify deeply with human beings as a whole.

_____ 11. have few but deep human relationships.

_____ 12. am not biased toward or against "classes" of people.

_____ 13. have a strong sense of ethics.

_____ 14. have a good sense of humor.

_____ 15. am spontaneously creative in my outlook on life.

_____ 16. am able to rise above the constraints of any culture.

_____ 17. have well-developed logical and analytical skills.

_____ 18. have well-developed interpersonal communicative skills.

_____ 19. can make good decisions quickly.

_____ 20. am put in positions of responsibility by other people.

To find out how you compare with *your view* of maturity, go back over this inventory and, in different-colored pen, categorize how you feel you express these characteristics (I FEEL I). If you can, have others fill out the scale as they see you (I FEEL YOU); then discuss the results to give insights into your behavior. As you continue through this book, the insights you gain should help you progress toward maturity.

Carol Puhl, an independent researcher on the effect of humanistic teaching on learning, has written an essay for this book discussing humanistic psychology's concept of maturity. Although no attempt is made to provide a prescription for maturity, Puhl has captured the very essence of maturity as the well-adjusted person would surely wish it to be. More than that, she has compared and contrasted the psychoanalytic, behavioristic, and humanistic-psychological conceptions of maturity, enabling the reader to evaluate the differing views that are (and may be) taken of the personal processes of maturation. As you read, please take special note of the numbered and italicized points.

Humanistic Psychology's Mature Person

Carol A. Puhl

The word "mature" as a descriptive term applied to human beings appears with great frequency in everyday language. Including its various structural forms, it is among the 1500 most frequently used words in American English (Kucera and Francis 1967). It appears as a decision-making dimension in newspaper want ads, on forms for giving a personal reference, and on job interview checklists (Bechtel, Inc.), and lack of maturity is suggested to the general public to be the leading cause of divorce (Nightingale 1968).

Several definitions of maturity form a basic construct of Eric Berne's last book, *What Do You Say After You Say Hello?* (1972, p. 183). He introduces four tests for it: first, trial by law, when a person is mentally competent and twenty-one years old; second, trial by parental prejudice, when he does things my way rather than his way; third, trial by initiation, when a person has passed certain tests, ranging from primitive rites of passage to earning one's driver's license. The fourth definition is trial by living, when a person moves out of a protected environment, and the world comes in upon him on its own terms. How well he succeeds here is the measure of his maturity.

With the idea of maturity as a familiar construct for making judgments about people and as an underlying quality relating to important social and personal human behavior, we might do well to examine what those who have studied people as their life's work have to say about the dimensions which comprise it, and along which it is assessed. Just what is meant by the term "maturity"?

In this paper we shall describe maturity as a construct of humanistic psychology, through development, contrast, and summary. Through development we shall examine the theoretical and empirical work of Maslow and Heath. By contrast, first we will examine maturity as seen by Freud, the founder of the psychoanalytic school of psychology, as well as the extension of this theory into the developmental stages by Erikson; and as seen by Skinner, the best-known representative of the behaviorist school. In the summary, we shall examine these works in relation to each other, with some additional observations.

First, let us begin the development by describing maturity as seen by the humanistic psychologist Abraham Maslow,

who spent most of his professional life studying healthy people to find out what they had in common and why they were so healthy. (We are using Maslow's term "healthy" as roughly equivalent to "mature.")

Maslow seems to see three categories of persons based on the level of development they have attained. At the first level is the person whose life is oriented to filling the basic needs common to the species (the need for life, for security, for belongingness, for respect). Trying [1] chiefly to preserve the status quo, he is motivated by deficiencies and engaged mainly in coping behavior. At the second level is the self-actualizer, who, his common basic needs filled, is oriented toward growth. He is positively using his capacities, is motivated by certain values (Maslow's B-values), and is engaged mainly in expressive behavior rather than coping behavior. At the third level is the transcender, who is a special kind of self-actualizer. Persons who have attained the second level and beyond are considered by Maslow to be mature.

What does this mature person look like? A description of the self-actualizer resulted from a study by Maslow (1970) of healthy people, about whom he lists fifteen clinically observed characteristics:

1. More efficient perception of reality and more comfortable relations with it. The self-actualizer can distinguish far [2] more than most the fresh, concrete, and idiographic from the generic, abstract, and rubricized.

2. Acceptance of self, others, nature. He shows a relative lack of crippling shame and anxiety. Any guilt he may feel is not about natural processes but about discrepancies between the way things are and the way they could be. He is not defensive.

3. Spontaneity; simplicity; naturalness.

4. Problem centering. His concerns focus on problems outside himself rather than on ego-centered problems. He lives in a wide frame of reference, concerning himself with basic issues rather than trivial ones.

5. Quality of detachment; the need for privacy. He needs time to be alone, possibly appearing objective or detached. He makes his own decisions rather than following the group.

6. Autonomy; independence of culture and environment; will; active agent. His satisfaction depends on his own potentialities and latent resources rather than on his environment. He can be serene in the midst of chaos.

7. Continued freshness of appreciation. He appreciates over and over, freshly and naively, the basic goods of life, with awe, pleasure, wonder, even ecstasy; things appear ever new to him.

8. The mystic experience; the peak experience. This is fairly common for him; the strong emotions get strong enough, chaotic, and widespread enough to be called mystic experiences.

9. Identifications with the human race. He has a deep feeling of identification with and affection for human beings in general, as if all are members of a single human family.

10. Interpersonal relations. These are more profound than for any other adults; his bonds are few but deep. He is capable of more fusion, greater love.

11. The democratic character structure. He is friendly with anyone of suitable character regardless of class, education, political belief, race, or color, Just being human is enough for respect from him. He is willing to learn from *anybody*.

12. Discrimination between means and ends, between good and evil. He is strongly ethical, with clear standards of right and wrong; he chooses good and avoids evil. He can appreciate the doing as well as the purpose.

13. Philosophical, unhostile sense of humor. He does not laugh at hostile humor, superiority humor, but at human beings in general when they are foolish or incongruous. His humor is more philosophical than brilliantly witty.

14. Creativeness. A universal for this group, his creativeness differs from special-talent creativeness of a composer. It seems to be a more spontaneous, less inhibited way of looking at life. Perhaps the self-actualizers only seem creative because others are so limited.

15. Resistance to enculturation: the transcendence of any particular culture. He falls well within the limits of apparent conventionality in choice of clothes, language, and food; yet he is not *really* conventional, certainly not fashionable or chic. But when yielding to conventions is too annoying, he does what he wants rather than what is prescribed. He weighs and tests the culture, and then makes his own decisions.

The self-actualizer, Maslow hastens to add, has his failings too; he has concluded that there is no perfect human being. The self-actualizer can be boring, irritating, and stubborn. Because he is strong, he is independent of the opinions of others; and he can put all his concentration in an impersonal world. On the other hand, his perceptiveness and kindness can lead him into mistakes, like letting others impose on him.

Self-actualized persons are not common; Maslow estimates them to be about 1 percent of the population! They are unlike one another, and yet more identified with humanity. They exemplify the humanness that can be realized when the person actualizes his potentials, when he fills his calling in life, when he knows and accepts himself, all with a constant trend toward integration and synergy within the person himself.

In addition to levels one and two, Maslow has tentatively distinguished two kinds of self-actualizing people: those described above, who were clearly healthy, but with little or no experience of transcendence, and those whose experiences of transcendence were important or central.

To describe these transcenders, he lists twenty-four characteristics, which will be presented in condensed form for the purposes of this paper. The transcenders value the peak experiences as the most important thing in life. They are more holistic about the world than the self-actualizers, seeing mankind as one, seeing all things sacred at the same time, with a whole-hearted love for all of reality. They can go out of their own egos easily. They seem to recognize other transcenders, and come quickly to a mutual understanding. As well as lovable, they are awe inspiring. They are far more likely to be innovators than the healthy self-actualizers, who are rather likely to do well what needs doing. They experience greater ecstasy, and they are more prone to a kind of cosmic sadness because they see so clearly the gap between the great possibilities in the world and the meager actualities.

In summary, Maslow's level-one person does not fully mature because he stops growing when his basic needs are met. The level-two person, the self-actualizer, matures to full humanness through continuous self-development; and the level-three person transcends maturity through his living at peak-experience level.

Maslow's method of investigation was clinical, studying in depth a great number and variety of healthy people, young and old, living and dead, in person and through biographical material. In contrast with his clinical method is that of Douglas Heath, whose methods of research and assessment admit data in quantifiable form as well. His conclusions do not differ substantially from Maslow's but he reaches them coming from a different direction.

Heath (1965, 1968) studied the maturing process and conditions that promote maturity in college men for a period of ten years. He found four structures of the maturity of self: intellectual skills, values, self-concept, and relations with men and with women; and five dimensions of maturing: symbolization, allocentrism, integration, stability, and autonomy. These specific theoretical constructs comprise his theory of maturity. The following material is a synthesis of his theory.

A. Maturity of Self-Structures

1. Intellectual Skills. Judgment, logical reasoning, analytical and synthetic thinking, and imaginativeness, the more important skills, enable man to transcend time and space; he is able to think about and reconstruct the past, as well as anticipate the future. Many educators use the extent to which these skills are developed as an index of a person's education. [3]

2. Values. A person's values, as well as his needs, motives, interests, and convictions, give him a sense of purpose and direction.

3. Self-Concept. What a person knows of himself determines how he adapts, what he will attempt or not attempt.

4. Skill in Interpersonal Relations. The development of the different parts of a person is inseperable from relationships with others (both male and female). Little ability to respond to others results in an inaccurate self-concept, underdeveloped intellectual skills, and values based on impulse.

These four structures seem to develop along a certain pattern—the five dimensions of maturing. Putting the structure and dimensions together would yield twenty hypotheses about how a person grows. (See Figure 1, a schematic conceptualization by this writer.)

B.   Dimensions of Maturity

Heath's dimensions of maturing seem to be universal, supracultural, invariant developmental trends that account for most of the phenomena pointed out by various theories. Heath describes each of them in both of his books, as well as the theoretical and empirical basis from which they come. (Note that these dimensions are expressed in terms of a continuum rather than a dichotomy or lock-step scale.)

1. Toward Increased Stability of Organization

This means to become more resistant to disorganization resulting from either internal or external sources. The maturing person maintains his identity over time. He knows better what he can do, what he believes, and what he wants, and these are similar to what they were yesterday and what they will be tomorrow. Decisions are easier, because one knows what is right. He has more energy available for solving problems and for relating to people. His relationships with both males and females become less impetuous and more steadfast, persisting even for a lifetime. He has attained a certain homeostasis in which behavior is less impulsive and more controlled by cognitive structures.

2. Toward a Progressive Integration of New Information

The person is an open system, constantly taking in new stimulation; he is curious, flexible, actively involved. Both his external environment and his internal environment are continually changing, requiring of him new adaptations and new syntheses. Like an open system, he changes toward greater complexity, greater differentiation; his thought processes become more subtle. Yet he continually integrates new information, reorganizing his cognitive structure to make this new information meaningful.

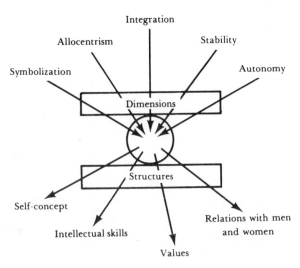

Figure 1   Aspects of maturation.

This accumulative integration can be called growth; it is a process which does not seem reversible. Persons whose thought processes are more integrative have been found to possess more accurate self-images and more control of their impulses; they are not alienated from others, and they are more quick, persistent, predictable, and realistic than persons whose thought processes are disorganized.

His values are more consistent, resulting in a way of life that gives him direction and purpose. He is less torn and divided by competing values. His self-image is more congruent. He sees himself as he thinks others see him, so he does not need to "play a role" to appear what he isn't, since he has no contradictory images of himself. He can act out of wholeness and thus be more spontaneous.

In his personal relationships, the person's growing intimacy and openness to others brings new interests, greater sensitivity to the thoughts and feelings of others, and an expanding internal environment as new information, carried by affection, is received into the self and integrated with old values and feelings. Integration fosters stability. For example, a child may respond to pain with a temper tantrum, where a more mature person, with his greater complexity, can find ways to reduce or avoid the pain without loss of stability. Instead of a reaction, he has more control.

3. Toward Increased Allocentrism

The mature person organizes his world more and more around internalized reality-given forms instead of inner need-dominated forms. To become more mature means to incorporate into oneself the social world which pushes and pulls at one. It means to incorporate into oneself the grammatical and logical structures of the culture, to organize one's private world around thoughts, memories, and wishes that involve others; to learn to take the viewpoint of the other person in seeing one's own ideas. However, allocentrism does not mean that the individual is a replica of his environment; his own temperament as well as his unique experiences modify the reality that he internalizes. He must find a viable accommodation between the demands of others and his own autocentric demands.

His world of others moves from his neighborhood to his city to the world. Differences of color, language, and culture are not barriers but different ways of seeing which generate greater sensitivity to and sympathy for others. The mature person is tolerant rather than authoritarian.

He values more aesthetic activities; but he does not get lost in narcissistic self-expression.

The mature person's ideas about himself are more allocentric. He sees himself as like most other persons in his hates, loves, fears, lusts, and pleasures. It is the immature person who believes that he is so unique and so isolated that he cannot possibly be understood. The mature person realizes that he has probably never felt or done things that most other people haven't felt or done as well. And he is increasingly able to care for others. The basic developmental trend is toward increased allocentrism.

4. Toward Increasing Symbolic Representations of Experience

The mature person develops the power to represent his experience as thoughts, words, or other symbols. Through this power to symbolize, he can mentally coordinate more and more of his internal and external worlds. He is freed of the restraints of time and place; he can go into the past and the future, the possible and the impossible. He can learn from the past, his own and that of the human race; he can explore alternative ways of behaving or of solving problems without making the mistakes of actual experience; he can anticipate and plan for the future. His imagination and his creative thinking are much more fertile.

He has a more accurate understanding of his own powers; he is more aware of his own beliefs and values. He can reflect on his personal relationships and why they are satisfying or draining. He is able to see why others feel and act as they do. Thus he is less likely to get caught blindly in repeated unhappy personal crises.

5. Toward Increasing Autonomy

A mature person is not under the domination of either his internal environment (his infantile wishes, drives, motivations) or his external environment (the situation, the people around him). He develops a buffer zone between the demands of the two. He is not compulsive; he can now postpone, delay, suppress, ignore, or otherwise deal with decisions in an appropriate way. He moves from situational influence to self-determination. Also, the area of rational conscious choice is expanded and the person becomes increasingly free from the influences of irrational and unconscious motivations. The locus of his choices is shifted from the environment and from the person's past history to his own self-structure.

Intellectually, the mature person can analyze information, even very personal information, without being unduly influenced by either his own desires or the opinions of others. He can be objective in his judgment even when his experience is contradicted by powerful public opinion. He can hold to his values as well when forced by severe opposition. He holds an autonomous self-image in that he is more selectively open to believable information about himself; he does not believe everything he takes in about himself, nor does he necessarily reject information that contradicts his self-image. A mature person sacrifices neither his independence in relations with others nor his own integrity to gain love and respect.

Autonomy is not in conflict with allocentrism. Through allocentrism he is able to see the world from another person's point of view, while retaining command of his own decisions.

Three other problems need to be dealt with (Heath 1968, pp. 17–19). First, development must happen reciprocally in all dimensions; too great a development of one may limit development of another. For example, too rigid a self-structure prevents new integration of information. A second problem concerns disorganization. The mature person can become disorganized when adaptation or his need to play requires it. He can allow himself to regress, for example, in admitting emotional chaos, or as a preliminary to a creative new synthesis, knowing he can pull himself out of this chaos at will. The third question concerns creativity; there is no evidence, and no research data so far to suggest, that mature persons are more intellectually creative than immature ones.

This model of maturing does not pretend to be definitive, but it does help to organize thoughts on maturing as well as suggest new theoretical relationships. And, more important, it predicts how actual students in a certain college may mature according to its constructs. Further, it puts the constructs of at least the humanist school of psychology in slightly different focus, operationalizing them so they can be measured. With a scale (his perceived-self questionnaire) to assess one's level of maturity, we may be able to establish clearer and more valid criteria for graduating into the world of adulthood, as well as discover what factors facilitate or retard the maturing process.

We have seen at length several dimensions which comprise the construct of maturity as developed by two researchers in the humanistic school of psychology. The humanistic school has come into being mainly in opposition to other approaches to the study of people; as Maslow says, "It has arisen as a reaction *against* the limitations (as philosophies of human nature) of the two most comprehensive psychologies now available — behaviorism (or associationism) and classsical, Freudian Psychoanalysis" (Maslow 1971, p. 223). Because of this, perhaps the work of Maslow and Heath can be brought even more sharply into focus by looking at the possible conceptions of maturity against which their orientation evolved. We shall now examine, by contrast, the mature person as seen by Sigmund Freud, the founder of psychoanalysis, and B. F. Skinner, the best-known spokesman of behaviorism.

Neither Freud nor Skinner have made direct statements on their concept of maturity, so it will have to be inferred from their view of man and from their general body of publications. Freud spent most of his life giving therapy and studying people who were hurting or troubled or "sick" who couldn't function in a way that would bring them reasonable satisfaction. To find Freud's idea of the mature person, let us consider the goal of psychoanalysis, his form of therapy, and describe the healthy or satisfactorily functioning person.

Man as Freud saw him is a hydraulic system with parts or structure (id, ego, superego) and processes among these parts regulating the flow of energy throughout the system. This energy (libido) derives mainly from the id's two basic instincts, sex and aggression. The id itself is seen as a seething mass of unorganized, blind, constant and inescapable instincts with no sense of time, nor of good and evil. It is dominated entirely by the pleasure principle, which drives the organism toward fulfillment of these instincts and discharge of the energy they generate. The uncontrolled id would destroy the person.

The superego, on the other hand, represents society's view of our behavior with its ideals that we try to live by, with its rewards (feeling "good") for "good" behavior and with its punishments (feeling "bad", inferior, guilty) for "bad" behavior. It enables the person to stand apart from himself and serve as his own critic. The language of "should," "ought," "must" often expresses the superego's demands. It can be primitive, harsh, and unbending, or reality tested, kind, and flexible, or anywhere in between. While the id blindly expresses only the person's needs, the superego expresses only society's views as perceived by that person.

The third structural conceptualization, the ego, is the compromiser among the demands of three masters: the pleasure-seeking id, the perfection-seeking superego, and external reality. The ego uses this reality principle to replace the pleasure principle, which in the long run offers the organism greater success and security. The ego is logical, synthesizing, tolerant of ambiguity and tension, and it channels the energy of the id by blocking it, diverting it, or letting it out gradually, according to the requirements of the superego and reality.

The balance held by the ego should maintain itself through each of the five psychosexual, instinctual developmental stages that Freud posits, though in different ways. To arrive at maturity, an individual must pass through the stages in sequence, dealing with the discoveries and conflicts appropriate to each and then, neither too comfortable to remain there nor too frightened to risk change, moving on as both nature and society ordain. Let us describe the stages briefly, after Pervin (1970).

The tensions of each stage focus around a particular erogenous zone of

6

the body (mouth, anus, genitals); the mental and emotional growth of the child depend on the social interactions, anxieties, and gratifications that occur relative to these zones. In the oral stage, the locus of excitation is the mouth, through feeding, thumb sucking, and other mouth movements, with the child chiefly passive and receptive. The anal stage concerns movement of the feces through the anal passageway, which involves conflicts between pleasurable expulsion and demands of society for delay, as well as conflict between simply retaining and letting go. In the phallic stage, the child learns psychological sexual differentiation based on genital biological differences, and identifies with the same-sex parent; sexuality at this stage concerns mainly the self. The latency stage shows no new developments. Finally, the genital stage, still located mainly in the genitals, deals with interactions, anxieties, and gratifications obtained with a person of the opposite sex, not just with self.

We carry the learnings at one stage along with us into the next, where they may be superseded or transformed but often remain within our behavior repertoire. Thus, the adult smokes, eats, chews gum (oral); is stingy or acquisitive (anal); proves manhood (phallic); loves others in intercourse (genital).

In summary, then, Freud would call a person mature who has successfully resolved the anxieties of the genital stage, experienced its gratifications, and worked through the appropriate social interaction (all of which implies having done these things appropriately at the earlier stages); who has done this by means of the ego-regulated balance among id, superego, and external reality; and who is not troubled by psychopathology from disorderly conflict and defense mechanisms. Barbara Hariton

(1973, pp. 39–40) describes Freud's ideal indicator of the healthy person: "He stressed . . . that the ultimate achievement of maturity and emotional health would be an unambivalent, tender relationship between the sexes, capped by mutual orgasm."

Freud's work has been extended by others, notably Erik H. Erikson, who concentrates more on the ego's development throughout the life cycle. Erikson takes from Marie Jahoda (Erikson 1968, p. 92) his idea of a healthy or vital or mature person as one who "*actively masters* his environment, shows a certain *unity of personality,* and is able to *perceive* the world and himself *correctly*" (emphasis his). He indicates that these relate to cognitive and social as well as sexual development. With this description as end product (though relative to each stage) of human growth, Erikson suggests that such maturity results from the successful resolution of the crisis of each stage. The specific content, which traces the ego's development, is evident from the list of stages below, which is a composite of charts from Erikson (1950, p. 234; 1968, p. 94).

7

Thus we see the Freudian concept of the mature person as a person in equilibrium who finds fulfillment in a heterosexual genital relationship; and we see an extension of his key concepts by a contemporary psychoanalyst, Erikson, who preserves the equilibrium, extends fulfillment beyond sexual to social spheres as well, and sees growth as extending far beyond childhood. Erikson's mature person, then, is the adult who has resolved the conflicts of growing up through stage eight.

In contrast with the Freudian view, as well as that of humanistic psychology, is the work of B. F. Skinner. Though perhaps Skinner's position is at the far end of the behavioristic continuum, his state-

	Stage	Crisis (successful if resolved in favor of first term)
I.	Oral Sensory	Trust vs. Basic Mistrust
II.	Muscular-Anal	Autonomy vs. Shame, Doubt
III.	Locomotor-Genital	Initiative vs. Guilt
IV.	Latency	Industry vs. Inferiority
V.	Puberty and Adolescence	Identity vs. Role Diffusion
VI.	Young Adulthood	Intimacy vs. Isolation
VII.	Adulthood	Generativity vs. Stagnation
VIII.	Maturity	Integrity vs. Disgust, Despair

ment of basic ideas common to "learning theorists" makes the contrast that much clearer.

For him, maturity as an attribute of the fully human being has no meaning. The concept of autonomous man, which says that man's behavior arises out of his inner feelings and needs and is initiated from within him, is diametrically opposed to Skinner's concept of the individual, which says that man's behavior arises as a result of the ways in which he has been reinforced by society. Instead of values and feelings being motives for behavior, they are concomitants; the real motives are whatever is reinforcing the behavior.

Skinner does not deny that there is a private piece of the universe inside the individual's skin, only that there is no proof that it is of a different nature from the world outside. Mental processes are not ruled out, and a complete account of human behavior must study self observation. He denies the existence of the person, who has traits of character, memories, and instincts; who uses his mind to think; who is free to be responsible and thus to deserve praise and blame; and who thus acts upon his environment. Rather, he says, the environment acts upon the individual, who is not really free but who is the product of the conditioning received from the environment. If he is not free, he is hardly responsible and thus hardly deserving of praise and blame. The individual's "thinking" results not from an innate cognitive faculty called mind but from a particular kind of environment. What stimuli he perceives have been determined by what he has experienced as "important". There are no traits of character, memories, or instincts belonging to a person inside a body; rather, the body *is* a person in that it displays a complex set of behaviors. The individual does not possess traits, memories, and instincts, but is himself a living product of his environment, a resultant of his experiences, a collection of habits.

Into this basic philosophy of man Skinner fits his definition of self as "a repertoire of behavior appropriate to a given set of contingencies" (1971, p. 189).

The individual as the product of his environment has been allowed to develop in a random way; but if one planned the environment by social, cultural, behavioral, and personal engineering as suggested in *Walden Two,* what would be the optimum final product?

Perhaps these traits can be summarized under four descriptors. The Skinnerian man as seen in *Walden Two* is self-controlled, secure, has an experimental spirit, and feels free.

Self-control is developed by setting up certain behavioral processes which will lead the individual to design his own "good" conduct at the proper time. He is programmed to "control himself" and this yields happiness and equanimity. It posits tolerance for annoying and frustrating situations and a sense of humor. It fosters the efficiency to stick to a job without suffering the aches and pains most of us go through.

The ideal man is secure, both emotionally, having had opportunity for acceptance and affection from hundreds of adults, and economically, having his needs supplied for a minimum of work. He is not competitive, seldom being compared with others, nor does he need to be to acquire fame and fortune, because these are meaningless in *Walden Two;* triumph over nature and oneself, yes — over others, never. When his basic needs are met, his artistic interests find expression. He knows the community would go on if he died, but he feels necessary to the extent that he is loved.

He has an experimental spirit, as opposed to wanting to control by power; he is willing to change, to approach life tentatively. His education is motivated by natural curiosity, by the motives in all human life. He understands himself and the motives of others.

He feels free. Skinner says no man is free, because he has been conditioned in some way; but his citizen of *Walden Two* does what he wants to do. He is never forced. Not only is his behavior engineered by the society, but the inclination to behave as well. He wants to behave in such a way as to observe the supporting code, and so in his behavior he feels free — a process not unlike that in present society in which the conditioning is random rather than engineered. The question of freedom is relevant only in the presence of restraint; when one feels free, it is not control that is lacking, but the objectionable control of force.

Maturity, then, can be described as self-control, security, experimental spirit, and a feeling of freedom, as determined by the society to fit in well with its goals.

Thus far, we have examined the humanistic approach to maturity as developed in the thinking of Maslow and Heath; and we have contrasted it with the mature person as seen by Freud and Erikson representing the psychoanalytic school and Skinner representing the behaviorists. There seem to be some points on which they agree and some on which they disagree.

They seem to be in agreement that the mature man is in balance, both within himself (intrapersonally) and in his relations with society (interpersonally). He is not easily disoriented, does not live by whim, and maintains a rather stable identity over time. He can live in society harmoniously. He is able to satisfy both his own inner demands and those of society.

The mature man is in process. His balance is that of an open system rather than a closed one: Skinner's experimental spirit, Maslow's self-actualizing, Heath's integration of new information. However, Freud's mature person is in the equilibrium of a hydraulic system, which more clearly resembles a closed system. He is in constant movement, but to reduce tension rather than to reach out to new ideas and experiences. Process for the mature person seems to be growth. A person grows because he or she reaches out to experience new things and integrate them into him- or herself. For Maslow, the process arises from an inner innate impulse; for Freud and Skinner, something has to happen to the person before he will grow (which describes Maslow's level-one person, who is deficiency-motivated rather than being-motivated). Skinner especially would see the process as response to stimuli from the environment; the organism deals with things as they impinge upon him, and thus he is as he is shaped to be.

Their mature man can symbolize, so that he is not locked into his immediate environment or his own experience. He thinks in terms of what could be as well as what is. Symbolizing helps him be aware of and deal with what is going on inside himself, especially knowing how he thinks and what he feels, because he can put them into words or some other symbolic expression. Freud and Maslow both give much importance to symbolic behavior; Skinner does not deal with this aspect of behavior in these terms, but his mature person could not understand himself and others, or feel free, unless he was capable of it, in Freud and Maslow's terms. Heath feels symbolizing is important enough to be one of his five dimensions of maturity.

Their mature person moves toward allocentrism. He is open to others, relating to them, understanding them, learning from them. Freud sees a full human relationship as the peak of maturity; Erikson extends the sphere of ego

development to include social matters; Skinner's mature person's security arises from relating to others; Maslow's self-actualizer relates profoundly; and Heath includes allocentrism as a dimension of maturity.

The points of disagreement about maturity seem to fall under two headings: autonomy and values. For Skinner, there is no autonomy; the individual acts as he has been conditioned to act. But Freud and Maslow both see mature people as able to make free choices, to control their own behavior, and to control enough of their environment to do basically what they want to do. *Indeed, the degree to which they are masters of their fate is an index of maturity.* Maslow's autonomous man experiences joy as he actualizes himself.

Related to the idea of autonomy is the issue of ability to structure one's work and one's play, to which perhaps too little attention has been given in this area of inquiry. Structuring of work requires the ability to set realistic goals, both long-range and proximate, and the ability to gather necessary materials, to put off unnecessary distractions, and to keep oneself proceeding steadily toward those goals. Maturity implies the self-control to achieve, to accomplish, to be fruitful, and to "generate," in Erikson's phrase, however productivity is defined in the individual's frame of reference. Maslow, Freud, and Skinner all agree that a mature person can so organize his work.

Structuring of play, besides the implication of simply allowing some time for it, can imply organizing it, as, for example, playing golf or improving one's batting average. An alternative implication involves *un*structuring of one's activity to permit spontaneity, or even allowing oneself to become chaotic, described by Maslow as peak experience and by Heath as indicating autonomy in that the person can allow chaos and yet

11

restore order in himself at will. Allowing oneself to be so unstructured is not mentioned by Skinner, whose mature person can pursue interests but not so intensely. Freud would see in such chaos unhealthy domination by the id. It seems that while all these schools allow the mature person to work, only the humanistic psychologists can allow him to play.

The issue of what the mature person values is perhaps the greatest point of disagreement. Skinner does posit certain values, such as aesthetics, but because values are concomitants rather than motives of behavior, they are largely irrelevant to the individual's development. For Freud, the main value of the mature person seems to be strong ego, which is the ability to reconcile opposing pressures satisfactorily. The mature person must be able to achieve his goals, with no suggestion as to what they might be.

But Maslow and others in the humanist school make some definite statements about what a mature person values. It is not enough that he be in balance, that he be able to think beyond his immediate situation. Hitler, for example, who had a certain personal balance and the ability to accomplish his goals, would not be called mature, because he valued genocide. Neither would the person who chooses friends because of their pretty legs or fancy cars be called mature. Maslow's list of characteristics of the self-actualizer includes positive values on several things: the basic goods of life, which are ever freshly appreciated; a feeling of identification with the human race; human beings themselves, regardless of race, culture, politics, education, or status; and for the transcenders, especially valuable is the peak experience, with its strong, chaotic emotions.

An alternative statement is given by Carl Rogers, who says these humanistic values are natural to man, valid across cultures, and concerned with the survival and development of the individual and others. He says the mature individual comes to value "such directions as sincerity, independence, self-direction, self-knowledge, social responsivity, social responsibility, and loving inter-personal relationships" (1967, p. 21). It is only by living out these values that a person comes to full human maturity.

REFERENCES

Berne, Eric. *What Do You Say After You Say Hello?* New York: Grove Press, 1972.

Chapline, James P., and Krawiac, T.S. *Systems and Theories of Personality*. 2nd ed. New York: Holt, Rinehart & Winston, 1968.

Erikson, Erik H. *Childhood and Society*. New York: W.W. Norton & Co., 1950.

———. *Identity and the Life Cycle*. Psychological Issues, vol. 1, no. 1. New York: International Universities Press, 1959.

———. *Identity: Youth and Crisis*. New York: W.W. Norton & Co., 1968.

Freud, Sigmund. *Collected Papers*. London: Hogarth Press & the Institute of Psycho-Analysis, 1950.

Hariton, E. Barbara. "The Sexual Fantasies of Women." *Psychology Today*, March 1973, pp. 39–44.

Heath, Douglas H. *Explorations of Maturity*. New York: Appleton-Century-Crofts, 1965.

———. *Growing Up in College*. San Francisco: Jossey-Bass, 1968.

Kucera, Henry, and Francis, W. Nelson. *Computational Analysis of Present-Day American English*. Providence, R.I.: Brown University Press, 1967.

Maslow, Abraham. *Motivation and Personality*. Rev. ed. New York: Harper & Row, Publishers, 1970.

———. *The Farther Reaches of Human Nature*. New York: The Viking Press, 1971.

12

―――. *Toward a Psychology of Being.* New York: Van Nostrand Reinhold Co., 1962.

―――. "Some Basic Propositions of a Growth and Self-Actualization Psychology," in *Personality: Readings in Theory and Research,* edited by Eugene A. Southwell and Michael Merbaum. Monterey, Calif.: Brooks/Cole Publishing Co., 1971.

Nightingale, Earl. Script no. 1771, "End of a Marriage," for "The Earl Nightingale Program: Our Changing World." Chicago: Conant Corporation, 1968.

Pervin, Lawrence A. *Personality: Theory, Assessment and Research.* New York: John Wiley & Sons, 1970.

Rogers, Carl. *Person to Person: The Problem of Being Human.* Lafayette, Calif.: Real People Press, 1967.

Skinner, B.F. *Beyond Freedom and Dignity.* New York: Alfred A. Knopf, 1971.

―――. *Walden Two.* New York: The Macmillan Co., 1948.

White, Robert W. *Ego and Reality in Psychoanalytic Theory.* Psychological Issues, vol. III, no. 3, monograph 11. New York: International Universities Press, 1963.

The preceding essay by Puhl has given us several end states which we might want to strive for. The mature person is certainly one who is in control of him- or herself, can function productively, and love deeply. Maslow gives us a hierachy of categories against which we can measure our station in life (1) and a detailed list of characteristics of the self-actualizer (2). How many of these characteristics do you have? How many do you want? What would a world of self-actualizers look like? Would you want to live in such a world? Can you move on into the self-transcendent stage?

Heath's characterization of the mature person is much closer to our world of academia. The interplay of his self-structure (3) and his dimensions of maturity (4) gives us a good picture of what the mature person looks like. We should note that each of his dimensions has a definite communicative aspect. The stable person gives a sense of consistency to the communication event. If we can integrate new information into our cognitive system, then we can be open-minded and "real" in our communication. Increased allocentrism indicates that we can look at ourselves realistically in light of our social structure and accept differences in others and social norms and maintain our sense of self. Thus we can bring a "cool head" to a communication event. At the same time, we are able to symbolize our experience and not react to the situation on a signal basis. We take time to consider the possible alternatives to any communication situation. Of course, none of this is possible without an increasing sense of autonomy. As Puhl says, "The degree to which they [people] are the masters of their fate is an index of maturity."

The contrast of the humanistic system with that of Freud (5, 6, 7) and Skinner (8, 9) leads to a succinct summary of the points of agreement (10): balance, process, symbolization, and allocentrism; and the points of disagreement (11): autonomy and values, with the sense of values (12) being the most important. From a humanistic point of view, the mature person values the person and a well-integrated life. This includes the ability to structure time and events to allow for both work and play.

Although the focus of this material is on the college-age student, it is applicable to other age groups too. This does not detract from the importance of the material, but gives it even more validity. Whether or not we are of college age, or have ever even attended college, we still encounter the stages of maturity described above. Regardless of our age or station in life, we all experience many of the same things and react to these experiences in much the same way—dictated in large part by the image we have of ourselves *at that time and in that particular situation.*

We have presented you with some very important information on the process of maturation. Here are some exercises to help you get a better grasp of this concept and to evaluate your own progress toward maturity.

ACTIVITIES FOR UNDERSTANDING MATURITY

For Individuals: (When individuals are asked to turn in these answers as part of their grade, they should be allowed to remain anonymous.)

1. Go back to the fifteen characteristics of the self-actualizer and evaluate yourself for each one of them. Where do you "measure up" the best? Where do you fall short? Can you think of ways to improve yourself? Do you really want to?
2. Consider the four structures of the maturity of self and Heath's five dimensions of maturing. Hows do you fare with these evaluators? Since these were found by working with college men, should you consider them as norms by which you should live? Why or why not?
3. Freud's concern with sex has been apparent throughout this book. Now he says that the climax of maturity is reached in a "tender relationship between the sexes capped by mutual orgasm." How do you feel about this philosophy of life? Is sexual activity that important to a relationship? Where have your ideas about this aspect of male-female relationships come from? Are you satisfied with your feelings about this subject? Whv?
4. How do you feel about your own state of maturity? By what do you measure it? Who has contributed the most to your present state of mind? Is maturity a state of mind? Why?

For Groups:

1. In a group, decide on the ten most important human values. Rank them in order of their importance to a "mature" individual. Then compare them with the values named by the rest of the class.

2. In a group, discuss the *sources* of the sexual norms and images in American culture. How are they changing? Why are they changing? Who is changing them? Is there a strong difference in the opinions of male and female members of the group? Decide on a statement for the class as to what role these norms play in the evaluation of a mature individual.

3. Within a group of no fewer than five of your classmates, reach *total* agreement on each of the following statements:

    a. Maturity may be considered a function of age.

    b. Resistance to change is a definite sign of immaturity.

    c. Becoming a self-actualizing person takes too much time when one considers the worth of self-actualization.

    d. Skill in interpersonal relationships is innate rather than learned.

    e. The mature person is always internally directed.

    f. Freud's concepts of the id, superego, and ego are no longer viable concerns for the study of human beings.

    g. Skinnerians clearly define the kind of environment which tends to manipulate people.

4. Form a group with five other members of your class and develop a definition of maturity. Then, rejoin the remainder of your class and attempt to define maturity so that all members of the class agree upon the definition.

Understanding Oneself through Human Relationships

We have considered the self-concept and the mature person. In both instances we have mentioned that these processes work in conjunction with interpersonal communication. The self develops through feedback from others, particularly significant others. With the development of a healthy self-concept comes the development of a mature person. From the characteristics enumerated by both Maslow and Heath we can see that there is a wide range for maturity as well as a number of different areas in which one may strive to mature.

We would now like to take a look at interpersonal relationships and their role in the understanding of oneself. If we find some attributes of human relationships that facilitate the development of the selves of the participants, then perhaps we will be able to actualize our own maturity (i.e., we may be able to develop the type of relationship that facilitates this growth). Then we will be able to "solve" some of the problems raised in Part 3 of this book. We will become more human, as will our partner, and thus the dehumanizing process will be reversed.

One point that seems to stand out in the development of mature, humanistically oriented persons is their ability to develop deep, intimate relationships. What does this mean to you? Some characteristics of relationships are given in Scale K. In front of each statement put a 1 for strongly disgree, 2 for disagree, a 3 for agree, or a 4 for strongly agree, to see how you feel about relationships.

SCALE K

Characteristics of Relationships

A DEEP, INTIMATE RELATIONSHIP EXISTS BETWEEN TWO PEOPLE ONLY IF:

_____ 1. There is strong mutual concern (caring) for the other's personal growth.

_____ 2. There is consistent agreement on intellectual matters.

_____ 3. There is strong mutual commitment to the potential of the relationship.

_____ 4. They have a reciprocal feeling for each other.

_____ 5. They can spend a majority of their time together.

_____ 6. There is a mutual depth of sharing of their experiences.

_____ 7. They consider each other as significant others.

_____ 8. There is openness and honesty in all their communication.

_____ 9. They are willing to bear the other's burdens in life.

_____ 10. They enjoy high, mutual sexual satisfaction.

You can also use this inventory as a point for discussion with your partner(s) in your own relationships. It might help you see where you agree or disagree on the meaning of a deep, intimate relationship.

As we have mentioned before, it is essential that there be negative as well as positive feedback in a human relationship. This means that we must be willing to accept such feedback and not terminate a relationship when something negative comes up. It also means that we must get into stage four of the intensity-of-involvement scale and be open to the personal dimensions of interpersonal communication if we expect to find out much about ourselves. We must always be open and honest with our partner, with the implicit assurance of a commitment to the *potential* of the relationship. Only when we are both open to each other can we trust and accept the other's evaluation of us.

There is a difficulty in all of this. We usually gravitate toward those who think and act the way we do. Can people who think the way we do give us a meaningful evaluation of our behavior? In one sense they are the only ones who can, but in another sense they may only be reinforcing our erroneous views. Perhaps we need this kind of feedback until our self-concept gets strong enough to withstand the attacks of opposing viewpoints without disintegrating. At this point, if we remain open, we can still change our attitudes and beliefs, given enough evidence to warrant it, but we will not be wiped out by an antagonist. A strong self-concept lets us mediate conflicting information (take time to consider alternative choices). It appears that a strong self-concept can best be developed through deep human relationships.

In an essay written for this text, Robert Eubanks — who has over twenty years of experience in counseling human relationships and is a strong advocate of the humanistic approach to education — considers some of the factors involved in human relationships and how they affect the relationships and the self-concepts. As you read, please take special note of the numbered passages.

Relationships: The Manifestations of Humanness

Robert E. Eubanks

As sociologist and psychoanalyst Hendrik M. Ruitenbeek notes in *The Individual and the Crowd,* the question "Do I belong?" is one of "the crucial questions man asks himself in modern mass society" (1965, p. 15). In his study of maturity, Douglas Heath emphasizes the importance of this question with these words: "The requirements most relevant to the maturity construct are those involving a person's relationships to himself, to others, and to his particular socio-cultural world" (1965, p. 329).

No one denies that the world in which we live has been brought closer together than anyone dreamed possible a few decades ago. Modern transportation, mass media, urbanization, and the population explosion have placed man in contact with his world, his nation, his neighbor, and himself in new and different ways.

Because of the increased contact he has with others, it would seem that man is in a position to transcend loneliness and find meaning for himself. He should be able to enjoy relationships which fulfill him as a person.

Man's environment is pregnant with possibilities for relationships. Communication situations are readily available. But just because the communication situation is available or even entered into does not mean that human communication will take place. Contact does not mean that the person has transcended loneliness, found meaning, or fulfilled himself. It does not mean that the person has come to feel that he belongs. The environment is not capable of fulfilling. As Rollo May has observed: "Actual personal communication is exceedingly difficult and rare. . . . our present fate as man is to exist in a world where communication between persons is all but destroyed" (1969, p. 22).

Ruitenbeek sums up the theme of many authors of recent years in these words: "Modern man is losing any genuine sense of belonging, and 'togetherness' signifies a longing rather than an achievement; something desired, not something possessed . . . feeling alone in an alien world is now the emotional property of everyman" (1965, p. 23). May reports the dream of a patient which might represent the depth feeling of many people in today's world: "I was in a crowd of people. They had no faces; they were like shadows. It seemed like a wilderness of people . . ." (1967a, p. 2).

In the midst of the crowd, man seems to be struggling to find meaningful relationships with his world, his neighbor, and himself. He seems to be groping for what we here term *human communication.*

Is it possible that man's struggle for meaning has been misdirected? Could it be that what he seeks cannot be found in the direction he seems to have taken? Is it possible that man must look within himself and within others to find the answers to his "crucial questions"? Can it be possible that man really is the key rather than the lock? Is it possible that the recognition of "self" and of others as a "self" in their own right is the point where meaningful relationships begin?

Will Herberg, in *The Writings of Martin Buber,* conveys this meaning of relationship (or *human communication*):

> The term I-Thou points to a relation of person to person, of subject to subject, a relation of reciprocity involving "meeting" or "encounter' while the term I-It points to a relation of person to thing, of subject to object, involving some form of utilization, domination, or control, even if it is only so-called "objective" knowing. The I-Thou relation, which Buber usually designated as "relation" par excellence, is one in which one can enter only with the whole of his being, as a genuine person. (1956, p. 14)

Quality of Relationships

It is the quality of a relationship that determines the measure of "human" communication which is achieved. Carl Rogers, the noted psychotherapist, oberserves that

> in a wide variety of professional work involving relationships with people — whether as a psychotherapist, teacher, religious worker, guidance counselor, social worker, clinical psychologist — it is the quality of the interpersonal encounter with the client which is the most significant element in determining effectiveness.

. . . . It is the quality of the personal relationship which matters most. I believe the quality of my encounter is more important . . . than scholarly knowledge, my professional training, my counseling orientation, the techniques. . . . (1972, pp. 85–86)

It is my observation that this is true in any relationship, regardless of its nature. When we try to determine the humanness of a relationship, we are speaking of the quality of an "encounter," "meeting," or "contact."

Essentials of a "Core"

As I have tried to develop and integrate the meaning of relationships in my own mind, I have become increasingly aware of similarities between different theorists' ideas regarding a core essential to all relationships which show the elements of humanness. By "relationships which show the elements of humanness," I am referring to those relationships which are "growth facilitating," "freedom promoting," "actualizing," "helping," and "caring."

Rogers pronounces the existence of a core on the basis of observations "in the experience of psychotherapy"have here the essential core of a process by which we might facilitate the production, through our educationl system, of persons who will be adaptive and creative, able to make responsible choices, open to the kaleidoscopic changes in their world, worthy citizens of a fantastically expanding universe" (1972, p. 50).

Perhaps it should be noted that, to this writer, Rogers tends to be behavioristic in his projected use of the core. The term "production" connotes the idea of acting upon others for a purpose rather than accepting others and letting them create their own lives. This direction toward

manipulation seems to run counter to the basic humanistic approach of his methodology and theory. In our attempt to synthesize, we are not projecting a model for the formation of persons. We are simply trying to identify some of those elements which help in establishing relationships as human.

The elements we identify in this paper as members of this core are: awareness, honesty, acceptance, and freedom. These elements, as we shall define them, seem to bring "quality" to the relationship of which they are a part. It might be well to note that they all relate to the inner resources of man, and not to the external environment. They exist within the individual. Man holds the key.

Awareness

The element of awareness, it would seem, is related to all the other elements in some way. Without awareness, the other elements lie dormant or even stand in the way of the development of the individual as a human being. Rogers uses the phrase "emphatic understanding" to define awareness. He describes the "climate" under which one "can blossom and grow": "When the therapist can grasp the moment-to-moment experiences occurring in the inner world of the client as the client sees it and feels it, without losing the separateness of his own identity in this emphatic process, then change is likely to occur" (1972, p. 49).

Milton Mayerhoff uses the word "knowing" to identify awareness. In order to care (be human in relationships), there must be more than "good intentions or warm regard. To care for someone, I must *know* many things. I must know, for example, who the other is, what his powers and limitations are, what his needs are and what is conducive to his growth; I must know how to respond to his needs, and what my own powers and limitations are" (1972, p. 13).

May, in speaking of a specific relationship, makes this helpful observation: "The essence of the relationship is that in the encounter both persons are changed. Relationship always involves a mutual awareness, and this already is the process of being mutually affected by the encounter" (1967a, p. 6). Heath (1965) states that "increasing maturity is defined by an increasing potential for bringing experience into awareness" (p. 335). He also links maturity and self-image together at this point: "The mature men tend to have more accurate self-images" (p. 335).

Whether one is speaking of an idea, an event, another person, or himself, "awareness" takes him beyond sensory information, toward the "inside." He is able to be more open to his experience. This ties in with another quality that flows through literature about relationships — honesty.

Honesty

The honest person, according to Rogers, "is able to take in the evidence in a new
5 situation, as it is, rather than distorting it to fit a pattern which he already holds" (1961, p. 115). Mayerhoff puts it in different words: "To care for the other, I must see the other as it is and not as I would like it to be or feel it must be" (1972, p. 19).

When speaking of the significant elements found in a growth-facilitating or freedom-promoting relationship, Rogers (1972) uses the term "congruence." A relationship has congruence when it is "genuine and without 'front' or facade. . . . [The] feelings and attitudes which at that moment are flowing *in* him [the person involved in a relationship]" are available to him. "He is able

to live these feelings, be them, and able to communicate them if appropriate" (p. 47). Rogers further points out that when this quality is developed in the individual "the more he is able to be the complexity of his feelings, without fear . . . " (p. 48).

The ability to see and be oneself, to deal with others as they are without "front" or facade, we define as honesty. Without it, man plays a game. With it, he reaches toward humanness.

In describing the mature person, whom we would say is more human, Heath sums up the qualities of awareness and honesty and opens the door to a third area for investigation: "Their thought processes are more reality oriented and less frequently coordinated by effect and drives. They are more aware of what other people think of them. Their valuators are centered around loving and caring relationships with others, and they are judged by their peers to be more empathic, altruistic and considerate of others" (1965, p. 335).

Acceptance

The relationship that helps man transcend the loneliness which is his lot does not seem to exist without the element of acceptance. Several ingredients can be
6 tied to this element. Mayerhoff defines patience and trust in such a way as to make them parts of the more ambiguous "acceptance." Of patience, he says: "I enable the other to grow in its own time and in its own way. . . . By being patient I give time and thereby enable the other to find itself in its own time. . . . Patience is not waiting passively for something to happen, but is a kind of participation with the other in which we give fully of ourselves" (1972, p. 17).

This idea is further developed by pointing out that patience is not bound by time and space. A better construct would perhaps be "room to live." Patience "enlarges the other's living room." It should be noted that patience must also be exercised toward self as well as toward the other.

When viewed from the position of a therapist, acceptance is perhaps best described by these words: "genuine willingness for the client to be whatever feeling is going on in him at that moment" (Rogers 1972, p. 48). Another way acceptance can be stated is to say that it is "unconditional positive regard."

Another term which might help us get inside the idea of acceptance is the term "trust." Trust develops as "the person increasingly discovers that his own organism is trustworthy, that it is a suitable instrument for discovering the most satisfying behavior in each immediate situation" (Rogers 1961, p. 118).

Mayerhoff links trust to caring. In doing this he gives meaning to trust in its relation to acceptance: "Caring involves trusting the other to grow in its own time and in its own way. It appreciates the independent existence of the other, that the other is other" (1972, p. 20). This kind of trust means that one does not force himself or others into a mold of preconceptions.

From another vantage point, we might view acceptance as understanding. Rogers captures the essence of understanding in his statement that "when someone understands how it feels and seems to be *me,* without wanting to analyze me or judge me, then I can blossom and grow in that climate" (1972, pp. 48-49).

These three elements — awareness, honesty, and acceptance — though not intended to be encompassing, do seem to form a core to which we can relate other aspects of the existent world of the truly human being. If one can assume the hypothesis that these form a core for structuring one way of looking at relation-

ships, then we can move into other related areas that share part of these elements.

Freedom

Truly "human" communication grows as one moves in the direction of the integration of this core into the realm of his personality. This movement is in the direction of freedom. May defines freedom and its relationship to the core we have described:

> Freedom is man's capacity to take a hand in his own development. It is our capacity to mold ourselves. Freedom is the other side of consciousness of self. . . . But by our power to be conscious of ourselves, we can call to mind how we acted yesterday or last month, and by learning from these actions we can influence, even if ever so little, how we act today. And we can picture in imagination some situations tomorrow. . . and by turning over in fantasy different alternatives for acting, we can pick the one which will do best for us. (1967b, p. 138)

The interaction between this freedom exercised and the consciousness of self or core is dynamic in nature, producing growth to both areas through the process. As the person participates in this interaction, he reaches the point where he no longer "sees himself as a being who can only submit to his experience and suffer" (Ruitenbeek 1965, p. 27). It is possible for him to grasp the reality of being able to choose his own way, to live his own life, to take his own stand. Shostrum sums up what happens at this point of development: "We must accept ourselves as we are, not regret that we are not gods. The paradox is that when we do accept ourselves we find ourselves growing and changing" (1967, p. 177).

Freedom Brings Risk

A person's growth—changing, freedom, participation in a fuller human experience—brings with it risks. Mayerhoff borrowed from Sören Kirkegaard when he made the observation that "trusting the other is to let go; it includes an element of risk and a leap into the unknown, both of which take courage" (1972, p. 21). This is also true when the person trusts himself and exercises the freedom described above. In "the moment" of the relationship he has invested himself in the act of being and has committed himself to the unknown.

Relationship exists only at "the moment" — "the instant." It cannot be experienced in the future or the past. Only our feeling about the past and the anticipated future give meaning to the relationship of the instant. At the same time, this which cannot be brought forth again is shaping our past and our anticipation of the future. To come to grips consciously with this relationship seems almost a beginning point for understanding. To be able, with this understanding of existence, to invest ourselves in the human potential of relationships is the start toward our goal. This beginning of investment in existence is the beginning of the journey toward a concept of wholeness. That journey ends for the truly human human being only when the potentials for relationships cease. When one moves along the continuum toward wholeness, risking, investing himself, he aspires to the "comprehension and the tolerance that find nothing alien in anything human" (Ruth Nanda Anshen in D'Arcy 1970, p. xviii).

Conclusion

As man finds himself "in relationship," he also finds that all the emotions, feelings, and actions available to the human organism can be brought into play. *The*

choices available are numberless, but the choices made are the expressions of the individual out of his own unique self.

A relationship, with all its variety of possibilities, forms the crux—the point—of being human. The awareness, honesty, acceptance, and freedom the individual exercises at this point of his existence is a good indication of his self-image and also a measure of his maturity and his humanness. But, as we look at others in this light, we should be aware of the possibility that the way we look is also indicative of the measure of the human that exists within us.

There must be recognition that our judgments are inadequate in any given situation. But their accuracy will improve as we become involved in the situation with the total being. An involvement that does not invest or commit our own interest or self in the experiment of humanity is incapable of evaluating the experience of the moment.

To the degree we: (1) understand all the alternatives, (2) invest ourselves in the moment, (3) are aware of that investment and the possibilities available to the others involved, (4) are willing to accept the outcome as an expression of our own and the other's humanness—to this degree we participate in relationships (communicate) and comprehend them as the expression or manifestations of humanness.

REFERENCES

D'Arcy, Martin C. *Humanism and Christianity.* Cleveland: World Publishing Co., 1970

Heath, Douglas. *Explorations of Maturity.* New York: Appleton-Century-Crofts, 1965.

Herberg, Will. *The Writings of Martin Buber.* New York: Meridian Books, 1956.

May, Rollo. *Existential Psychotherapy.* Toronto: CBC Publications, 1967a.

———. *Love and Will.* New York: W. W. Norton & Co., 1969.

———. *Man's Search for Himself.* New York: Signet, 1967b.

Mayerhoff, Milton. *On Caring.* New York: Harper & Row, Publishers, 1972.

Rogers, Carl R. "The Interpersonal Relationship: The Core of Guidance," in *Person to Person: The Problem of Being Human,* edited by Carl R. Rogers and Barry Stevens. New York: Pocket Books, 1972.

———. *On Becoming a Person.* Boston: Houghton Mifflin Co., 1961.

Ruitenbeek, Hendrik M. *The Individual and the Crowd: A Study of Identity in America.* Nashville, Tenn.: Thomas Nelson, 1965.

Shostrom, Everett L. *Man, the Manipulator.* Nashvile, Tenn: Abingdon Press, 1967.

The preceding essay puts the cap on this section of the book. All of self and maturity are combined in the process of relating. The way in which we relate to others, and others to us, is a good measure of our self-concept and our level of maturity. Are we treated, and do we treat others, as equals, dependents, superior, children, inferior, or responsible? Are we lonely, with or without friends, aggressive, shy, understanding, intolerant, patient, or exciting to be with? Do we see ourselves as others see us? In short, are we living up to our ability to relate, and is this level of relating what we find desirable? Are we over- or underinvolved?

The present condition is usually described as one of loneliness (1), and as was brought out in Rollo May's article (Part 3), this is in part due to our inability to feel. The schizoid world May describes is the basis for Eubanks's remarks about the quality of a relationship (2). We cannot overemphasize the importance of the quality of a relationship. It has been seen as the major factor in the development both of a healthy self-concept and of a mature individual. The attributes that form the core of relationships — awareness, honesty, acceptance, and freedom (3) — appear to be the discriminating factors. If they are there, then quality can develop; if not, the relationship is limited.

In discussing the ability to be aware of ourselves and others (4), Eubanks indicates that this is a universal characteristic of human growth, for "whether one is speaking of an idea, an event, another person, or himself, 'awareness' takes him beyond sensory information, toward the 'inside.' " Getting "inside" oneself seems to be the only way we can understand how we are relating to others. It is not a sufficient condition for a quality relationship (for we all know people who are so inside themselves that they can't relate), but it is a necessary condition. Without this awareness we cannot know enough about ourselves and others to ever get to the personal level of sharing.

The other attributes are also necessary but not sufficient (5, 6, 7). Quality relationships only develop if all attributes are reciprocal — if both parties share them. Thus, one does not risk (8) without knowing that there is mutual trust and understanding in both participants.

There is little doubt that man finds himself in innumerable situations in which relationships are possible. The potentialities for such relationships as to type and level seem incalculable. Eubanks has suggested the manner in which the truly human being is going to approach and interact in such a relationship. This seems *not* to be a "laying down of laws" for what has come to be known as a successful relationship—instead, his paper constitutes a philosophical statement of the necessary attributes of those persons most interested in establishing truly human relationships with other persons. It provides suggestions for a framework in which an individual is able to give of herself as she is and accept others as she finds them. It asks people to understand the alternatives, be aware of the investment of all involved, and accept the outcomes, for "the choices available are numberless, but the choices made are the expressions of the individual out of his own unique self."

Having looked at relationships philosophically, now let's look at them pragmatically. The following activities are presented to stimulate your thinking, analysis, evaluation, and assessment of your own relationships.

HUMAN RELATIONSHIP ACTIVITIES

For Individuals: (When individuals are asked to turn in these answers as part of their grade, they should be allowed to remain anonymous.)

1. Think about your relationships. Can you rank them in terms of their quality? What are the distinguishing characteristics of your good and bad relationships? What do you contribute to them? What can you do to increase the quantity of your relationships? What can you do to increase the quality of them? Why don't you do this?

2. Compare what you know about your best friend and a casual acquaintance. What level of sharing (Table 2, p. 76) do you operate on in each relationship? Do you have the openness you desire with your best friend? Is it easier to be open with friends of the same sex or opposite sex? Why? What problems does your sense of awareness give you?

3. Are you completely honest with your friends? Are there times when tact and discretion must outweigh honesty? If so, when? How do you feel when you aren't "real" with a friend? When you are "caught" not being yourself? Do you think others ever know? Can you tell when your friends are "playing games"? Can you confront them with this? What would happen?

4. Do you accept your friends for what they are or do you try to change them? What behaviors in others make you tend to mistrust them? Do you have any of these characteristics? Do your friends understand you? How do you feel about one who tries to change you? If you accept someone for what he is, how can you convince him that you really care?

5. How free do you want to be in a relationship? If your friends put no constraints on you, what tells you that they care? How much risk are you willing to take? In your best relationship, who sets the limits of your freedom? How important are the limits of freedom in your relationships? What does this say about your feeling of dependence-independence?

For Groups:

1. Each of us is involved in what we consider to be "good relationships" and "bad relationships." With a group of your classmates, come to a consensus on a one-sentence definition of what each of these relationships might involve.

2. In a group, come to a consensus on how relationships would or should differ between the following persons and how they might be the same or very similar: (a) parent and child, (b) husband and wife, (c) friends of the same sex, (d) friends of opposite sex, (e) boyfriend and girlfriend, (f) employer and employee, (g) fellow workers, (h) college roomates.

3. In a group, discuss the pros and cons of the double standard in light of the four attributes of human relationships presented in the Eubanks essay. Come to a consensus on a statement you can present to the class of your feelings about male-female equality in a relationship.

THOUGHT QUESTIONS

These questions are answerable from this text.
1. In a three-page paper, discuss what you consider to be the main differences among the three schools of psychology's view of the concept of self.
2. How do the five types of noise enter into the process of maturing?
3. How do the four attributes of humanness in relationships contribute to the character of the humanistic communicator?
4. How would a mature person (use Heath's dimensions) function in a schizoid world?
5. Interrelate the four stages of involvement with the development of a healthy self-concept.
6. Discuss the similarities and differences between the values of Rogers (Part 3) and the characteristics of Maslow's self-actualizer.

RESEARCH QUESTIONS

You will need outside sources for these.
1. Choose a religious leader (e.g., Abraham, Moses, David, Christ, Confucius, Buddha) and evaluate him or her according to the standards reported in this section (i.e., Maslow's fifteen characteristics or Heath's nine elements of structure and dimensions of maturity).

2. What role does the self-concept play in drug abuse? For instance, see Mary Clare Higdon, *Personality Characteristics of Marijuana Users* (Nashville, Tenn.: Dede Wallace Center, 1973), and Janice S. Robinson, *The Self Concept of Drug Abusers* (Nashville, Tenn.: Dede Wallace Center, 1973).

3. What other behaviors can we correlate with various types of self-concept? To get you started, see:

   Fitts, William H. *The Self Concept and Behavior: Overview and Supplement.* Nashville, Tenn.: Counselor Recordings and Tests, 1972.

   ———. *The Self Concept and Performance.* Nashville, Tenn.: Counselor Recordings and Tests, 1972.

   ———. *The Self Concept and Psychopathology.* Nashville, Tenn.: Counselor Recordings and Tests, 1972.

   Fitts, William H., and Hamner, William T. *The Self Concept and Delinquency.* Nashville, Tenn.: Counselor Recordings and Tests, 1972.

4. Look into the characteristics of love relationships. What are the present-day values and commitments? To get you started, see:

   Masters, William, and Johnson, Virginia. *The Pleasure Bond.* Boston: Little, Brown & Co., 1974.

   McCary, James Leslie. *Freedom and Growth in Marriage.* Santa Barbara, Calif.: Hamilton Publishing Co., 1975.

   Reik, Theodor. *The Need to Be Loved.* New York: Bantam Books, 1963.

   Toffler, Alvin. *Future Shock.* New York: Random House, 1970.

REFERENCES

Allport, G. W. *Becoming.* New Haven: Yale University Press, 1955.

———. *Pattern and Growth in Personality.* New York: Holt, Rinehart & Winston, 1961.

Borislow, B. "Self Evaluation and Academic Achievement." *Journal of Counseling* 9 (1962): 246–54.

Brookover, Wilbur B.; Thomas, Shailor; and Paterson, Ann. "Self-Concept of Ability and School Achievement," *Sociology of Education* 37 (1964): 271–78.

Buhler, Charlotte, and Allen, Melanie. *Introduction to Humanistic Psychology.* Monterey, Calif: Brooks/Cole Publishing Co., 1972.

Calkins, M. W. "The Self in Scientific Psychology." *The American Journal of Psychology* 26 (1915): 295–324.

Campbell, P. B. "Self-Concept and Academic Achievement in Middle Grade Public School Children." *Dissertation Abstracts* 27 (1966): 1535–36.

Carlton, L., and Moore, R. H. *Reading, Self Directive Dramatization, and Self-Concept.* Columbus, Ohio: Charles E. Merrill Publishing Co., 1962.

Coleman, James C. *Personality Dynamics and Effective Behavior.* Glenview, Ill.: Scott, Foresman & Co., 1960.

Combs, A. W., and Soper, D. W. "The Self, Its Derivate Terms, and Research." *Journal of Individual Psychology,* 13 (1957): 134-45.

Davidson, H. H., and Lang, G. "Children's Perceptions of Their Teacher's Feelings toward Them Related to Self-Perception, School Achievement and Behavior." *Journal of Experimental Education* 29 (1960): 107-18.

Erikson, E. H. "The Problem of Ego Identity." *Journal of the American Psychoanalytic Association* 4 (1956): 56-121.

Felker, D., and Kay, R. "Self-Concept, Sports Interests, Sports Participation and Body Type of 7th and 8th Grade Boys." *The Journal of Psychology* 78 (1971): 223-28.

Fink, M. B. "Self-Concept as It Relates to Academic Achievement." *California Journal of Educational Research* 13 (1962): 57-62.

Fox, R.; Luszki, M. B.; and Schmuck, R. *Diagnosing Classroom Learning Environments.* Chicago: Science Research Associates, 1966.

Frick, Willard B. *Humanistic Psychology: Interviews with Maslow, Murphy, and Rogers,* Columbus, Ohio: Charles E. Merrill Publishing Co., 1971.

Gergen, K.J. *The Concept of Self.* New York: Holt, Rinehart & Winston, 1971.

Hall, D.S., and Lindzey, G. *Theories of Personality.* 2nd Ed. New York: John Wiley & Sons, 1970.

Hamacheck, D. E. *Encounters with the Self.* New York: Holt, Rinehart & Winston, 1971.

————. *The Self in Growth, Teaching and Learning.* Englewood Cliffs, N. J.: Prentice-Hall, 1965.

Havighurst, R. J.; Robinson, M. Z.; and Dorr, M. "The Development of the Ideal Self in Childhood and Adolescence." *Journal of Educational Research* 40 (1946): 241-57.

Horney, K. *Neurosis and Human Growth: The Struggle toward Self Realization.* New York: W. W. Norton & Co., 1950.

James, W. *The Principles of Psychology.* Vol. 1. New York: Dover Publications, 1890.

Jersild, Arthur T. *In Search of Self.* New York: Columbia University Bureau of Publications, 1952.

Keen, Sam. *To a Dancing God.* New York: Harper & Row, Publishers, 1970.

Kelley, E. C. "The Fully Functioning Self," in *Perceiving, Behaving, Becoming: A New Focus for Education,* edited by A. W. Combs. Washington: Association for Supervision and Curriculum Development, 1962.

Kopp, Sheldon B. *If You Meet the Buddha on the Road, Kill Him!* Ben Lomond, Calif.: Science & Behavior Books, 1972.

Lundberg, G. A.; Schrag, C. C.; Larson, O.; and Catton, W. R., Jr. *Sociology.* 2nd ed. New York: Harper & Row, Publishers, 1968.

Maslow, A. H. *Toward a Psychology of Being.* New York: Van Nostrand Reinhold Co., 1962.

May, Rollo. *Love and Will.* New York: W. W. Norton & Co., 1969.

Mead, G. H. *Mind, Self and Society.* Chicago: University of Chicago Press, 1934.

Moustakas, C. E., ed. *The Self.* New York: Harper & Brothers, 1956.

Murphy, G. *Personality: A Bisocial Approach to Origins and Structure.* New York: Harper & Brothers, 1947.

Raimy, Victor C. "Self Reference in Counseling Interviews." *Journal of Consulting Psychology.* 12 (1948): 153-63.

Rogers, Carl. *Client-Centered Therapy.* Boston: Houghton Mifflin Co., 1951.

————. "Toward Becoming a Fully Functioning Person," in *Perceiving, Behaving, Becoming: A New Focus for Education,* edited by Arthur W. Combs. Washington: Association for Supervision and Curriculum Development, 1962.

Rosenberg, M. "Psychological Selectivity in Self-Esteem Formation," in *Attitude, Ego-Involvement and Change,* edited by C. W. Sherif and M. Sherif. New York: John Wiley & Sons, 1967.

Ruch, F. L. *Psychology and Life.* 6th ed. Chicago: Scott, Foresman & Co., 1958.

Sherif, M., and Cantril, H. *The Psychology of Ego-Involvements.* New York: John Wiley & Sons, Inc., 1947.

Wattenberg, W. W., and Clifford, C. "Relation of Self-Concepts to Beginning Achievement in Reading." *Child Development.* 35 (1964): 461–62.

Wylie, R. *The Self-Concept: A Critical Survey of Pertinent Research Literature.* Lincoln, Nebr.: University of Nebraska Press, 1961.

*I know of no more encouraging fact than the
unquestionable ability of man to elevate his life by a
conscious endeavor. It is something to be able to paint a
particular picture, or to carve a statue, and so to make a
few objects beautiful; but it is far more glorious to carve
and paint the very atmosphere and medium through which
we look, which morally we can do. To affect the quality of
the day, that is the highest of arts. Every man is tasked to
make his life, even in its details, worthy of the
contemplation of his most elevated and critical hour . . . .
I went to the woods because I wished to live deliberately, to
front only the essential facts of life, and see if I could
not learn what it had to teach, and not, when I came to die,
discover that I had not lived. I did not wish to live what
was not life, living is so dear; nor did I wish to practise
resignation, unless it was quite necessary. I wanted to live
deep and suck out all the marrow of life, to live so sturdily
and Spartan-like as to put to rout all that was not life, to
cut a broad swath and shave close, to drive life into a
corner, and reduce it to its lowest terms, and, if it proved
to be mean, why then to get the whole and genuine
meanness of it, and publish its meanness to the world; or if
it were sublime, to know it by experience, and be able to
give a true account of it in my next excursion.*

Henry David Thoreau, Walden

Part 5

On Becoming a Humanistic Communicator

Upon completion of this section you should be able to:
1. Understand the implications of choosing your own lifestyle.
2. Understand the process of personal decision making.
3. Describe the behavior of a self-actualizer.
4. Ascertain your own degree of freedom from society's control.
5. Differentiate between the need for love by self and love from others.
6. Ascertain your hierachy of values.
7. Ascertain your self-esteem.
8. Ascertain your areas of high and low self-assertion.
9. Understand what it feels like to become a humanistic communicator.
10. Understand the basic characteristics of a "good" relationship.
11. See some of the effects of "game playing" on a relationship.
12. Ascertain your feelings about specific characteristics of the opposite sex.
13. Differentiate between addictive and facilitative relationships.
14. Make the decision to be or not to be a humanistic communicator.

We began this book with a poem proclaiming our control over our own lives:

I am the master of my fate
I am the captain of my soul.

We now begin the last section with the same message from Thoreau. His conviction that we are in control of our lives is clear in his attempt to wrestle with life in all its manifestations — to experience both its good and bad moments. We are responsible for our own lives, but how this responsiblity is played out is different for each person. The only universal characteristic is "the unquestionable ability of man to elevate his life by a conscious endeavor." This statement has been the underlying theme of our book. In this final section we shall explore some of the ways by which this process may be realized.

On Choosing to Be or Not to Be a Humanistic Communicator

Thoreau is one who chose his own lifestyle because that was how he wanted to live. He felt others should develop their own individuality and that they could find themselves best in solitude. To facilitate this for his friend, Ralph Waldo Emerson, he built a log house in the woods in back of Emerson's home for him to study and be alone in. Emerson in return had a bedroom in his house set aside for Thoreau whenever he wanted to visit. They were very close friends, yet very different in their lifestyles. Being different didn't hinder their relationship: it strengthened it because they both accepted the other as a unique person, thus allowing each to bring more to the relationship. It was this feeling of uniqueness that led Thoreau to write: "Why should we be in such desperate haste to succeed, and in such desperate enterprises? If a man does not keep pace with his companions, perhaps it is because he hears a different drummer. Let him step to the music which he hears, however measured or far away. It is not important that he should mature as soon as an apple-tree or an oak. Shall he turn his spring into summer?" *(Walden,* 1960, p. 216).

It is easy to imagine people pointing at Thoreau and calling him "weird." He had a very strong internal locus of evaluation, allowing him to pursue his own goals rather than those of society. We all know people like this. Sometimes they irritate us because they don't "fit in" the conventional, normative mold. And sometimes they are obnoxious in their differences. We do not advocate the latter way of behaving, but we do hold to the former position that we should be our own person.

As you have probably guessed, there are hazards involved in maintaining your own individuality. As we saw in Part 1 of this book, most of our institutions are built on the normative behavior of individuals who have been conditioned (taught, coerced, bribed) into this type of behavior. Jourard said it well in the quote at the beginning of Part 3. By emphasizing the expected norms, society essentially eliminates the individual's will to be accepted as a unique person. Fear of being different, of being responsible for our behavior so dehumanizes us that we become the passive, controlled respondents the behaviorists tell us we are. The idealism of the humanistic psychologists, then, can only been seen as an illusion. That we can be active, information-seeking, autonomous individuals (as we were as children) is more of a dream than a reality to most of us. Yet, the presence of such people in the world and the good feelings we have when we act out of our own self-direction tells us that it is both possible and rewarding to be our own person.

In Part 4 of this book you were given a glimpse of the development of a strong self-concept and the value of this inner structure in the process of maturing and the development of human relationships. It was seen that people who feel they are in control of their own lives are better able to meet crises and realize their potential in their everyday living. Many of you have wanted this feeling of self-control and, perhaps, have been given quick and easy methods for obtaining such control. Invariably these methods have consisted of games you can play to fool others into believing you are in control of your own destiny. If you have tried these ploys you may have found that you don't feel any better, because now you no longer feel real — you have become a false person in a false world.

In Part 3 we presented some evidence to show that the world in general is schizoid. People have become so enamored of science that they feel if we can just objectify everything and treat it scientifically we can solve all our problems. The process of objectifying is the process of dehumanization — the loss of feeling and concern for other human beings. The activities presented in that section should help identify this syndrome, and as the last two readings indicate, help us pull ourselves out of this dehumanized state. Bugental's humanistic ethic with its five phases and Rogers's valuing process with its ten value directions of personal growth gave us an indication of what it meant to be a maturing individual — a fully functioning person.

We would now like to take a closer look at one of the primary processes of the healthy individual: self-actualization. We believe very strongly that no one can make you into a fully functioning person. You must do this yourself. Others may be able to facilitate this growth, but they cannot cause it, nor can they grow for you. However, if you have the desire or even if you only have an uneasy feeling about your present state of affairs, you have what is needed to begin the development of a strong inner locus of evaluation and control.

Hopefully others around you may facilitate this growth once the desire or the growing becomes evident.

SELF-ACTUALIZATION

How does one go about realizing one's potential? Sir William Osler once said that natural man has only two wants in life: "to get and to beget." Although this is an obvious oversimplification, there appear to be certain and specific needs and desires behind every human belief or act. Commonly, we have come to classify such needs into five basic categories or what has often been referred to as the "hierarchy of needs" defined by Abraham Maslow (1970) :

$$\uparrow \begin{array}{c} \text{Self-actualization} \\ \text{Esteem Needs} \\ \text{Love Needs} \\ \text{Safety Needs} \\ \text{Physiological Needs} \end{array} \uparrow$$

By way of general explanation, one nearly always attempts to meet one's physiological needs first. Such needs include food, drink, shelter, avoidance of pain, avoidance of injury, discomfort, disease, and fatigue. It is important to note that, if any of the needs on the lower portion of this "ladder of needs" have not been dealt with satisfactorily, none of those higher on the ladder will be of major concern until such time as those lower ones are satisfied. In other words, if physiological needs are not satisfied, they are stronger in their motivation than any higher needs (i.e., persons with empty stomachs do not care much about esteem or self-actualization).

Safety needs, the second level on the hierarchy ladder, include personal safety as well as a feeling of security resulting from the knowledge that society has police departments, fire departments, a welfare system, insurance programs, armed forces, and so on. It is understandable that when one's safety is being threatened those items higher on the ladder of hierarchies (love, esteem, self-actualization) lose their motivating power over the individual.

Fundamentally, love needs fall into two separate categories. The first includes love of family (spouse, children, parents), while the second involves the need to belong (to groups and clubs, for example). When either of these needs is thwarted, people feel rejected and somewhat isolated — feelings which are often accompanied by mistrust and suspicion toward others.

Concern for the self, reputation, recognition, prestige, and attention from others falls into the category reflecting esteem needs. There is little doubt that such needs are stronger in certain areas of the world than others. The United States is certainly an area in which such needs hold a prominent position.

Finally, one must take into consideration the highest of man's needs — the fulfillment of individual capabilities and potentialities. Surely, most lives are replete with such cases: when one wants to play the piano better than anyone else, have the most beautiful gown at the Junior-Senior Prom, hit .459 for the season in Little League, gain a full professorship by age thirty, etc. There is little doubt that such needs as we find on this level (self-actualization) will demand little effort or attention until all levels below it have been satisfactorily dealt with. In any effort to better understand man (or to better understand oneself) it is important to consider such needs, their respective "position" on the hierarchy, and the need for them to be met in turn.

What exactly is self-actualization? We have already recognized self-actualization as the "final stage" in the need hierarchy of the human being. It should also be regarded as a level to which one aspires — a goal individuals attempt to achieve in their lifetimes. For one person, it may be obtaining a high school diploma — as a goal at least for a certain period of time. For someone else, self-actualization may mean running a sub-four-minute mile, owning a car, or walking on the moon. It may involve owning material things, making a great deal of money, achieving personal goals, or "just" being happy. It may involve other persons or be something that the individual realizes totally on his or her own. Few recognize the achievement of self-actualization as an end in itself — as a matter of fact, once a goal which could be considered self-actualizing is achieved, it very often ceases to be a goal and a new level of self-actualization is instituted to replace that which has been reached or achieved.

Additionally, it is important to note that the schema presented on page 202 is highly simplistic. Admittedly, the human being is *not* so simple as this might suggest. The functioning human cannot so clearly differentiate among these levels but rather finds needs, wants, desires, and goals crossing many lines and boundaries and finds countless more areas of consideration than those mentioned in this highly simplified five-step hierarchy. Functioning humans should not be led to believe that as soon as they have enough to eat they must rush to buy a new record album so they can begin developing aesthetic tastes. It would be misleading to even suggest that such is the case.

Finally, one must not expect self-actualization to occur at a certain age. There seems to be few criteria to suggest that self-actualization is achieved by the rich, the young, or the intellectual any faster than by their respective counterparts, the poor, the old, and the slow learning. As a matter of fact, when one stops to consider the fact that one individual's idea of self-actualization may be of little concern to another, it is not difficult to see how and why self-actualization may well be achieved at different times by people having different roles in life. *Self-actualization is, quite frankly, a very personal matter.*

In this light, it is not surprising that one who attempts to achieve certain levels of self-actualization might well be exposed to specific social pressures. It is not uncommon for society to place on an individual who is striving to reach certain goals (which this individual considers to be self-actualizing) certain sanctions or restrictions. We have, historically, been exposed to persons who believed they wanted to live differently from the general population. In particular, those who want to live as hermits have been looked at as odd, different, or weird because they had felt the need, apparently, to "do their own thing." How many persons in our society have felt that to really reach a goal of self-actualization they must "do their own thing"? How many times have we put a type of social pressure on an individual (or group of individuals) for dressing a special way, living a certain way, even eating a certain type of food? In general, how many times do we find ourselves applying *pressures* in an effort to get others to conform to certain unwritten laws of society as we interpret them?

In a similar vein, how many persons can honestly say they have never been exposed to such pressures? How many persons can reply that they have been able to adequately withstand such pressures and still live the kind of life they have chosen to live? How many people have not buckled under social pressures? It may well be that achieving a level of self-actualization is just that: *doing your own thing;* doing those things that you most want to do with your life that give you a feeling of *inner satisfaction.* How many of us are willing to suffer the "slings and arrows of outrageous fortune" and go ahead with our "thing"? How many of us have decided what our "thing" really is and then failed to even attempt it out of fear of social chastisement? The admissions, we think, would be staggering, and we could not exclude ourselves.

To achieve self-actualization is crucial and necessary to the development of the fully functioning individual—to the healthy personality. But it is quite possible that the *achievement of the goal* is at least partly in the *attempts to achieve* the goal. Our main concern should be with the self-actualizer—one who is attempting to realize his or her goals—rather than with self-actualization—the obtaining of these goals. Our main concern should be *the process rather than the product.*

Maslow seems to approach self-actualization from a process point of view. Go back and reread his fifteen dimensions of self-actualization presented in the essay on maturity by Puhl (pp. 169–170) and see how many of them you usually display. The first thing to remember when you do this is that the results are *your* perceptions of yourself and you could very easily be wrong in either a negative or positive way. This exercise will tell us how we feel about ourselves, and if we are honest with ourselves, we will probably find we do not measure up very well to the ideal—less than 1 percent do. Then what happens? We may resolve to develop self-actualizing behaviors, we may be satisfied with what we have, or we may resign ourselves to a feeling of inferiority or inadequacy. The first two are probably healthy attitudes; the last one leads to self-deprecation.

Does it matter if you have an unfavorable opinion of yourself? Many of us seem to hate ourselves with a passion. We see others as having it "all together," but we are *always* operating on three cylinders, with two out in the bottom of the ninth, our mainsail in shreds, standing in the middle of quicksand, behind the eight ball, trying to put a square peg in a round hole, and not being able to see the forest for the trees (you can probably mix in some more metaphors). In short, we don't feel good about our behavior, and so we don't feel good about ourselves. Wrestling with these feelings takes so much time and energy that for every step we take forward we slip back two. The amazing thing, however, is that when we talk to those people who seem to have it "all together," we find that they have failures in their lives too. That they don't let these failures get them down is a matter of mental attitude, their psychological frame of reference.

Related to the above problem but less intense is the condition of misevaluating ourselves. We all carry around intellectual, emotional, and physical images of ourselves. How close are these to reality? (Check back to your experiences with activities 2-4 on page 91.) If we see ourselves as dumb, sensitive, and fat, what effect will this have on our communicative behavior? If we feel that what we do is, usually, intellectually inadequate, how will this affect our performance on examinations and scholastic activities? Teachers who are sensitive to this characteristic can facilitate significant growth in a student just by giving encouraging, positive feedback. It makes both the teacher and the student feel a little more human and the student feel a little better. Of course we cannot give incorrect feedback, but whether the work is actually inferior or not, the attention one gives it must spring from a genuine interest in the growth of the other person. With this interest as a guiding principle, we can facilitate the self-actualizing of the other.

Perhaps we should take a closer look at the self-actualizer. You have re-read Maslow's fifteen characteristics and checked yourself out on them. Did it occur to you to ask: Do these characteristics make me a self-actualizer? Or is it because I am a self-actualizer that I, to some degree, manifest these fifteen characteristics? There is a great deal of difference between these two questions. The first assumes a behavior pattern that can be assimilated into our "normal" behavior through conscious practice; the second assumes an attitude, belief system, self-concept from which these characteristics emanate as a way of life. We should not confuse the two, for they are as different as the behaviorists are from the humanists. The former would strive to create an environment where self-actualization was the normative behavior and would condition people to behave this way. The latter would encourage people to seek their own fulfillment and allow self-actualization to become a way of life.

These two approaches exemplify two basic theories in psychology, both of which can be shown to be true, but which appear to be contradictory (Bem 1970, pp. 54-69). One says that our attitudes are shaped by our behavior;

when we see what we are doing, we change our attitudes to come in line with this behavior. This is usually done by saying, "I must have believed this all along." For example, we may pride ourselves on being a kind, giving-type human being. Then we find ourselves driving by a person who is obviously in need of help on the highway. We may excuse our behavior the first few times with the conventional excuses: "I don't have time"; "There are other people whose duty it is to take care of these things"; or "It's too dangerous to stop on a busy highway like this." But after seeing ourselves do this a few times we may realize (or bring ourselves to believe) that we really aren't the helpful type — at least in that situation. Similar excuses can be made for our behavior when we mistreat minorities (but we are not prejudiced) or take the traditional male-female roles (but we are not sexist).

The theory that behavior follows attitudes (i.e., that we behave according to our beliefs) is the more accepted way of looking at our lives. In fact, we would explain the above behavior by saying that our beliefs in each case were just subconscious and these behaviors brought them to light. It is not surprising that we intuitively feel that attitudes come first, since most of our cultural institutions are built on this principle. Perhaps the most obvious example is our Judeo-Christian heritage. In the book of Proverbs (23:7) we read, "For as he [man] thinks in his heart, so is he." And Christ said in Matthew 12:34, "Out of the abundance of the heart the mouth speaks." Eventually our inner self will be made known through our communicative behavior. The importance of this concept (behavior follows attitude) is made even stronger by the insistence on Christian conversion. The mind must first be converted to the Christian beliefs; then Christian behavior will follow.

Perhaps you are now expecting us to preach a sermon to convert you to self-actualizers! Sorry, but we have no sermon. Maybe this is because we feel it takes more than conversion to become a self-actualizer, since many already believe in this way of life but cannot put it into action. It also takes less than conversion because we all have the seeds of self-actualization in us and need only to cultivate them. If you are unsure of this, we suggest you read Everett L. Shostrom's book, *Man, the Manipulator* (1968), in which he takes you from normal phony manipulative behavior to the genuineness of actualizing behavior. The actualizer's behavior is contrasted with the manipulator's behavior in Table 3 on page 207 (Shostrom 1968, pp. 23-24).

This table indicates the basic differences between these two types of people. Self-actualizers or fully functioning persons are in control of their behavior; their locus of evaluation is within the self. They are aware of society, its norms and restrictions, but they do not let it control them. Shostrom has developed a 150-item personal orientation inventory (POI) which is reported to differentiate between self-actualizers and non-self-actualizers. It has also been shown that "sensitivity training may result in increased inner directiveness" (Coelho, Hamburg and Adams 1974, p. 358).

TABLE 3*
Fundamental Characteristics of Manipulators
and Actualizors Contrasted

Manipulators	Actualizors
1. Deception (Phoniness, Knavery). The manipulator uses tricks, techniques, and maneuvers. He puts on an act, plays roles to create an *impression*. His expressed feelings are deliberately chosen to fit the occasion.	1. Honesty (Transparency, Genuineness, Authenticity). The actualizor is able honestly to be his feelings, whatever they may be. He is characterized by candidness, *expression,* and genuinely being himself.
2. Unawareness (Deadness, Boredom). The manipulator is unaware of the really important concerns of living. He has "Tunnel Vision." He sees only what he wishes to see and hears only what he wishes to hear.	2. Awareness (Responsiveness, Aliveness, Interest). The actualizor fully looks and listens to himself and others. He is fully aware of nature, art, music, and the other real dimensions of living.
3. Control (Closed, Deliberate). The manipulator plays life like a game of chess. He appears relaxed, yet is very controlled and controlling, concealing his motives from his "opponent."	3. Freedom (Spontaneity, Openness). The actualizor is spontaneous. He has the freedom to be and express his potentials. He is master of his life, a subject and not a puppet or object.
4. Cynicism (Distrust). The manipulator is basically distrusting of himself and others. Down deep he doesn't trust human nature. He sees relationships with humans as having two alternatives: to control or *be* controlled.	4. Trust (Faith, Belief). The actualizor has a deep trust in himself and others to relate to and cope with life in the here and now.

Thus far we have tried to summarize some of the conditions of the individuals we have described in the previous sections of this book, indicating that the person does have ultimate control over his or her fate. However, there is another important theory that suggests that we only have control over the "trivial" aspects of our life but not the major guiding principles. Eric Berne (1972) developed a therapy called script analysis, which functions on the belief that "each person decides in early childhood how he will live and how

* This table is reprinted from *Man, the Manipulator* by Everett L. Shostrom, copyright © 1967 by Abingdon Press.

he will die, and that plan, which he carries in his head wherever he goes, is called his script. His trivial behavior may be decided by reason, but his important decisions are already made: what kind of person he will marry, how many children he will have, what kind of bed he will die in, and who will be there when he does. It may not be what he wants, but it is what he wants it to be" (p. 31). He defines a script as "an ongoing life plan formed in early childhood under parental pressure. It is the psychological force which propels the person toward his destiny, regardless of whether he fights it or says it is his own free will" (p. 32).

A person is like a movie. Many times the plot is well concealed, and only the director knows for sure how it will end; at other times it is obvious from the beginning. It has a definite beginning (birth), a short development of the plot (childhood), various acts and scenes (adulthood), all revealing the plot to some degree, and a conclusion (death). Some of those looking on may never know what the plot was; to others it will be obvious. Berne was quite definite in his belief that people follow these scripts unerringly, usually without knowing it, but at the same time feeling the pressure of the plot. This suggests a predetermined lifestyle, one that is predictable and manipulatable. He answers this charge by stating that "it is not our intention in this book to reduce all human behavior or all human life to a formula. Quite the contrary. A real person may be defined as one who acts spontaneously in a rational and trustworthy way with decent consideration for others. One who follows a formula is a no-real, or unreal, person. But since these seem to constitute the bulk of humanity, it is necessary to try to learn something about them" (p. 32).

Even with such a strong theory, there are allowances for those who are self-actualizers — real people. Although he states categorically that we are motivated and predestined by and through our scripts, Berne does not propose a wholly deterministic model of man. As he stated in the last sentences of our first two quotes, we have *chosen* our script. It is our way of reconciling dissonant beliefs. Berne gives the following example (pp. 31–32):

> Magda was a devoted wife and mother, but when her youngest boy got very sick, she realized to her horror that in the back of her mind was an idea, a picture, or perhaps even a wish that the much-loved son would die. It reminded her of the time when her husband was overseas with the army and the same thing had happened. She was haunted by an eerie wish that he would get killed. In both cases she pictured herself in terrible grief and affliction. This would be her cross to bear, and everyone would admire the way she bore it.
>
> Q. What would happen after that?
> A. I never got that far. I'd be free, and then I could do what I wanted to. Start over.
>
> When Magda was in grade school she had had many sexual adventures with her classmates, and the guilt of that had been with her ever since. The death of her son or husband *would be* a punishment or an expiation for this, and would free her from her mother's curse. She would no longer feel like an outcast. People

would exclaim: "Isn't she courageous!" and acknowledge her as a fullfledged member of the human race.

Throughout most of her life she had had this tragic cinema planned out and pictured in her mind. It was the third act of her life drama, or script, as written in her childhood. Act I: Sexual Guilt and Confusion. Act II: Mother's Curse. Act III: Expiation. Act IV: Release, and a New Life. But in reality she was leading a very conventional life, in accordance with the teachings of her parents, and doing what she could to keep her loved ones healthy and happy. This was counter to the plot of her script—a counterscript—and was certainly not as dramatic or exciting.

Our everyday lives, then, are lived in a counterscript, one that fits into society's norms or into our conscious directing. It is no wonder that we feel frustrated and trapped in our existence. Our scripts are unconscious forces directing us toward our destiny, and our counterscripts are our ways of expressing the self in light of society's demands. This sounds very much like the deterministic model Freud proposed (see pp. 11-17). This constant internal strife has a profound effect on our sense of happiness, productivity, and tranquility.

If we are locked into these scripts, as Berne indicates, is there anything we can do about it? Claude Steiner (1974, p. 77) gives us an answer:

> There are three basic ways in which people's autonomous lives are thwarted and distorted into scripts. Looking over the many unhappy life styles that have come to my attention, and taking their extremes, I find that people can either become depressed to the point of suicide, go mad, or become addicted to some sort of drug. Depression, madness, and drug addiction are the three basic life disturbances and I call the scripts that correspond to these disturbances Lovelessness, Mindlessness, and Joylessness; or, for short, No Love, No Mind, and No Joy scripts.

The No Love script stems from lack of adequate stroking when a child and very effectively cripples "the growing child's normal tendencies and skills for getting strokes. The result is various degrees of depression with feelings of being unloved and/or unlovable" (p. 77). With the No Mind script people live in continual fear of going crazy, and it results in an "incapacity to cope in the world, the feeling that one has no control over one's life." It "is based on early childhood injunctions which attack the child's capacity to think and to figure out the world" (p. 78). The No Joy script stems from the fact that "people are, from early in their lives, prevented from experiencing their bodies and from knowing what will feel good or bad to them" (p. 78). Steiner continues:

> These three life scripts—No Love, No Mind, No Joy—are, as I said earlier, exemplified in their extreme form by being completely and catatonically depressed, by going crazy, or by becoming addicted to a drug. Much more common in everyday life, though, is some intermediate outcome, such as going from one unsuccessful loving relationship to another, eventually living alone as an "old

maid" or bachelor; or being a hardened, unfeeling, cigarette and coffee addicted, hard-drinking, unhappy person; or being constantly in the throes of crises due to incapacity for managing everyday problems. These banal manifestations of the three major scripts can also be mixed so that a person can be under the influence of a Loveless as well as Joyless script, or under the influence of a Loveless and Mindless script, or under the influence of all three.

Each of these three oppressive scripts is based on very specific injunctions and attributions which are laid down by parents on their children, and each of these three scripts can be effectively analyzed and given up in a group therapy situation.

Generally speaking, every person is affected in some degree by every one of these three scripts, even though he may manifest one of them most prominently. People can work through the early childhood injunctions, attributions, and decisions that affect their loving capacities, their capacities to experience their bodies fully, and their capacities to experience and control the world, and free themselves of these oppressive scripts. (pp. 79–80)

So it is possible to change our scripts. We can become what we want to become if we can find our what our scripts are. However, becoming aware of our scripts is very difficult, especially when most of us don't even believe they are there. We are much more likely to believe that we are operating under information overload (too many things to do, decisions to make, information to process). Pressures are brought about by the economy, the government, our church, our schools, our kids, our parents, our friends. It's amazing that we can cope at all. On top of all of this, we must meet the norms of society. Since these norms are more implicit than explicit, we usually are not conscious of them. Yet, we find that we are constantly striving to meet something, always pushing, trying to "get ahead."

In his book *Compassion and Self-Hate,* Theodore Rubin explores our social code as a total myth: "Many of these concepts [social values] contain erroneous ideas about human characteristics, human relationships and human expectations, which dictate a rigid, choiceless and self-destructive lifestyle. In setting puristic, extreme and conflicting standards, they obscure reality, denigrate the human condition, and produce a confused state, in which we forget what it is to be a person" (1975, p. 229). Again we come back to the need to become an autonomous human being, to cast off the burden of meeting someone else's expectations.

Rubin says that we can rid ourselves of self-hate, Steiner says that we can change our life scripts, Shostrom says we can change from a manipulator to an actualizer, and Thoreau says that we can elevate our life through conscious effort. Still, we ask, are we really free to do this? Thomas Harris explores that question in *I'm OK — You're OK* (1969, pp. 86–88) : *

---

* The following passage is quoted by permission of Harper & Row, Publishers, Copyright © 1967, 1968, 1969 by Thomas A. Harris, M.D.

Can man really change if he wants to, and if he can, is even his changing a product of past conditioning? Does man have a will? One of the most difficult problems of the Freudian position is the problem of determinism versus freedom. Freud and most behaviorists have held that the cause-and-effect phenomenon seen in all the universe also holds true for human beings, that whatever happens today can theoretically be understood in terms of what has happened in the past. If a man today murders another man, we are accustomed by Freudian orientation to look into his past to find out why. The assumption is that there must be a cause or causes, and that the cause or causes lie somewhere in the past. The pure determinist holds that man's behavior is not free and is only a product of his past. The inevitable conclusion is that man is not responsible for what he does; that, in fact, he does not have a free will. The philosophical conflict is seen most dramatically in the courts. The judicial position is that man is responsible. The deterministic position, which underlies much psychiatric testimony, is that man is not responsible by virtue of the events of his past.

We cannot deny the reality of cause and effect. If we hit a billiard ball and it strikes several more, which then are impelled to strike other billiard balls in turn, we must accept the demonstration of the chain sequence of cause and effect. The monistic principle holds that laws of the same kind operate in all nature. Yet history demonstrates that while billiard balls have become nothing more than what they are as they are caught in the cause-and-effect drama, human beings have become more than what they were. The evidence of evolution — and of personal experience — convinces us that man has become more than his antecedents.

Will Durant has commented on how nineteenth-century French philosopher Henri Bergson relentlessly pressed the issue of determinism to absurdity:

> Finally, was determinism any more intelligible than free will? If the present moment contains no living and creative choice, and is totally and mechanically the product of the matter and motion of the moment before, then so was that moment the mechanical effect of the moment that preceded it, and that again of the one before . . . and so on, until we arrive at the primeval nebula as the total cause of every later event, of every line of Shakespeare's plays, and every suffering of his soul; so that the sombre rhetoric of Hamlet and Othello, of Macbeth and Lear, in every clause and every phrase, was written far off there in the distant skies and the distant aeons, by the structure and content of that legendary cloud. What a draft upon credulity. . . . There was matter enough for rebellion here; and if Bergson rose so rapidly to fame it was because he had the courage to doubt where all the doubters piously believed.[1]

The answer lies not in refuting the cause-and-effect nature of the universe or of man's behavior but in looking elsewhere than in the past for cause. Man does what he does for certain reasons, but those reasons do not all lie in the past. In a television interview I was asked my opinion as to why Charles Whitman climbed a tower at the University of Texas and shot scores of people on the ground below.

---

[1] Will Durant, *The Story of Philosophy* (New York: Simon and Schuster, 1933), pp. 337-338.

After a recount of a number of possible reasons I was asked, "But why do some people do a thing like this and others do not?" This is a valid question. If our position is that we simply don't know enough about the past history of an individual, then we still hold to the position that somewhere "back there" lies an answer.

There is an essential difference, however, between a man and a billiard ball. Man, through thought, is able to look to the future. He is influenced by another type of casual order which Charles Harteshorne calls "creative causation."[2] Elton Trueblood elaborates this point by suggesting that causes for human behavior lie not only in the past but in man's ability to contemplate the future, or estimate probabilities:

> The human mind . . . operates to a large extent by reference to final causes. This is so obvious that it might seem impossible to neglect it, yet it is neglected by everyone who denies freedom in employing the billiard ball analogy of causation. Of course, the billiard ball moves primarily by efficient causation, but man operates in a totally different way. Man is a creature whose present is constantly being dominated by reference to the nonexistent, but nevertheless potent, future. What is *not,* influences what *is.* I have a hard problem but the outcome is not merely the result of a mechanical combination of forces, which is true of a physical body; instead I think, and most of my thought is concerned with what might be produced, provided certain steps could be taken.[3]

Ortega defines man as "a being which consists not so much in what it is as in what it is going to be." Trueblood points out

> . . . it is not enough to say that the outcome is determined even by one's previous character, for the reality in which we share is such that genuine novelty can emerge in the very act of thinking. Thinking, as we actually experience it daily, is not merely awareness of action, as it is in all epiphenomenalist doctrine, but is a true and creative *cause.* Something happens, when a man thinks, which would not have occurred otherwise. This is what is meant by self-causation as a genuine third possibility in our familiar dilemma.[4]

[2] See "Causal Necessities, an Alternative to Hume," *The Philosophical Review,* 63 (1954), pp. 479-499.
[3] Elton Trueblood, *General Philosophy* (New York: Harper, 1963) .
[4] J. Ortega y Gasset, *What is Philosophy?* (New York: Norton, 1960).

So, since we are thinking beings, we are also changing beings. If we know our condition and want to change it, we can. We have given you abundant evidence of what the present human condition is and what it might be. You should now know something about where you stand and whether that is where you want to be. This has all involved a great deal of communication on the part of all of us. To make a decision as important as changing oneself will require even more, so before we get into that stage, let us look at the decision-making process in light of the human communication model we have proposed.

HUMANISTIC DECISION MAKING

Humanistic communicators, as described in Part 2, make their decisions based on a set of constructs or values which they have developed from their view of reality. The important point is that each one of us develops our own set of values. They are not given to us by our parents or by society, though these forces may have a great influence on their development. Furthermore, values do not result from the events we experience, but rather from the way in which we assimilate these experiences into our memories, our cognitive structures. Thus, one person may have feared the authority of a religious organization and another the authority of a dominant father. These are certainly not the same events, nor do they suggest the same experiences, but we may have developed similar feelings about authority. On the other hand, others may have experienced similar events but, because they were able to assimilate these into their cognitive structures differently, have an entirely different feeling about authority.

Obviously no two people have the same values nor the same priorities for the feelings they share. This has very far-reaching ramifications in the area of compatibility, likes and dislikes, learning ability, and maturation. Far too often we look at people's behavior and fail to ask *why* they make the choices they do. Usually we look at their choices in the light of our values and judge them accordingly, never stopping to think that they chose between alternatives that we may not even recognize. Even if we like what we perceive in someone, this does not mean that he or she shares our values. For example, you may not engage in premarital sex because of religious convictions, while your boyfriend or girlfriend may not because of a fear of VD. Since neither of you desire this behavior, you may feel that you are very compatible. On further investigation, however, you may discover that you are really hurt by the implications of your friend's thoughts about you and VD, and that your friend may be turned off by your religious conservatism.

Milton Rokeach has written much on beliefs and values. He separates them into terminal values (those which we hold as ideal states to strive for in our lifetime) and instrumental values (those which are desirable ways of behaving). The latter may be the means of obtaining the former. Terminal values may be further divided into personal and social, and instrumental values may be divided into moral and competence. In his work (1973, p. 28) he has isolated thirty-six values, eighteen terminal and eighteen instrumental. These are given in Scale L on page 214 in a form that allows you to rank them in your order of preference by numbering them from 1 (most desirable) to 18 (least desirable).

Now, if you like, discuss your rankings with a friend who has also ranked them. If you disagreed on some of the rankings, why did you disagree? Which one of you was quicker to change your rankings? Why? Would you be as changeable or would you rank them the same way if the values were opera-

SCALE L

Terminal and Instrumental Values

Terminal Value	*Instrumental Value*
_____ A comfortable life (a prosperous life)	_____ Ambitious (hard-working, aspiring)
_____ An exciting life (a stimulating, active life)	_____ Broad-minded (open-minded)
_____ A sense of accomplishment (lasting contribution)	_____ Capable (competent, effective)
_____ A world at peace (free of war and conflict)	_____ Cheerful (light-hearted, joyful)
_____ A world of beauty (beauty of nature and the arts)	_____ Clean (neat, tidy)
_____ Equality (brotherhood, equal opportunity for all)	_____ Courageous (standing up for your beliefs)
_____ Family security (taking care of loved ones)	_____ Forgiving (willing to pardon others)
_____ Freedom (independence, free choice)	_____ Helpful (working for the welfare of others)
_____ Happiness (contentedness)	_____ Honest (sincere, truthful)
_____ Inner harmony (freedom from inner conflict)	_____ Imaginative (daring, creative)
_____ Mature love (sexual and spiritual intimacy)	_____ Independent (self-reliant, self-sufficient)
_____ National security (protection from attack)	_____ Intellectual (intelligent, reflective)
_____ Pleasure (an enjoyable, leisurely life)	_____ Logical (consistent, rational)
_____ Salvation (saved, eternal life)	_____ Loving (affectionate, tender)
_____ Self-respect (self-esteem)	_____ Obedient (dutiful, respectful)
_____ Social recognition (respect, admiration)	_____ Polite (courteous, well-mannered)

_____ True friendship   _____ Responsible
      (close companionship)   (dependable, reliable)

_____ Wisdom (a mature   _____ Self-controlled
      understanding of life)   (restrained, self-disciplined)

---

tionalized into a concrete behavior (e.g., saying you enjoyed the party [polite] when you really were bored stiff [honesty])? This exercise may activate some cognitive processes that will help you form a better picture of yourself.

As we have said, our dominant evaluative characteristic is identified by the sets of values we bring to decision-making situations. At the same time these values are developing, we are experiencing different decision-making situations and seeing which values "work" the best. A child's first conscious valuing process may reflect only the good-bad dimension, but subconscious feelings involving such qualities as wet-dry, pleasant-unpleasant, and hot-cold may have been in use for some time. We assume that children begin to develop their personal values by internalizing purely physical feelings such as hot-cold and wet-dry, and progress to abstract symbolic values such as good-bad and honest-dishonest as their conceptual abilities grow. The clustering of specific feelings in relation to various events is interpreted as fear, desire, trust, and the like. Each of these states may be expressed as a specific cognitive construct (i.e., fearful-fearless, desirable-undesirable, and trustworthy-untrustworthy). However, any given decision-making process is not definable by these specific feelings alone. Our choices in any real-life situation must be operationally defined in terms of a cluster of personal feelings, since we are not usually single-dimensioned people. We don't help or not help a friend because the action is good or bad; there are many other dimensions involved, such as time, depth of relationship, projected outcome, and the like.

There is another aspect of the decision-making process that is important for the humanistic communicator to consider. When confronted with a decision, what are the possible actions that can be taken? What are the do-ables, or sayables, that I have at my command? The three variables that must be considered then are (1) the effect or end product, (2) all possible actions that might facilitate this effect, and (3) which of these actions will fit into *my* cognitive structure. For example, a man takes his best woman friend to a party. There he meets an old male friend whom he has not seen for several years. He must make a decision as to how much time he can spend talking to his old male friend without upsetting his woman friend. The desired end product here is a good feeling among all concerned. It will be based on communicating sufficiently with each one of his friends to satisfy each of their expectations as well as his own desires.

What are the do-ables? Well, there are a great number. Each reader can probably list ten or more. A few might be: The man could sit with his male friend between dances and let the conversation and time dictate how much they catch up on each other's experiences since last they met. Or the three of them could leave the party and go to his place, where they can talk in a quieter atmosphere. Or he could excuse himself from his woman friend and spend the evening with his male friend. Or he could make a date to see his male friend at some other time and carry on the evening as planned. Or . . . etc., etc. In each case different values are given priority, both for what he wants to accomplish and what best fits his way of doing things. Of course, if other variables are introduced—such as the male friend having an eye on the woman friend, or the male friend having with him his sister whom the man used to date, or the woman friend seeing another male at the party whom she knew and wanted to get better acquainted with—decision making can be very complicated, and there is almost never a situation in which the process has clear-cut dimensions and values on which it can be made.

Let's take another example. You are an employee of a firm and are in charge of hiring. Suppose your boss wants to play the role of "boss" and continually checks up on your hiring procedures. If you feel you are doing a good job, are competent, and responsible, what will your reaction be? More to the point, if you get steamed over his behavior, what would you do about it? What are your do-ables? You might confront him head on and tell him to stay out of your business; you might go deeper inside yourself, bitch to your friends about it, get an ulcer, but never mention it to him; or you might try to be open and discuss the problem with him, let him know how you feel. Be tactful, but assert yourself. He may not even realize what he is doing. If he doesn't, he will probably change. If he does, then you must be willing to take the consequences. You have to be responsible for your behavior.

A situation that is coming more and more into prominence now is that of the woman who works, is married, has children, and wants her husband to share the household chores. Suppose her husband is unwilling to do his share: what are her do-ables? Can you think of six possible solutions to this problem? Work out a feasible plan of action for each of these options. Keep this example in mind as we proceed through this part of the book.

In a situation where you are thinking about making a decision that will affect your whole life, such as becoming a humanistic communicator, you must consider the variables involved very closely. What are the effects or products you want to result from this decision? What are the do-ables in this situation? And what are your priorities for these do-ables? The last two questions are, on the surface, rather easily answered. First, you can either choose to become a humanistic communicator or choose not to become one, and, of course, by doing nothing you are making the latter choice. Since you may be well on your way toward being such a communicator, you may have already made this choice without even knowing it. Thus, the choice only becomes a problem if you now want to become a humanistic communicator but have not yet started.

The reasons for your not having started may be difficult to pin down. Perhaps you aren't sure how to start, what to do, or whether you really want to or not. We will help you solve the first two problems later in this book; the last one is really the basic question we are concerned with now. Why are you undecided? Perhaps it is because you do not know what the results might be. We have painted a positive picture of the humanistic communicator, but you may have detected some adverse aspects as well. Your projections about the results of deciding to be a humanistic communicator may be highly inflated or critical and as such you are not willing to accept them. Perhaps it would be good to look at some of the results that might occur if you make the choice to become a humanistic communicator.

First of all, why should you choose to become such a communicator? Maybe you are happy with the way things are, so why upset them? No reason—if you are happy with the status quo, then you should stay with it. Perhaps your present state is as humanized as you care to get it, for we must remember that we are talking about a continuum, not a dichotomous, either-or situation. We all make attempts at being "human" to some degree at some time. To make a conscious effort to maintain this way of life continuously at a deeper level than you are now on, however, has implications for both you and the people you interact with. In your present state you may be able to rely on many of society's norms to give you direction and fulfillment. If you decide to become a consciously autonomous person, many of these guidelines may be cut loose and you will have to build your own guidelines within your own cognitive structure. This situation is illustrated well in the following excerpt (Mebane-Francescato and Jones 1973, pp. 31–32):

> An oriental fable tells of a man who was entered by a serpent while he was asleep. The serpent settled in the man's stomach and took over control of his life so that the man no longer belonged to himself. One day, after a long period of domination, the serpent finally left; but the man no longer knew what to do with his freedom. He had become so used to submitting his will to that of the serpent, his wishes and impulses to those of the beast, that he had lost the capacity to wish, to strive, or to act autonomously. Instead of freedom he found only the "emptiness of the void," for the departure of the serpent had taken with it the man's new essence—the adaptive fruit of his occupation. He was left with the awesome task of reclaiming, little by little, the former human content of his life. . . . through the same actions of prevarication and violence by which the serpent destroyed the man, our system breeds "mental illness" by forcing the unwary individual to incorporate and submit to the very enemy who destroys him. . . . *all* of us who participate in society are slaves of the serpent, and if we do not struggle to destroy or vomit it, we will lose all hope of regaining our human dignity.

These are strong words, but we endorse them completely. It is only by relieving ourselves of the restrictive norms of society that we are able to grow into the responsible persons we have the potential to become. The term "responsible" is very important here. Removal of society's restrictions is not a license for "unbridled gratification of our sexual and aggressive urges," to hark back to an earlier section. Rather it is an opportunity to develop our own inner structures through which we can control our own behavior and develop our own mature way of life. We shall have more to say about this way of life later in this section. Now we would like to consider one more aspect of this decision-making process.

What can you expect to happen if you decide to be your own person and this decision leads you to violate one or more of society's norms (e.g., dress codes or male-female-interaction norms)? We have suggested several possibilities in Table 4, and, again, they are on a continuum in either a positive or negative direction.

TABLE 4
Behavioral Expectations of Violating
Society's Norms

Negative	Positive
1. Become the butt of jokes.	1. Go unnoticed.
2. Be ridiculed.	2. Be commended for your behavior.
3. Be discriminated against.	3. Have your behavior adopted by others.
4. Be attacked.	4. Be made a hero by society.

To illustrate this continuum, let's have you wear cutoffs to church on a warm Sunday morning. People might laugh and make fun of you for not "knowing" the proper dress for this situation (e.g., "Did your valet have the day off?"), or they might not even notice how you are attired. If your dress is a little more offensive to them, they might ridicule you by saying, "Don't you know where you are?" Or if they are sympathetic to your behavior, they might say, "You really look comfortable." On the next level you might get remarks like, "Why don't you go over to the Fifth Avenue Church next Sunday?" Or on the other side, others in the congregation might show up wearing more casual dress, including cutoffs, the next warm Sunday. On the most reactive level, we can imagine someone (maybe the minister) preaching against such "looseness" or maybe even bodily forcing you out of the building. On the other side, we can see someone mounting a crusade for less formal dress in the house of worship and citing you as a hero.

The extent of the reaction to your violation of society's norms depends to a great extent on the personalities of those involved. If you are aggressive and obnoxious in your behavior, it will probably trigger like behavior in others, either pro or con. If you are assertive but tactful, others may be less inclined to take a strong stand, pro or con. However, if you insist on doing your thing, you must be willing to take the consequences. This is probably the greatest deterent to individuality; our parents, our peer group, or society in general objects to our deviating from their norms, or they accept our behavior, publicize it, and make it into the norm. We seem to be afraid of those who are not like us, so we either fight them or join them.

We have given you some ideas of the possibilities and implications of becoming a humanistic communicator. The following activities will allow you to explore these two aspects a little more.

TO-BE-OR-NOT-TO-BE ACTIVITIES

1. What is self-actualization? In a group, arrive at a definition of self-actualization upon which everyone can agree. You should consider values, very basic issues that confront most people — questions of ethics, morals, and the inevitability of ever achieving self-actualization (e.g., is it a goal we *achieve* or is it a *process?*).

2. What aspects of self-actualization must be considered in making your decision to strive for this goal? In a group, list ten pro and ten con aspects of self-actualization and rank them according to their priority in making such a decision. Each member of the group should now participate in a debate, or class presentation, on this issue.

3. Before individuals can become self-actualizers (or self-actualizing persons), they must have other persons around them. Comment on this statement and why you would agree or disagree with it. In a group, decide on the necessity for a person to have other persons around to reach a stage of self-actualization. Can a man, for example, on a desert island, achieve self-actualization if he never sees another person during his lifetime?

4. What scripts do we live by? Three scripts were given in the text. In a group, look at the themes of nursery rhymes, novels, and movies and see what other "scripts" you can use to classify human behavior. Role-play some of your scripts for the class.

5. What are the mythical norms (codes) of our society? In a group, come up with as many of these as possible. Rank them in the order of their importance to your behavior. Now rank them as a group. How close are you to the group feeling? How does this affect you?

6. What are the do-ables? In a group, decide on an important decision that must be made at your university (to raise tuition, integrate sports). List

all of the do-ables the group can think of. Sort them according to their practicality. What were the bases for this sorting? Do these represent real or mythical codes of behavior?

7.   Basic needs. List the things you feel you must have in order to live life the way you want to. Are all of these attainable in your present situation? How would they change your situation? Are they really worth the change? How many of them depend on someone else? A specific person? Are you self-transcendent enough to change your priorities to maintain the above relationship? (This does not mean "giving up" your priorities for some-one else's. It means having sufficiently abstract goals to allow for their fulfillment in non-situation-specific events.)

8.   How free are you to choose your own fate? Get inside yourself and list the social norms that affect your personal life. What would you or wouldn't you do? Think of things all the way from missing class to rebuking your parents to walking around in the nude. How much does society control your behavior? Are you satisfied with this level of control? If not, how do you plan to change your level of satisfaction? *Is it up to you?*

Developing the Humanistic Communicator Intrapersonally

If it should happen that you decided to become a humanistic communicator, how would you go about it? What are the basic principles that need to be con-sidered when making this choice? Probably the most basic principle is the satisfaction of your needs, and the most basic one in this case is the need to be loved. Theodore Reik (1963) suggests that this is the most basic and universal need of all humans — male or female. Though there seem to be basically dif-ferent reasons for this need in males and females, the need is there never-theless. One of the three life scripts suggested by Steiner develops from the lack of fulfillment of this need in early childhood. He calls it stimulus hunger, and it leads to the No Love script.

THE NEED FOR LOVE

There are two manifestations of this basic need. One is the need to be loved by others: the other is the need to be loved by oneself. We touched on the latter characteristic earlier in this section, but we should say a little more at this point. As we mentioned, most of us suffer from self-hate; thus we do not ful-fill this basic need in ourselves. As a substitute we may seek love from a greater number of others, thinking that this will fill the void left by our inability to love ourselves. We have not learned the more basic truth that we must love ourselves before we can expect fulfillment of the need to be loved by others. Of course this can be carried to extremes also, and we can love ourselves so much that we cannot find anyone else's love adequate. Thus, the first principle we must consider is how we feel about ourselves. We have included some scales in this section to help *you* decide how *you feel about yourself.* If you are interested in this, you should fill out Scale M at this time.

Put an *x* on the dash closest (depending on the strength of your feelings) to the adjective that *you* feel best describes *you*.

SCALE M

How I Feel about Myself (1)

I THINK I AM:

Good_____Bad

Beautiful_____Ugly

Hard_____Soft

Strong_____Weak

Dirty_____Clean

Valuable_____Worthless

Unpleasant_____Pleasant

Deep_____Shallow

Sad_____Happy

Tense_____Relaxed

Brave_____Cowardly

Delicate_____Rugged

Healthy_____Sick

Unlovable_____Lovable

Independent_____Dependent

Fast_____Slow

Dull_____Sharp

Active_____Passive

Fat_____Thin

Honest_____Dishonest

Since there are no norms for this scale (in fact, there are many items on it that cannot be given a positive or negative value) you can only use it to evaluate *yourself*. If you were *honest* with yourself, you can go back over it at any time and see how you felt about yourself at this time. Now, to get an idea of your need to be loved by self, go back over this scale and mark each set of adjectives with a ✓ as you would like to feel about yourself (I WOULD LIKE TO FEEL THAT I AM) . Is there much difference? If there is, then you know where you need to change *your* image of *yourself*. It may be of interest to know that just the fact that you have filled out this scale will start the process of changing your self-image.

If you have *good* friends, you may want to make a copy of this scale (*without* your marks on it) and ask them to fill it out as they think you feel about yourself (I THINK *YOU* FEEL YOU ARE). By comparing their ratings with yours and discussing the differences, you can get an idea of how you project your feelings about yourself. This may also help you get a more realistic image of yourself.

The need to be loved by self and others may be separated into several different feelings. Scale M gave us *evaluative·* feelings—feelings of being evaluated positively or negatively according to those adjectives. Now you may want to fill out Scale N on page 223 to see if you can differentiate among other types of feelings. Again, this scale has no norms, as it is *your* feelings about *yourself*. Try to think of the slightly different aspects of your feelings that each pair of these verbs represents.

Notice that the concept you are to have in your mind as you fill out this scale is slightly different from the previous one. For each set of characteristics, put an *x* on the dash closest (depending on the strength of your feelings) to the one you think best describes how you feel about yourself.

Now you may want to go back through this scale and put a ✓ on the dash that best depicts how you would like to see yourself (I WOULD LIKE TO FEEL THAT I AM _____ BY MYSELF). If there are differences, then you know where you have to work on your self-image. Again, since *you* have actively engaged in evaluating yourself, you have taken the first step in changing your image. If you have a friend fill out this scale as he or she thinks you feel (I THINK THAT YOU FEEL THAT YOU ARE _____ BY YOURSELF), you can discuss any differences and get a more realistic image of yourself.

Your need to love yourself should be apparent now. Of course only you know if you have been honest on these scales. But then you are the only one it matters to, if it matters at all. The other need, the need to be loved by others, is more difficult to reveal, but Scales M and N can be of some help. Using different marks or different-colored x's and ✓'s, fill out Scale M to reflect how *you think* others feel about you (OTHERS THINK I AM) and how *you would like* others to feel about you (I WOULD LIKE OTHERS TO THINK I

SCALE N

How I Feel about Myself (2)

IN GENERAL I FEEL THAT I AM ____
BY MYSELF:

Valued ___ ___ ___ ___ ___ Abhorred

Ridiculed ___ ___ ___ ___ ___ Respected

Understood ___ ___ ___ ___ ___ Misunderstood

Detested ___ ___ ___ ___ ___ Adored

Accepted ___ ___ ___ ___ ___ Rejected

Disliked ___ ___ ___ ___ ___ Liked

Admired ___ ___ ___ ___ ___ Loathed

Mocked ___ ___ ___ ___ ___ Idolized

Appreciated ___ ___ ___ ___ ___ Unappreciated

Hated ___ ___ ___ ___ ___ Loved

AM). Then, if you trust your friends, have some of them fill it out as they think you think they think you are. Wow!! What you are trying to get here are their perceptions of how you perceive others' feelings about you (I FEEL YOU THINK I FEEL YOU ARE). You should try to discuss any differences you find in the perceptions measured on this scale in order to better understand the conflicting feelings you and others may have about how they feel about you.

Now you may want to do the same for Scale N. If you change BY MYSELF to BY OTHER PEOPLE and use different marks or colors, you can fill out this scale as you feel others feel (IN GENERAL I FEEL THAT I AM _____ BY OTHER PEOPLE), and as you would like others to feel (IN GENERAL I WOULD LIKE TO FEEL THAT I AM _____ BY OTHER PEOPLE). Then you might also have some of your friends fill it out to get their impressions (IN GENERAL I THINK YOU FEEL THAT YOU ARE _____ BY OTHER PEOPLE). By discussing any differences you can then get a better image of your need to be loved by others.

There are two other processes that these scales can be used for. We caution you on using them this way, because if you get negative results, it may be very hard to take. On the other hand, if you really want to know how others feel about you, then we suggest you change the heading on Scale M to I THINK YOU ARE and the heading on Scale N to IN GENERAL YOU ARE ____and ask some of your friends, your acquaintances, and "others" to fill them out. (If they do this anonymously, it will be easier to get the general picture.) With these findings you should now have a pretty good idea of how others feel about you and your love needs. Again, the fact that you have gone through these processes indicates that you have already begun to change in your desired direction.

We all have other values that play a major role in our development. When we communicate with others we not only say something about how we feel about ourselves, but we also reveal these other values. By doing this, others begin to get a symbolic picture of us, and we begin to see where we agree or disagree with others—that is, if we are aware of our communicative behavior! The process of revealing our values can be extremely difficult because it usually means that we will be evaluated by the person we are communicating with according to his or her value system. If that person is a significant other (one whom we feel we must please)—and to some of us everyone is a significant other—we are very apprehensive about stating our position before we find out what his or her position is.

Do you find that you are hesitant to disagree with another's position whether you have to make it known or not? If so, this may stem from the mistaken belief that our values must never change, either over time or across subjects. Thus, we feel very reticent about revealing our values to others for fear they may find an inconsistency. However, if we were to look closely at our values, we would find that many of them are in direct contradiction when viewed from some vantage points. For example, we may be liberal in our views on education and politics (free schools, socialized medicine), but conservative in our views on sexual mores and family structure (sex for reproduction only and male dominance in the home). Yet these values may exist side by side with no trauma attached. How can this be?

Daryl Bem explains it in terms of opinion molecules. These are essentially isolated molecules of beliefs that have their basis in fact and are reinforced by knowing others who believe the same way. He says, "Opinion molecules serve such a simple function that psychologists have usually ignored them. They are conversational units. They give us something coherent to say when a particular topic comes up in conversation. Accordingly, they do not need to have logical interconnections between them, and they are notoriously invulnerable to argument because of their isolated, molecular character. I suspect that the majority of our knowledge comes packed in little opinion molecules like these, just waiting for the topic to come up" (1970, p. 39). We cannot argue with the fact that we can hold contradictory values without noticeable discomfort. However, one of the best ways to get to know ourselves is by looking at our values and comparing them with others — *but* with the strong resolution that we want to find out where we stand. We can then come away from this experience with a better understanding of ourselves, the values we hold, and the strength of our convictions.

In defining your values you are also defining your needs:

> Man is the only animal that can be meaningfully described as having values. Indeed, it is the presence of values and systems of values that is a major characteristic distinguishing humans from infrahumans. Values are the cognitive representations and transformations of needs, and man is the only animal capable of such representations and transformations.
>
> This proposition is not the whole story, however: Values are the cognitive representation not only of individual needs but also of societal and institutional demands. They are the joint results of sociological as well as psychological forces acting upon the individual — sociological because society and its institutions socialize the individual for the common good to internalize shared conceptions of the desirable; psychological because individual motivations require cognitive expression, justification, and indeed exhortation in socially desirable terms. The cognitive representation of needs as values serves societal demands no less than individual needs. Once such demands and needs become cognitively transformed into values, they are capable of being defended, justified, advocated, and exhorted as personally and socially desirable. For example, the need for sex which is so often repressed in modern society may be cognitively transformed as a value for love, spiritual union, or intimacy; needs for dependence, conformity, or abasement may be cognitively transformed into values concerning obedience, loyalty, or respect for elders; aggressive needs may be transformed into values concerning ambition, honor, family or national security. Needs may or may not be denied, depending on whether they can stand conscious personal and social scrutiny, but values need never be denied. Thus, when a person tells us about his values he is surely also telling us about his needs. But we must be cautious in how we infer needs from values because values are not isomorphic with needs. Needs are cognitively transformed into values so that a person can end up smelling himself, and being smelled by others, like a rose. (Rokeach 1973, p. 20) *

In knowing ourselves and others symbolically we begin to develop a sense of the sociological and psychological needs and values of the human species. The values that you ranked (pp. 214-215) reflected some of the needs you felt for society and self. If we could take a more macroscopic view of life and of reality as you see it, we would probably see that they fit into the overall structure that functions in your life. This structure is often difficult to be seen either by us or a therapist, but that we all have one is sure. That we are able to use it to actualize our own life processes is not sure, for we often find ourselves striving to realize the myths of society rather than trusting our own inner

---

* Quoted from *The Nature of Human Values* by Milton Rokeach, copyright © 1973, The Free Press. Reprinted by permission of MacMillan Publishing Company, Inc.

structure. Viktor Frankl (1963, pp. 167–168) talks about this problem in terms of an existential vacuum:

> The existential vacuum is a widespread phenomenon of the twentieth century. This is understandable; it may be due to a twofold loss that man had to undergo since he became a truly human being. At the beginning of human history, man lost some of the basic animal instincts in which an animal's behavior is embedded and by which it is secured. Such security, like Paradise, is closed to man forever; man has to make choices. In addition to this, however, man has suffered another loss in his more recent development: the traditions that had buttressed his behavior are now rapidly diminishing. No instinct tells him what he has to do, and no tradition tells him what he ought to do; soon he will not know what he wants to do. More and more he will be governed by what others want him to do, thus increasingly falling prey to conformism.

Since we now have to make choices, instead of taking the responsibility we often fall back to conforming to society's norms. In this passive behavior we find great trauma; we are not able to reach the mythical goals and thus hate ourselves for our inadequacies. However, the fact that we can see this disparity should give us hope. According to Frankl (1965 p. 45):

> No man is justified in insisting upon his own inadequacies — that is, in demeaning his own potentialities. No matter how discontented with himself a person may be, no matter how he torments himself with brooding on his own failings and how sternly he sits in judgment upon himself — the very fact that he is doing so proves that he is not so poor a creature as he thinks he is. Just as deploring the relativity and subjectivity of all knowledge and values assumes the objectivity of knowledge and values, so a man's moral self-condemnation assumes an ideal of personality, his private ought-to-be. Thus the man who judges himself harshly has caught sight of a value and is taking part in the world of values. The moment he is able to apply the standard of an ideal to himself, he cannot be entirely valueless any longer. For by that fact he has reached a level of ethical values by which he is redeemed from worthlessness.

What does all of this mean? Are we turning the tables on you by saying that if you deviate from the norm you're not bad, inadequate, or a loser? That is partly true, but more correct is the statement that by seeing your differences from your friends in values and needs you are seeing your uniqueness, your humanness, and your ability to use your cognitive processes. If you couldn't see some way that you differed from others, then we would be concerned. Frankl (1963, p. 172) puts this in terms of logotherapy and the search for meaning:

> One should not search for an abstract meaning of life. Everyone has his own specific vocation or mission in life; everyone must carry out a concrete assignment that demands fulfillment. Therein he cannot be replaced, nor can his life be repeated. Thus, everyone's task is as unique as is his specific opportunity to implement it.

As each situation in life represents a challenge to man and presents a problem for him to solve, the question of the meaning of life may actually be reversed. Ultimately, man should not ask what the meaning of his life is, but rather must recognize that it is *he* who is asked. In a word, each man is questioned by life; and he can only answer to life by *answering for* his own life; to life he can only respond by being responsible. Thus, logotherapy sees in responsibleness the very essence of human existence.

To be responsible for one's life (taking the initiative, the praise and the blame) is the goal of the humanistic communicator. It will result in a self-actualizing, fully functioning, and self-transcending person.

SELF-AWARENESS

You cannot take responsibility for your life unless you are aware of yourself and the choices you make. We have given you some opportunities to develop self-awareness, but there are other ways as well:

All studies show evidence that can be interpreted as indicating the critical importance of the opinions of others on the individual's self-evaluation. Furthermore, the importance of others has been shown to be in some sense a direct function of the frequency of interaction with those others and an inverse function of the extensity of interaction with alternative others. There is some evidence that the others with whom the individual interacts are not all equally important in determining self-evaluation, and the term "significant other" has been given to those who are considered to be most influential. However, the characteristics of a significant other have not been spelled out in detail, either conceptually or in terms of empirical evidence. In addition to forming the self, others have been shown to be important both for maintaining a given self-evaluation and for producing change in the level of self-evaluation. Finally, the research by Israel and by Maehr indicates that two of the important scope conditions for demonstrating the effects of others' opinions on the self are a high level of attraction to the others and a high level of motivation, either to learn one's own level of achievement or to attain a high level of achievement.

All studies reviewed have implicitly or explicitly conceptualized the self as a cognitive entity, that is, as a set of self-referent ideas that are held by the individual and of which he can be aware. Second, although the self seems to be sensitive to changes in the evaluations received from others, it is not infinitely flexible, nor is it constantly changing to be in perfect agreement with every modification in evaluations. In other words, a semipermanent *structure* seems to arise as the result of the evaluations received, and the type of structure that arises partly determines the effect of subsequent opinions. Thus it is possible to talk of two individuals—one who possesses a high self-evaluation as the result of having received a large number of positive evaluations and another who possesses a low self-evaluation as the result of having received a large number of negative evaluations—*and* it is possible to assert that the effect of a given subsequent evaluation will not be the same for both these individuals.

Jones's research indicates one major consequence of a given level of self-evaluation: an individual who receives many positive evaluations at a particular task is more likely to attempt future performances than an individual who receives many negative evaluations. This suggests that one consequence of a high self-evaluation may be an increased willingness to perform in the future, and by extension, that a consequence of a low self-evaluation may be a decreased willingness to perform.

A second consequence of a high self-evaluation that appeared in several of the studies is a greater willingness to evaluate one's own future performances positively and a greater willingness to rank oneself highly within the group. If this result suggests a more general tendency for subjects with high self-evaluations to place themselves first in a variety of contexts and to think they are right when there is no objective reason to do so, among other diverse consequences, then it is important to form a precise concept of the tendency. Whether this is the case cannot be determined from the studies so far examined. However, the results of these studies indicate that the possibility merits further examination. (Webster and Sobieszek 1974, pp. 28–29) *

The influence of others cannot be denied. Thus, we would like to emphasize the point that we made earlier — when people see you as different from them, this does not make you any more deviant than they are, for they cannot act out of your cognitive structure any more than you can act out of theirs. At the same time we must realize that they are a very important source of information to us. By utilizing this information we can better establish our own sense of self, our direction and meaning in life.

This sense of direction, or meaning, Buhler and Allen (1972, p. 44) call intentionality, which "implies both a person's focussing on a subject which means something to him and his directing himself toward that subject." Thus, intention has a commitment within it, and the saying "the road to Hell is paved with good intentions" does not refer to the humanistic concept, implying as it does only wishful thinking and not commitment to carry out intentions. If we are constantly falling short of our goals, then we probably are aware of some of the variables involved in our behavior. Awareness of our own behavior patterns, our desires, and our potentialities will allow us to put them together in such a way as to realize our intentions. This may mean reevaluating our intentions and making them more realistic.

To develop realistic intentions requires an in-depth awareness of ourself. Among other things, this means bringing our locus of evaluation back inside us, centering the evaluative process for any decision in our feelings and values and not in the feelings and values of others. It takes the "I shoulds" and "I oughts" out of decision making and puts the "I wills" in. It also brings the acceptance of the responsibility for our behavior back to the person. Along with moving the locus of evaluation back inside us, we also must move the locus of

---

* Quoted from *Sources of Self-Evaluation: A Formal Theory of Significant Others and Social Influence* by Murray Webster, Jr., and Barbara Sobieszek, copyright © 1974, John Wiley & Sons, Inc. Reprinted by permission of John Wiley & Sons, Inc.

control back inside us, the feeling that we are not pawns in a huge chess game but rather that we have some control over our actions. Frankl (1963, pp. 206-207) puts it this way:

Man is *not* fully conditioned and determined; he determines himself whether to give in to conditions or stand up to them. In other words, man is ultimately self-determining. Man does not simply exist, but always decides what his existence will be, what he will become in the next moment.

By the same token, every human being has the freedom to change at any instant. Therefore, we can predict his future only within the large frame of a statistical survey referring to a whole group; the individual personality, however, remains essentially unpredictable. The basis for any predictions would be represented by biological, psychological or sociological conditions. Yet one of the main features of human existence is the capacity to rise above such conditions and transcend them. In the same manner, man ultimately transcends himself; a human being is a self-transcending being.

As we stated before, to have this ability one must be aware of oneself. To become aware of something may be a painful experience. If you have done the exercises and activities in this book so far, you have probably become more aware of your own thinking and behavior. Some would say that you could better reach this awareness by joining a sensitivity or T-group. This fad became very big in the United States during the last decade. It is still a strong movement in some areas, but since it is not the cure-all people expected it to be, it is becoming less publicized. We would rather you become aware through self-reflection, introspection, and open discussion with close friends. That is why our exercises have been focused in that direction.

We have tried to bring to an awareness the various needs we all have. As we continue this process we would like to introduce you to a model of interpersonal behavior that may help you to become more aware of your own communicative behavior. It is called the Johari Window (Luft 1969, p. 13) and is shown in Figure 5.

The four quadrants represent the total person in relation to other persons. The basis for division into quadrants is awareness of behavior, feelings, and motivation. Sometimes awareness is shared, sometimes not. An act, a feeling, or a motive is assigned to a particular quadrant based on who knows about it. As awareness changes, the quadrant to which the psychological state is assigned changes. The following definitions and principles are substantially the same as those in *Group Processes* (Luft, 1963, pp. 10-11). Each quadrant is defined:

1. Quadrant 1, the open quadrant, refers to behavior, feelings, and motivation known to self and to others.
2. Quadrant 2, the blind quadrant, refers to behavior, feelings, and motivation known to others but not to self.
3. Quadrant 3, the hidden quadrant, refers to behavior, feelings, and motivation known to self but not to others.

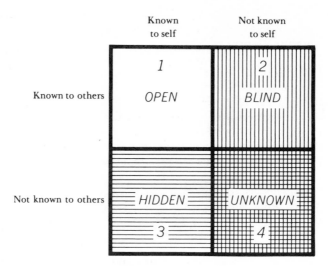

Figure 5   The Johari awareness model.

4. Quadrant 4, the unknown quadrant, refers to behavior, feelings, and motivation known neither to self or others.*

As we become more and more open to others, quadrant 1 gets larger and quadrant 3 gets smaller. As our awareness of ourself and sensitivity to others increases, quadrant 2 gets smaller; and as we mature and realize more of our potential, quadrant 4 gets smaller. Thus, we can characterize people by the size of their quadrants. We should hasten to add that we are *not* suggesting that everyone should be completely open to everyone else at all times. In fact, that would lead to a very chaotic society. All of us have the right to privacy and none of us wants to know everything other people know about us. If there were no blind and hidden areas, friendship and love would lose their meanings.

We do advocate, however, the awareness of what is in quadrant 3, and as small a quadrant 2 and 4 as possible. To facilitate this we have worked out a modification of the Johari Window for the individual. It consists of taking a large piece of poster board and making a collage on one side representing how you think people see you (quadrant 1). Cut out pictures, sayings, cartoons, jokes, etc., from magazines and paste them on the poster board in a way that expresses your own creativity. You may want to do some drawing and other creative work as well. On the other side, do the same for quadrant 3, the way you see yourself (the way you *really* are?). By paying this much attention to these two quadrants and putting this much effort into illustrating them, you should gain a better awareness of yourself.

* Figure and description reprinted from "The 'Johari' Window" in *Of Human Interaction* by Joseph Luft, by permission of Mayfield Publishing Company, formerly National Press Books. Copyright © 1969 by the National Press.

So far we have been concerned primarily with awareness of self and our own feelings. There is another side of the coin, however. That is the expression of ourself and our communicative behavior. We probably behave overtly as we see ourselves covertly (e.g., if we see ourselves as shy and introverted, we will communicate less assertatively than if we see ourselves as confident and extroverted). However, one can be assertive without being extroverted. Even though the common belief is that assertiveness is the same as aggressiveness and goes along with loud, boisterous behavior, this is not necessarily the case. You can be very assertive without even raising your voice. Assertive behavior goes along with confident, independent, mature thinking. It is the product of high self-esteem.

One of the major variables in self-concept development is the development of high self-esteem. To develop this you must be aware of yourself and have faith in your own abilities. Your decisions must come from your feelings and you must be willing to take the responsibility for your actions. To get a better indication of what self-esteem is and your estimate of what yours is, we have included a self-esteem inventory as Scale O (Barksdale 1972, pp. 6-7). Remember, this is how *you feel about yourself.* To get your score, add the individual scores of all even-numbered statements and subtract from this the sum of all the odd-numbered statements. The highest possible score is 75. If you think your net score is too low, then go back over the items to see where you can improve it. Being aware can automatically move you toward increased self-esteem.

To obtain an indication of your prevailing self-esteem, score the following statements as follows: 0 if not true, 1 if somewhat true, 2 if largely true, 3 if true.

SCALE O

Test for Self-Esteem

Score	Statement of Action or Condition
1	1. I feel inferior to others.
0	2. I feel warm and happy toward myself.
0	3. I feel inadequate to handle new situations.
2	4. I feel warm and friendly toward all I contact.
0	5. I usually condemn myself for my mistakes and shortcomings.
1	6. I am free of any shame, blame, guilt or remorse.

_2_ 7. I have a driving need to prove my worth and excellence.

_2_ 8. I have great enjoyment and zest for living.

_0_ 9. I am concerned about what others think and say of me.

_3_ 10. I can let others be "wrong" without attempting to correct them.

_1_ 11. I hunger for recognition and approval.

_2_ 12. I am free of emotional turmoil, conflict and frustration.

_1_ 13. Losing usually causes me to feel resentful and "less than."

_2_ 14. I anticipate new endeavors with quiet confidence.

_0_ 15. I am prone to condemn and wish to punish others.

_3_ 16. I do my own thinking and make my own decisions.

_0_ 17. I often defer to others on account of their wealth or prestige.

_2_ 18. I willingly take responsibility for the consequences of my actions.

_0_ 19. I am inclined to exaggerate and lie to maintain an image.

_2_ 20. I am free to give precedence to my own needs and desires.

_1_ 21. I tend to belittle my talents, possessions and achievements.

_2_ 22. I am free to speak up for my own opinions and convictions.

_0_ 23. I deny, alibi, justify or rationalize my mistakes and defeats.

_2_ 24. I am poised and comfortable among strangers.

_0_ 25. I am critical and belittling of others.

_2_ 26. I am free to express love, anger, hostility, resentment, joy, etc.

_0_ 27. I am vulnerable to others' opinions, comments and attitudes.

_1_ 28. I rarely experience jealousy, envy or suspicion.

_0_ 29. I am a " professional people pleaser."

2 30. I am unprejudiced toward racial, ethnic and religious groups.

0 31. I am fearful of exposing my "real self."

2 32. I am considerate, sincere and generous with others.

0 33. I often blame others for my handicaps, problems and mistakes.

3 34. I rarely feel uncomfortable, lonely and isolated when alone.

0 35. I am a compulsive "perfectionist."

2 36. I accept compliments and gifts without embarrassment or obligation.

1 37. I am often compulsive about eating, smoking, talking or drinking.

2 38. I am appreciative of others' achievements and ideas.

0 39. I shun new endeavors because of fear of mistakes or failure.

2 40. I make and keep friends without effort.

0 41. I am often embarrassed by the actions of my family or friends.

1 42. I readily admit my mistakes, shortcomings and defeats.

2 43. I experience a strong need to defend my acts, opinions and beliefs.

2 44. I take disagreement without feeling "put down," or rejected.

1 45. I have a strong need for confirmation and agreement.

2 46. I am eagerly open to new ideas and proposals.

0 47. I judge my self-worth by comparison with others.

2 48. I am free to think any thoughts that come into my mind.

0 49. I frequently boast about myself, my possessions and achievements.

2 50. I accept my own authority and move on my own initiative.

_____ NET SCORE OF SELF-ESTEEM INDEX

48
10 odd   27.   27. even
―――
38   26.

As we increase our self-esteem, we will also increase our assertiveness. Knowing where we are "coming from" will help us "tell it like it is." Fensterheim and Baer (1975, p. 8) list four characteristics of the truly assertive person:

> He feels free to *reveal himself.* Through words and actions he makes the statement, "This is me. This is what I feel, think, and want."
>
> He can *communicate* with people on all levels—with strangers, friends, family. This communication is always open, direct, honest, and appropriate.
>
> He has an *active orientation* to life. He goes after what he wants. In contrast to the passive person who waits for things to happen, he attempts to *make* things happen.
>
> He acts in a way *he himself respects.* Aware that he cannot always win, he accepts his limitations. However, he always strives to make the good try so that win, lose, or draw, he maintains his self-respect.

These are very close to what we have been calling the characteristics of the self-actualizer, the humanistic communicator, or the fully functioning person. To find out how you see yourself, Fensterheim and Baer give an assertiveness inventory (Scale P) in which you can spot some of the difficulties *you feel* you may have in asserting yourself. If you want to fill out this inventory, put a 1, 2, 3, or 4, in front of each item, depending on whether the answer is always, often, sometimes, or never.

SCALE P

An Assertiveness Inventory
(Modified from Fensterheim
and Baer, 1975, pp. 36–37)

__4__ 1. Do you buy things you don't really want because it is difficult to say no to the sales clerk?

__4__ 2. Do you hesitate to return items to a store even when there is a good reason to do so?

_____ 3. If someone talks aloud during a movie, play, or concert, can you ask him to be quiet?

__3.__ 4. Can you begin a conversation with a stranger?

__3__ 5. Do you have trouble maintaining conversations in social situations?

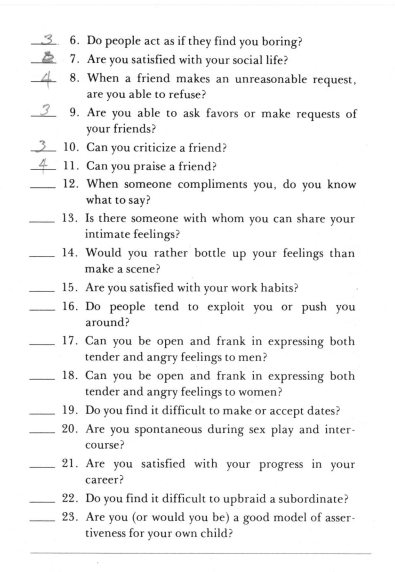

_3_ 6. Do people act as if they find you boring?

_2_ 7. Are you satisfied with your social life?

_4_ 8. When a friend makes an unreasonable request, are you able to refuse?

_3_ 9. Are you able to ask favors or make requests of your friends?

_3_ 10. Can you criticize a friend?

_4_ 11. Can you praise a friend?

_____ 12. When someone compliments you, do you know what to say?

_____ 13. Is there someone with whom you can share your intimate feelings?

_____ 14. Would you rather bottle up your feelings than make a scene?

_____ 15. Are you satisfied with your work habits?

_____ 16. Do people tend to exploit you or push you around?

_____ 17. Can you be open and frank in expressing both tender and angry feelings to men?

_____ 18. Can you be open and frank in expressing both tender and angry feelings to women?

_____ 19. Do you find it difficult to make or accept dates?

_____ 20. Are you spontaneous during sex play and intercourse?

_____ 21. Are you satisfied with your progress in your career?

_____ 22. Do you find it difficult to upbraid a subordinate?

_____ 23. Are you (or would you be) a good model of assertiveness for your own child?

Now you can see where *you feel you have problems.* To alleviate these problems Fensterheim and Baer suggest a behavior modification program. We endorse their method, and if you feel you would like to try it, we strongly suggest you get their book and work through it. Having found what you think are some of your problem areas, if you have any, you can now work on them as you see fit. One thing we do suggest is that you have a friend answer the questions in Scale P as he or she sees your behavior, and then get together and discuss the differences, if any.

As you can see by the last few pages in this book, we are really getting into human communication. Since that is where it is at — that's where our apprehensions, failures, successes, and peak experiences occur — perhaps we should make a few more explicit suggestions. In his introduction to *The Winner's Notebook* (1969), Theodore Rubin says, "Are you a winner or a loser? A winner is a person who relates successfully to himself and to other people. A loser does not! Relating successfully to ourselves and to other people means a richer, more rewarding and happier life in all areas of human existence and endeavor." Since to communicate is to relate, "winning" or "losing" may be the result of our communicative behavior. Rubin concludes his book with a more detailed list of the characteristics of winners and losers (pp. 204-205):

> There is no absolute winner and no absolute loser. But there are relative winners and their capacity to win grows and grows. These are some general criteria.
>
> They are people who are happy with who they are, at least sometimes.
>
> They like to be alone and they like to be with other people.
>
> They listen to other people and they decide for themselves.
>
> They are capable of self-assertion rather than having a need for compliance, rebellion, or running away.
>
> They enjoy sex, food, entertainment, work — without guilt and without making a claim on others for fulfillment.
>
> They enjoy today and look forward to tomorrow.
>
> They are capable of spontaneous feelings.
>
> They can give and receive love. They can tolerate the anger of others and get angry and they can forgive and forget.
>
> They know who they are — in limits, in assets, in values, in likes and dislikes — and they are capable of enjoying individuality.
>
> They can invest emotion and enthusiasm in people, causes and things.
>
> They know the difference between real self-fulfillment and fleeting glory.
>
> They care about this world and they appreciate their role and responsibility as part of it.
>
> Ownership of assets; clarifying muddles; knowing the enemy; knowing yourself and how to make it with Max;* knowing where and how and who to get help from, if necessary — are formidable allies in becoming a winner. Practice and application are necessary. There are bumps in the road. But the road winds on to wonderful goals. You have an opportunity to be responsible for your own life, in achieving self-fulfillment and in becoming a happier person as a winner.

* Here and there I shall refer to "Max." Max will at times be a boy friend or girl friend, wife or husband, boss, colleague, client, audience or anybody else with whom you have or desire to have a relationship.

Thus we see the winner as the self-actualizer, the self-assertive person, the fully functioning person — the humanistic communicator. If you feel the necessity, you may want to pick up Rubin's book and work through it. It can't help but make you more aware of the human communication process and what it means to be a humanistic communicator.

INTRAPERSONAL ACTIVITIES

On the preceding pages we have given you some activities to show you what it is like to *become* a humanistic communicator intrapersonally (getting inside yourself). We would like to emphasize again that this is a process, not a product. How do you feel about becoming such a person? Perhaps the following activities will help you clarify your feelings.

1. In a group, come to a consensus on the relative importance of the characteristics of love as depicted on Scales M and N by ranking the items on each scale from most to least important. How do these rankings agree with your own? Why do people disagree with you on these rankings? What does this say about the sameness and uniqueness of the individual?

2. In your group, or for the class, present your Johari Window collage. Did this presentation help you to get a better picture of yourself? What new feelings about yourself did you discover?

3. In a group, come to a consensus on the rankings of the values given in Scale L. How do these fit in with your rankings? If you have to give concrete examples of the values in order to rank them, what does this do to the values?

4. In a group, content analyze the fifty items on the self-esteem inventory (Scale O). Put all of the questions together that refer to relatively the same area of concern (e.g., authority, self-worth). How many groups are there? Are there as many positive as negative statements in each group? You can now get individual scales for each area of self-esteem. Does this help you understand yourself?

5. Look back to your replies on the self-assertion inventory (Scale P). Give a reason (example) for each of your ratings. For example, if you put a 3 in front of item 10 ("Can you criticize a friend?"), an example might be, "I despise some of the things Hank does, but I just can't tell him about them." This should help you look deeper into yourself.

6. In a group, rank in order of importance the characteristics of a winner (see p. 236). How does this ranking agree with yours? What does this say to you? Should it matter?

7. What is self-esteem? In a group, define this concept to everyone's satisfaction. Now come to a consensus on the following: What does failure or success do to a person's feeling of self-esteem? Is a relatively high, positive level of self-esteem necessary before one can become a self-actualizing person? How are these two constructs related?

8. All of us have seen people we think don't think very much of themselves or have a very high opinion of themselves. In a group try to draw a character sketch of these two types of people. List the characteristics of people you think exhibit a low opinion of themselves; then make a contrasting list for the individuals who think quite highly of their ability to accom-

plish things. Be sure to differentiate between the individual who is what we call *conceited* and that person who is *confident*. What makes this distinction obvious to us as perceivers?

Developing the Humanistic Communicator Interpersonally

In the last section, on intrapersonal communication, we developed some of the needs and behaviors that were important in the personal development of the humanistic communicator. If you wanted to strive to become this type of person, these were some of the variables you had to be concerned with. As we progressed through this section we found that we were getting more and more away from the autonomous individual and more into a person's relationships with others. In this section we will look at some of the problems and risks as well as the growth and fulfillment one might encounter in human relationships, while striving to become a humanistic communicator. In other words, we have seen what a humanistic communicator looks like as an individual and how one can develop toward being such a person, and now we would like to explicate some of the differences between "normal" relationships and the types of relationships the humanistic communicator would foster and which would facilitate self-realization, self-actualization, self-fulfillment, and the further development of the fully functioning person.

We have touched on relationships in each section of this book, trying to make it clear that the relationships we enter into have a great deal to do with our own personal development. We opened Part 3 with Rollo May's pronouncement on the condition of society as a schizoid world, indicating that we were becoming unable to feel and to attain and maintain meaningful relationships. Some sociologists ascribe this condition to the transience of our population. Alvin Toffler (1970, pp. 87-88) summarizes this feeling in his concept of Modular Man:

> Consciously or not, we define our relationships with most people in functional terms. So long as we do not become involved with the shoe salesman's problems at home, or his more general hopes, dreams and frustrations, he is, for us, fully interchangeable with any other salesman of equal competence. In effect, we have applied the modular principle to human relationships. We have created the disposable person: Modular Man.

Rather than entangling ourselves with the whole man, we plug into a module of his personality. Each personality can be imagined as a unique configuration of thousands of such modules. Thus no whole person is interchangeable with any other. But certain modules are. Since we are seeking only to buy a pair of shoes, and not the friendship, love or hate of the salesman, it is not necessary for us to tap into or engage with all the other modules that form his personality. Our relationship is safely limited. There is limited liability on both sides. The relationship entails certain accepted forms of behavior and communication. Both sides understand, consciously or otherwise, the limitations and laws. Difficulties arise only when one or another party oversteps the tacitly understood limits, when he attempts to connect up with some module not relevant to the function at hand.

Toffler goes on to suggest that the decline in the *average* duration of human relationships is a likely corollary to the increase in the number of such relationships.

All of us approach human relationships, as we approach other kinds of relationships, with a set of built-in durational expectancies. We expect that certain kinds of relationships will endure longer than others. It is, in fact, possible to classify relationships with other people in terms of their expected duration. These vary, of course, from culture to culture and from person to person. Nevertheless, throughout wide sectors of the population of the advanced technological societies something like the following order is typical:

Long-duration relationships. We expect ties with our immediate family, and to a lesser extent with other kin, to extend throughout the lifetimes of the people involved. This expectation is by no means always fulfilled, as rising divorce rates and family break-ups indicate. Nevertheless, we still theoretically marry "until death do us part" and the social ideal is a lifetime relationship. Whether this is a proper or realistic expectation in a society of high transience is debatable. The fact remains, however, that family links are expected to be long term, if not life-long, and considerable guilt attaches to the person who breaks off such a relationship.

Medium-duration relationships. Four classes of relationships fall within this category. Roughly in order of descending durational expectancies, these are relationships with friends, neighbors, job associates, and co-members of churches, clubs and other voluntary organizations.

Friendships are traditionally supposed to survive almost, if not quite, as long as family ties. The culture places high value on "old friends" and a certain amount of blame attaches to dropping a friendship. One type of friendship relationship, however, acquaintanceship, is recognized as less durable.

Neighbor relationships are no longer regarded as long-term commitments — the rate of geographical turnover is too high. They are expected to last as long as the individual remains in a single location, an interval that is growing shorter and shorter on average. Breaking off with a neighbor may involve other difficulties but it carries no great burden of guilt.

On-the-job relationships frequently overlap friendships, and less often, neighbor relationships. Traditionally, particularly among white-collar, professional and technical people, job relationships were supposed to last a relatively long time. This expectation, however, is also changing rapidly, as we shall see.

Co-membership relationships—links with people in church or civic organizations, political parties and the like—sometimes flower into friendship, but until that happens such individual associations are regarded as more perishable than either friendships, ties with neighbors or fellow workers.

Short-duration relationships. Most, though not all, service relationships fall into this category. These involve sales clerks, delivery people, gas station attendants, milkmen, barbers, hairdressers, etc. The turnover among these is relatively rapid and little or no shame attaches to the person who terminates such a relationship. Exceptions to the service pattern are professionals such as physicians, lawyers and accountants, with whom relationships are expected to be somewhat more enduring.

This categorization is hardly airtight. Most of us can cite some "service" relationship that has lasted longer than some friendship, job or neighbor relationship. Moreover, most of us can cite a number of quite long-lasting relationships in our own lives—perhaps we have been going to the same doctor for years or have maintained extremely close ties with a college friend. Such cases are hardly unusual, but they are relatively few in number in our lives. They are like long-stemmed flowers towering above a field of grass in which each blade represents a short-term relationship, a transient contact. It is the very durability of these ties that makes them noticeable. Such exceptions do not invalidate the rule. They do not change the key fact that, across the board, the *average* interpersonal relationship in our life is shorter and shorter in duration. (pp. 90–92)

Though the length of our relationships may be measured and their quantity recorded, this information will give us only limited insight into the *quality* of our relationships. At the same time, it does give reason to assume that, if we expect a particular relationship to be of short duration, we probably won't try to develop it to any great depth. Yet, we know that it is through relationships that we are able to evaluate ourselves and develop into the mature person we want to be. Relationships are absolutely necessary. More than this, since all societies continue to exist through procreation, it is necessary that some kind of male-female relationships exist. In the American society today the most common male-female relationship, marriage, is also losing its durability. Yet, many point to this relationship as the ultimate for self-realization.

In the preface to his book *Freedom and Growth in Marriage* (1975), James McCary says:

It does not seem unreasonable that all people should experience the fullest and most satisfying lives possible without, of course, those experiences adversely affecting the lives of others. Such experiences when one is living alone cannot be nearly as satisfying and fulfilling as they are when shared in a loving relationship. The Book of Genesis contains a profoundly prophetic statement to this effect by its declaration that it is not good for a person to live alone, and that each person should have a helpmate. Marriage is the best solution developed to this date to the dilemma of aloneness. Because most people do marry, and spend most of their lives in the married state, the hope for satisfying the goals of personal maturity and emotional fulfillment would seem to lie within marriage. When that hope is not reached within a particular marriage, that marriage has failed, whether there is a divorce or not. Conversely, when full and satisfying lives are lived within the marital framework, one will usually find that the relationship has allowed maximum freedom and growth for both partners.

He goes on to say

that individuals reach their greatest potential and experience their fullest humanity when they are involved in a close relationship with another person with whom they can share their triumphs and failures, to whom they can open themselves and be unconditionally accepted, with whom they can experience honest conflict that is either resolved satisfactorily or accepted as unresolvable, and toward whom they can fearlessly express the tenderness, eroticism, dependency, nurturance, admiration, and anger that all who live intimately together feel toward one another.

Without such relationships, human beings would be closed in upon themselves, living solitary emotional lives, always peripherally involved with others, and never deeply involved. We would become a society that relied on sensory experiences alone to define ourselves. Our emotional responses of compassion, love, desire, and empathy would be denied full expression. Rather than becoming more fully human, we would become less human and less aware of ourselves and of others. For most human beings, the closeness of a rewarding relationship is best realized in a union of a man and a woman who live together with the sanction of society, and this is a **Marriage.** (pp. 3-4) *

Thus, to McCary, marriage is the answer to our needs. It is the relationship that will fulfill us and let us develop into the fully functioning persons that we should be.

You should keep in mind the characteristics of the marriage relationship he has described. When you review in your mind various marriages you are familiar with, how many of these characteristics do they have? In your own male-female relationships, whether they have progressed to the marriage stage or not, how many of these characteristics are present? It should be clear, then, that the relationship that McCary describes is an ideal one, that of two humanistic communicators. What do we find if we look at real relationships?

MANIPULATIVE RELATIONSHIPS

There are several obvious alternatives to the mutual-growth-and-fulfillment ideal established by McCary. One is the dependency relationship that we are all familiar with. One member (or in some cases both) is so tied to the other that he or she psychologically smothers the other person. This is the opposite of the relationship pictured by Gibran on pages 77–78. In a recent work, Stanton Peele (1975) equates this type of relationship with drug addiction.

* Quoted from *Freedom and Growth in Marriage* by James L. McCary, copyright © 1975, Hamilton Publishing Co. Reprinted by permission of John Wiley & Sons, Inc.

He makes a very good case for the fact that in such relationships one person (or both) is addicted to the other — complete with withdrawal symptoms if the partner should ever leave the relationship. He develops six criteria for judging the addictiveness of a relationship (pp. 83-84):

> In Fromm's notion of integrity in love and Greer's emphasis on self-actualization and personal pride, we have the elements of a positive concept of love. By contrasting this model with that of addictive love, we can develop specific criteria for assessing the character of our relationships. These criteria follow from our more general standards for distinguishing between the addictive and nonaddictive approach to life. They are points at which a relationship either expresses health and the promise of growth, or leans toward addiction:
>
> 1. Does each lover have a secure belief in his or her own value?
> 2. Are the lovers improved by the relationship? By some measure outside of the relationship are they better, stronger, more attractive, more accomplished, or more sensitive individuals? Do they value the relationship for this very reason?
> 3. Do the lovers maintain serious interests outside the relationship, including other meaningful personal relationships?
> 4. Is the relationship integrated into, rather than being set off from, the totality of the lovers' lives?
> 5. Are the lovers beyond being possessive or jealous of each other's growth and expansion of interests?
> 6. Are the lovers also friends? Would they seek each other out if they should cease to be primary partners?
>
> These standards represent an ideal, and as such they cannot be fulfilled completely even by the healthiest relationships. But given that every relationship is bound to contain some elements of addiction, we can still tell what makes one predominantly addictive. This occurs, as in drug addiction, when a single overwhelming involvement with one thing serves to cut a person off from life, to close him or her off to experience, to debilitate him, to make him less open, free, and positive in dealing with the world.
>
> Interpersonal addiction need not be a one-to-one affair. An addict may form successive or simultaneous relationships, either because he or she never allows himself to become seriously involved, or because he can't find a partner who completely accepts him. In all cases, however, addiction has at its center a diminished sense of self. The addict uses relationships to seal off his inner self from a frightening environment. In the process, the already weakened self ceases to develop, and the addict's life contracts further.

How do your relationships measure up on these criteria? If you can answer a partial yes to all six questions, you have a very healthy nonaddictive relationship. If you cannot, then perhaps you should look deeper into the reasons for this to see why it is not as facilitating as it could be (i.e., one that a humanistic communicator would strive for which would allow personal growth for both parties).

The addictive marriage is only one side of the coin. On the other side we have those marriages that exist because a license has been obtained and an "official" has pronounced the couple "husband and wife." At the time, there was probably great purpose in this relationship, great happiness, hopes, and expectation; even, perhaps, great fulfillment. But something went wrong, or the script you were living said that you "live happily ever after," and no real effort was made to maintain the relationship. What happens with these "existence-type" relationships? One answer is given by Gilbert Bartell (1971, pp. 209-211) in the study he did on the "swinging" phenomenon:

> While our data was collected in mid-America, other researchers, such as the O'Neills in New York and the Smiths in California, have told us that the same phenomena can be found in suburbs on the East and West coasts. The most consistent of these findings is "boredom with marriage." When couples reported this complaint, they did not mean that they had an unhappy marriage, but rather the dilemma that *Philadelphia Magazine* neatly summed up in a 1969 (158) survey of swinging in its area:
>
>> "Married sex, if left alone, rapidly becomes stale. It takes a very imaginative married couple willing to play games with each other to maintain a viable sex relationship after a period of time in marriage. That's why so many married men seek the excitement of conquest outside of marriage, or else they redirect their sexual energy to other activity and become like the businessman who gets so caught up in his work he has no time for anything else."
>
> We believe that this applies to females as well as males. . . .
>
> This finding is not nearly as incongruous as it may appear to the uninitiated. Swinging couples are drawn together, first of all, because they are continually replaying the mating game. They can relive their youth, and for many this is advantageous. They can get dressed up, go out together and attempt a seduction. It is a form of togetherness that they have never had before, and it certainly goes well beyond the togetherness promoted by *McCall's* magazine. Each partner wants to reinforce in the other the idea that the other is sexually more enjoyable than any swinger they encounter. There is a general increase in the sexual excitement of both partners because they are stimulated to think about new types of sexual experiences and there is opportunity to translate these thoughts into action. The woman receives a great deal of positive reinforcement if other swingers consider her even the least bit desirable. She is actively committing men to her. The same principle operates for the opposite: if a fifty-year-old man can "make it" with a twenty-two-year-old girl with relatively little risk of rejection and no legal or emotional repercussions, it is likely to be a source of tremendous satisfaction to him.

What transparent behavior! Admittedly, this is only one segment of the population; however, it may very well be the more creative of those relationships on this side of the coin. Most end up in a state of coexistence, not even having the energy or creativity to seek something better. There are many reasons for this—a family, the double standard myth, jobs, money, etc. In almost every case the woman is treated as an object to revolve around the man. In most of these cases she accepts this second-class status with only a twinge of uneasiness about not being fulfilled. Many times she is not even aware of not being fulfilled since she has borne children, kept the house, and cleaned up after her husband, sometimes while also working eight to five at a paying job.

Do you ever wonder why men treat women this way? James Keys (1971, p. 25) says:

> To put it bluntly, it looks as if the male is so afraid of the fundamentally different order of being of the female, so terrified of her huge magical feminine power of destruction and regeneration, that he daren't look at her as she really is, he is afraid to accept the difference, and so has repressed into his unconscious the whole idea of her as *another kind of being,* from whom he might learn what he could not know of himself alone, and replaced her with the idea of a sort of second-class replica of himself who, because she plays the part of a man so much worse than a man, he can feel safe with because he can despise her. . . . And because it is the man's business to be articulate, not the woman's, when the man forgets who the woman is, then so does the woman.

That's not a very nice picture. It certainly doesn't lead to a loving relationship in which both parties have room to grow and be fulfilled. No wonder we have so many sex-related crimes.

Our feelings about the opposite sex are developed over a long period of time but come primarily from our early childhood training in sex roles. As a result we grow up with set assumptions and expectations (cultural variables) about how we are to act in our particular sex role. The two sexes come from as different cultures as a Frenchman and an Irishman, or people from any other two cultures. Psychological and cultural noise (see Part 2) exert tremendous pressure on the communication processes between the sexes. How do you in general see a person of the opposite sex? To find out, you might want to fill out Scale Q on page 245 as you really feel about the general, normative person of the opposite sex.

Then, using a different mark, fill it out as you would ideally like the opposite sex to be (I FEEL A PERSON OF THE OPPOSITE SEX SHOULD BE). How do your marks compare? On which dimensions do you see differences? Now think of your best friend/lover of the opposite sex and using a different mark fill out the scale again as you feel he or she is (I FEEL MY BEST FRIEND/LOVER IS). How do these marks compare to the previous ones? Does your lover/friend compare more closely with the norm or the ideal? How do you feel about this? Do you think the two of you can have a fulfilling relationship? *Remember,* all of the marks you put down are how *you feel* and are only as *accurate* as you are *honest.* Thus, you now only know what you wanted to reveal to yourself.

The above exercise may have indicated a lack of openness and desire to know the real person in your relationship. The report on swinging makes it abundantly clear that, instead of getting deeper into their marriage relationship, the swingers were masking their own problems by playing games and trying to introduce novelty into a deteriorating relationship. Although they say swinging gives them a new sense of openness and excitement in their own

SCALE Q

Feelings about the Opposite Sex

I FEEL A PERSON OF THE OPPOSITE SEX (MALE OR FEMALE) IS:

Rough __ __ __ __ __ __ __	Delicate
Open __ __ __ __ __ __ __	Closed
Soft __ __ __ __ __ __ __	Hard
Strong __ __ __ __ __ __ __	Weak
Insensitive __ __ __ __ __ __ __	Sensitive
Communicative __ __ __ __ __ __ __	Noncommunicative
Shallow __ __ __ __ __ __ __	Deep
Assertive __ __ __ __ __ __ __	Nonassertive
Slow __ __ __ __ __ __ __	Fast
Chaotic __ __ __ __ __ __ __	Ordered
Complex __ __ __ __ __ __ __	Simple
Relaxed __ __ __ __ __ __ __	Tense
Subtle __ __ __ __ __ __ __	Obvious
Dynamic __ __ __ __ __ __ __	Static
Emotional __ __ __ __ __ __ __	Rational
Remote __ __ __ __ __ __ __	Intimate
Vague __ __ __ __ __ __ __	Precise
Kind __ __ __ __ __ __ __	Cruel
False __ __ __ __ __ __ __	Real

marriage, it has proven to be a deficient exercise for those who are sensitive and aware of real human relationships. Bartell (1971, p. 216) reports that "these people feel that the practice of more or less indiscriminate swinging is much too mechanistic; that there is a loss of identity, and absence of commitment; and that this total noninvolvement — at least to them — represents the antithesis of sexual pleasure and satisfaction." The substitution of sex for genuine human communication does not make for the fulfilling relationship one is looking for. Instead it seems that it is a case of objective manipulation for an end goal, usually the woman as the object of trade (pp. 216-217):

We believe that, initially, most women are more or less "strong-armed" — psychologically and on occasion even physically — into the swinging scene by their male partners. The overt insistence that swinging partners are really "friends" would seem to indicate a desire to establish a brotherhood and authentic intimacy. In fact, we believe that the "friendship" theme is a rationalization, a way for swingers to say to themselves and everyone else involved: "We are not callous enough just to want to screw anybody. We only do it with friends."

Beyond this, we have come to conclude that most male swingers are, in effect, bartering their women. True, these couples do not like the term "wife-swapping." It seems to show that the women are not equal to the men. Nevertheless, the facts are that men almost invariably initiate swinging; that they exchange pictures of their nude or seminude women with other couples, and that they circulate such pictures much more readily than pictures of themselves together with their mate. The male who sends out his mate's picture is saying to another male, "Look what a luscious tid-bit I have for you. Do you have anything equally good for me?" All that the male usually says about himself is something that amounts to the message, "I'm well-endowed and I can french."

On numerous occasions, male swingers looked over my wife's figure and then said to me, "You won't have any trouble getting any woman you want." We consider this a further indication that swingers generally swing for purely mechanical, sexual reasons.

To us, this sounds like Machiavellian behavior which "has come to designate the use of guile, deceit, and opportunism in interpersonal relations. Traditionally, the 'Machiavellian' is someone who views and manipulates others for his own purposes" (Christie and Geis 1970, p. 1). This description of the Machiavellian-type person fits in well with the above picture. Three of Christie and Geis's four characteristics of the Machiavellian personality are applicable here (pp. 3-4):

1. *A relative lack of affect in interpersonal relationships.* In general, it seemed that success in getting others to do what one wishes them to do would be enhanced by viewing them as objects to be manipulated rather than as individuals with whom one has empathy. The greater the emotional involvement with others, the greater is the likelihood of identifying with their point of view. Once empathy occurs, it becomes more difficult to use psychological leverage to influence others to do things they may not want to do.

2. *A lack of concern with conventional morality.* Conventional morality is difficult to define, but we were thinking here in terms of the findings that most people think lying, cheating, and other forms of deceit are, although common, reprehensible. Whether manipulators are amoral or immoral is a moot problem, and one which probably concerns them less than those who are manipulated. The premise here is that those who manipulate have a utilitarian rather than a moral view of their interactions with others.

3. *Low ideological commitment.* The essence of successful manipulation is a focus upon getting things done rather than a focus upon long-range ideological goals. Although manipulators might be more involved in tactics for achieving possible ends than in an inflexible striving for an ultimate idealistic goal.

Is this the type of person who generates and facilitates open, genuine communication upon which solid, deep interpersonal relationships can be formed? The strategies of this type of person are those described by Berne as the games people play to achieve their goals:

> A game is an ongoing series of complementary ulterior transactions progressing to a well-defined, predictable outcome. Descriptively it is a recurring set of transactions, often repetitious, superficially plausible, with a concealed motivation; or, more colloquially, a series of moves with a snare, or "gimmick." Games are clearly differentiated from procedures, rituals, and pastimes by two chief characteristics: (1) their ulterior quality and (2) the payoff. Procedures may be successful, rituals effective, and pastimes profitable, but all of them are by definition candid; they may involve contest, but no conflict, and the ending may be sensational, but it is not dramatic. Every game, on the other hand, is basically dishonest, and the outcome has a dramatic, as distinct from merely exciting, quality. (1964, p. 48)

The practice of deception to obtain a desired goal certainly does not lead to understanding, trustworthiness, and fulfillment. Even when the goal is achieved, the victory is tainted. Berne gives many examples of many different kinds of games, and we suggest you read his analysis of this behavior.

One of the "games" that so many of us play is that of accommodation. Unable to bring ourselves to be open and honest, we accommodate our partner, hoping to make a good impression. A very explicit example of an encounter between two such people is given by George Bach and Ronald Deutsch (1970, pp. 89-96):

> In the beginning, it seems only politeness. No one wants to appear indifferent to a partner's wishes, after all, or self-centered about his own. It is only the courteous thing to put another's comfort or pleasure first.
>
> So no alarm bells go off when accommodation begins to meet the intimate anxiety of hiding real feelings from a partner. And once accommodation begins, it is hard to stop.
>
> Will and Carol, who have been dating for some weeks, have had an exhilarating day on the beach. Their dates have been good-time expeditions and the conversation has been limited to trifling subjects. They have been physically affectionate, which was very stimulating to both, but until now they have not gone to bed.
>
> At the beach they touched a great deal, in the water and on the sand, and both became excited. They had dinner at a seaside place, and a couple of drinks raised their sexuality and frankness. Will finally asked Carol to spend the night at his apartment, and, she agreed. Impatiently, they started the long drive home.
>
> Half way, they began to feel the fatigue that follows too much sun and sea and wine. It is Sunday, and both must be at work early next day. They begin to regret their plan — but only in secret. Now their real personalities start to show.
>
> WILL (stretching behind the wheel, he groans just a little, uncomfortably):

CAROL:

Is something wrong?

WILL:

Oh, nothing much. (Bravely) I guess I got some sunburn. Quite a lot in fact.

CAROL:

Well, I wish you'd have let me put some lotion on you. I asked you, remember? Maybe if you put something on it as soon as you get home . . .

WILL (a little annoyed. He wanted sympathy, not medical advice. He frequently wants sympathy for his many minor complaints.):

Yes, I will. I'm not sure it's just sunburn, actually. I sort of have a cramp in my back, and I —

CAROL:

Is that the right time on the dashboard clock?

WILL (more annoyed):

Why? Are you very tired? You really won't be getting any sleep tonight, I'm afraid, by the time we get home. I'll be all right, but —

CAROL (looking at him to try to read his expression):

Well, you won't get any more sleep than I do. (She forces a smile.) Aren't you tired? I'll be fine.

WILL:

Well, if you don't *want* to, Carol — I mean, I'll understand. I want to, but I don't *have* to, tonight.

CAROL (her competitive streak showing through):

Maybe *I* have to. (She forces a smile.) You can't get out of it.

WILL:

As if I want to!

Both would really prefer to go home and to sleep. But they are trapped. They do not want to seem inadequate for one another. When they finally reach Will's apartment, they are sleepy and dulled, but they proceed. Now they have been having intercourse for several minutes. They are tired, but they continue to embrace with all the show of passion they can muster.

THEY SAY	THEY THINK
WILL: Carol, darling —	*I hope she can come soon. My back is ready to break, and I don't know how much longer I can wait. What if I lose control? Maybe if I show more passion, she'll get more excited.*
CAROL: Oh, Will, darling!	*Oh! My sunburn!*
WILL: I love you, Carol!	*My left leg is cramping.*
CAROL: Yes, yes!	*I can't come. I know it. I'm too tired.*
WILL: I could go on all night!	*Please come. You said you could. I don't want to lose control. I remember what you said about men who were selfish and immature in bed.*

THEY SAY	THEY THINK
CAROL: Yes! Yes! Harder!	*Well I can't go on all night, I'm losing all sensation. I wish you'd just go ahead and come. Please.*
WILL (complying): Like this?	*As if it wasn't tough enough to hold back before. Two plus two are four; four plus four are eight. Eight and eight —*
CAROL: Yes! More!	*I think he's weakening. If he'll only come, he won't think I'm frigid. I know I'll come with him another time. Maybe I could even fake it. I bet he couldn't tell.*
WILL: Oh! Carol, I-Can-can you-make-it?	*Please say yes. I'm at the end of my rope.*
CAROL: Yes! Yes I can! The minute you-do!	*Damn, I'm closing up or something. It's starting to hurt. I'll just have to fake and hope for the best.*
WILL: I hate to have it end.	*Thank heaven! But for her sake, I'll hang on another minute. Sixty-four and —*
CAROL: Now, darling! Oh, Will!	*For pity's sake, get it over with. Is he? I'm almost sure. Well, I'll try to be convincing.*
WILL: AH!!	*At last!*
CAROL: OH!!	*Hallelujah. I thought he never would.*

(THERE IS A MOMENT
OF SILENT RELIEF)

WILL: Did you?	
CAROL: Did I ever? Was it nice for you, Will?	*That's not an actual lie. And I will some other time. I really hope he liked me.*
WILL: Did I like it? Silly girl! Was it really all right for you?	*I wonder if she'd be awfully hurt if I just went to sleep. Burke is coming in for that meeting very early tomorrow.*
CAROL: Oh, Will. (She sighs.) I knew you'd be a real man. Are you always so strong?	*I hope he doesn't want to talk long. I have to do something with my hair before I can go to work.*
WILL: I think I could be for you. I didn't get too rough for you at the end, I hope?	*She wants to talk a while. Well, I don't really mind.*
CAROL: No, you'd never hurt me. But you are quite a man.	*He wants to talk. Oh well. He would. He's really a fine lover, but it's so late.*

THEY SAY	THEY THINK
WILL (beams): Am I? Of course, what else could I be with that wonderful body of yours? (He strokes it.)	*I'm glad she feels that way. I can see how important sex is for her.*
CAROL: And I love *your* body. (She caresses him.) Most men just want to go to sleep.	*I know I'll need at least an hour for my hair. It's so salty.*
WILL: I'm not most men. Besides, I've waited so long to touch you.	*She really is special. If only Burke weren't coming so early — I don't want to seem crude. Women need after-play; it says so in the books.*
CAROL: Oh, Will! (She reproves.)	*I know I'm supposed to want this, and it's sweet. But the time is — Hey! I really like for him to touch me there, but — hey!*
WILL: I'm not hurting you?	
CAROL: No, I like that.	*Except at three in the morning. I really should return the gesture.*
WILL: Oh, Carol; you'll turn me on. Oh, Carol —	*It is now three A.M. Burke is due at eight-thirty. Maybe she's trying to tell me she needs more. I wonder if I could —*
CAROL: Do you want to again, dear?	*I may as well hear the news.*
WILL: I want to, but you must be so tired —	*What can I say?*
CAROL: I'm not too tired if you need me —	*What am I saying? But after all he's said about cool, unsexed women —*
WILL: Really?	*Does that mean she expects more?*
CAROL: Really.	*I knew once wouldn't be enough for him.*
WILL: Darling. Do you like this?	*It's a flat offer. I can't refuse.*
CAROL: Oh, yes. And do *you* like *this?*	*I do, but why now?*
WILL: Oh . . .	*If she keeps that up, I just might make it.*
CAROL: Darling, now!	*Let's get it over with.*
WILL: You're wonderful, the way you can say things right out so frankly. Is this what you have in mind?	*Let's get it over.*
CAROL: Oh . . .	*And he'll expect me to come.*

THEY SAY	THEY THINK
WILL: Oh . . .	*And she'll expect me to come.*
CAROL: Aaah . . .	*There's no choice. I'll just have to fake it again.*
WILL: Aaah . . .	*I'm sure I can't come. It's a miracle that I can do anything at all. I wonder if she could tell if I faked coming?*

> It is fairly obvious what is going to happen next. A mutually unwanted sexual experience is about to end in a mutually nonexistent orgasm. And mutually unreal pleasure will surely be expressed.

Wouldn't it have been better all the way around to just own up to their true feelings? How often do you find yourself accommodating others? How do you feel afterwards? Will you be more aware of this behavior in both yourself and others now?

We have seen some of the difficulties of what we would call a poor relationship. Unfortunately these are what constitute the majority of marriages and male-female relationships in the United States today. Robert Ravich and Barbara Wyden (1974, pp. 2-4) have done extensive research in the area of pair relationships (marriage as well as other types of pairs) and find that they "can be classified into eight patterns of interaction." More than this, it can be predicted very early in their existence which ones will be

> exciting, rewarding pairings; which will spawn extramarital sexual liaisons; which will be rather pleasant but dull; which will be sheer hell, but (unless terminated almost immediately) will seldom break up; which will inevitably end in separation or divorce; and which pairs have an excellent chance of living happily enough ever after.
>
> I say "happily enough," because I am convinced that one of the almost irresistible stresses our culture places on the institution of marriage is the expectation that this pairing should result in a "happily ever after." It won't. This is too much to expect of any relationship and too much of a burden to place on marriage. Marriage cannot and should not guarantee instant or perpetual happiness. To hope to be "happy enough" is a healthier approach.

Ravich and Wyden go on to say that

> One person can have many intimate relationships and may in each one exhibit very different aspects of his personality—indeed, so radically different that the other persons in these relationships, were they to exchange information among themselves about him, would have great difficulty in believing that they were talking about the same individual.

From this we get the definite feeling that relationships depend on the interactions of the selves participating in these relationships. In their diagnostic work, Ravich and Wyden determine how these selves interact and can then predict what the eventual outcome will be. This agrees very well with Berne's script analysis.

There are two basic assumptions in this operation. The most obvious is that these "selves" will not change appreciably in this relationship. (The script will be adhered to.) The self is more stable than the relationship. Thus, we maintain our life scripts, although we may try to hide them to various degrees, and try to force the relationship to conform to them. We seek the fulfillment of our own needs and desires with little or no concern for the growth of the other or of ourself. Our primary commitment, then, is to our past; the immediacy of the present and the anticipated continuation of this behavior into the future effectively rule out any growth in our relationship. We are satisfied with the status quo.

Thus, the second assumption, that people in general are not self-transcendent, that there is a greater commitment to the uniformity of our self-expression than to the potential of the relationship. This says that in these relationships there is really no appreciable communication as we have defined it. True, there may be a great deal of interaction from the mechanistic point of view, but in terms of sharing (which is necessary for growth) these relationships are severly anemic. A humanistic communicator could not remain a part of them, for they seldom if ever get into the first three dimensions of involvement (see p. 76).

GROWTH-FACILITATING RELATIONSHIPS

What is it that makes for a good "human" relationship then? David Viscott (1974) suggests that it is in the agreement two people make when they decide to live together. The emphasis is on change, potential growth, and synergy — the fact that the potential for human development in the relationship has to be greater than this potential for either person alone; the whole is greater than the sum of its parts. The strength and stability of a relationship is not dependent on the strength or stability of the individuals alone. Too often we equate these characteristics with stubbornness, and this has very little place in a "human" relationship, for a relationship must assume growth in both parties. This means that it is the relationship itself that is its primary strength.

We must learn to transcend our own selves and facilitate growth in others. Of course this cannot be done to the continual detriment of the participating person, but neither can we expect growth to occur if the plant is discarded at the first sight of a wilted leaf. We must feed, water, and cultivate if we expect growth. Sharing ourselves through communication may be as helpful to psychological health as donating our blood is to physical health. Analogies such as the above two can be used to great advantage in describing and analyzing human relationships.

William Masters and Virginia Johnson (1974) have done extensive research on the effect of sexual relations on interpersonal relationships. Their conclusions about what constitutes a healthy relationship appear to be extremely germane to what we have been saying about the facilitating of growth in any human relationship. First of all, if a relationship exists because it is decreed by some outside force (such as a marriage license and ceremony), it has very good possibilities of *not* being a growth-producing or continuing relationship. Their view is that "the word 'marriage' means more than the existence of a license. Throughout this book [*The Pleasure Bond: A New Look at Sexuality and Commitment*], a man and woman are considered united in the true sense of the word, whether or not they have a license to live together, as long as each is committed to the other. They are not committed because they are married; they are married because they are committed" (p. xiii). Thus, commitment from within must come first. It is a major way for one to *assert* the self.

A second point is that through true "human" communicating, the sharing of each self, two individuals become more than just two individuals. The results of a humanistic relationship facilitate the growth of each individual toward greater self-realization. They become actualized through open, honest relating. According to Masters and Johnson (p. 87), "what a man and a woman achieve together benefits both — the very quality of life, *as it is individually experienced,* can be immeasurably augmented by a fully shared partnership."

It is not only that communication is facilitated by a relationship, but that this must be one of the goals of a relationship:

> If one theme seems to repeat itself today, it seems to me to be that each of you understands the importance of communicating, of keeping in touch, of constantly making the effort to reach out to your partner. And you seem to realize that this is not a goal that you will eventually reach or an achievement of some kind. It's a process — the circulatory system of marriage. As long as it continues, a marriage stays very much alive. (p. 229)

Thus, a humanistic communicator facilitates growth-producing relationships, which facilitate the development of a more humanistic communicator, who facilitates more growth-producing relationships, which . . . etc., etc. This we saw presented in Bugental's article in Part 3.

Finally, we must realize that the type of commitment a humanistic communicator has to a relationship is quite different from that of most people. Masters and Johnson speak to several aspects of commitment in the marriage relationship (pp. 251–258):

> A commitment is a pledge to do something. One person tells another, "I promise," and the promise is kept, the obligation fulfilled. Trust has been asked for; trust has been given; and trust has been repaid.

This is the basic meaning of commitment. It is the cement that binds in-dividuals and groups together. Without the ability of one person to rely upon another, the social bond could not exist. Even a legal contract depends, in the final analysis, on the keeping of a pledge. For if a contract is broken, the commitment not kept, the law can penalize the person who failed to perform as he had promised, but penalizing him leaves the obligation unfulfilled, the job undone, the need unmet.

That is all there is to commitment insofar as it relates to associations that exist for practical purposes. When the association is for emotional reasons, however, the meaning of commitment changes. It can still be defined as a pledge to do something, but the pledge possesses a radically different dimension. "I promise," one person tells another, "because I care about you."

Caring—which is defined as paying attention, being concerned, solicitous and protective—flows from two related but different kinds of feelings. One is a feeling of being *responsive to* someone, of *caring for* that person; the other is a feeling of being *responsible for* someone, of wanting to *take care of* him or her. These feelings are generated in entirely different ways. Responsiveness occurs spontaneously, before the mind is consciously aware of what is happening—a sudden surge of interest and attraction, triggered by another person's physical presence. Responsiblity is consciously, though often unwillingly, invoked by the mind—an acknowledgment of obligation.

Masters and Johnson say that mutual pleasure

is the foundation on which all future affectionate relationships will be constructed. The search for pleasure—and pleasure is an infinitely deeper and more complex emotional matter than simply sensual gratification—continues throughout life. The quality of marriage is determined by whether the pleasure derived exceeds the inevitable portion of displeasure that human beings must experience in all their associations. When there is more displeasure than pleasure in a marriage, a husband and wife are more aware of the obligations of marriage than they are of its rewards. It may clarify the subject if their bond is characterized as a commitment of obligation.

In contrast, there is the commitment of concern, a bond in which a man and a woman mutually meet their obligations not because they feel *compelled* to but because they feel *impelled* to do so. They do so in response to impulses, desires and convictions that are deeply rooted within themselves, not all of which do they fully understand. When they act in each other's best interests, even though this may at the time be in conflict with their own immediate wishes, they are saying to each other, in effect: "I care very much about your feelings—because your feelings affect mine. Your happiness adds to mine, your unhappiness takes away from my happiness, and I want to be happy."

. . . Each partner, to protect his or her own happiness, tries to sustain the other partner's happiness so that their relationship will flourish; and these reciprocal efforts intensify the satisfactions they find in living together—which further strengthen their wish to remain a couple. *They live according to the commitment of mutual concern, and pleasure is the bond between them.*

They expect to be faithful because they want to be. Furthermore they realize that if either or both of them must seek sexual satisfaction with other partners, the circle of commitment will have been broken. The more satisfactions they find with other people, the fewer satisfactions do they need from each other; and the less they need from each other, the easier it is for them to go their separate ways. Beyond all rationalization, extramarital affairs would demonstrate two things: first, that they were incapable of meeting each other's most basic physical and emotional needs, and second, that they did not consider each other unique, and therefore irreplaceable, sources of satisfaction and pleasure.

To make an emotional commitment to someone is to be on his or her side, a steadfast ally; it is essentially an expression of loyalty. This is what most people have in mind when they speak of commitments; to some extent, commitments involve obligations and responsibilities but they are obligations that have been voluntarily chosen.

But there is another dimension to commitment. Becoming committed to someone is, by definition, to entrust one's physical and emotional well-being to that person; it is an act of faith and an acceptance of vulnerability. This is the opposite side of the coin of commitment. If, for example, a woman has had sufficient evidence that a man has made a commitment to her, that she can trust him to be concerned about her welfare and to be there when she needs him, she will then, no matter how slowly, allow herself to become committed to him—that is, to become openly, emotionally vulnerable and sexually responsive.

This vital distinction between *making* a commitment and *becoming* committed is obscured by the English language, which fails to provide words that differentiate one emotional dimension from the other. To say that a man and woman are committed to each other, for instance, in no way indicates the nature of their bond. A woman may be committed to her husband in the sense of being his loyal wife, his cooperative partner in maintaining a family—and yet *not* be committed to him in the sense of trusting him with her deepest feelings, of becoming emotionally vulnerable.

Because this distinction between making a commitment and becoming committed has not been widely appreciated and generally goes unremarked, considerable confusion results among people. They believe that until they have made a mutual commitment no commitment exists. They tell each other that although they are having an affair, neither one is committed to the other. This is self-deception. Becoming committed happens of itself, as part of an emotional evolution that follows its own course. Not infrequently men and women discover to their astonishment that they have become committed in spite of themselves and without ever openly making a commitment.

When the "two become one" by sharing in the growth of their relationship and thus facilitate the growth of each other, then we can safely say they exemplify the "human" in human communication.

By now you have seen the ideal relationship that results from the commitment of two humanistic communicators to the development of their growth potential. We hope that reading this book has had a positive effect and that you are actively pursuing a humanistic orientation to your life. The following activities should help you see more clearly the effects of such an orientation.

INTERPERSONAL ACTIVITIES

1. Using McCary's characteristics of a marriage relationship, evaluate the marriages of (a) your parents, (b) two other relatives, (c) a friend, or (d) your own marriage or friendship.
2. Look back into your friendships. See if you can name five friends for each of Toffler's four durations. What are the three outstanding characteristics of each group of friends? Would you have preferred to move some of your friends from one group to another? Why?
3. What are some of the major differences between the husband-wife relationship and the relationship between two lovers living together but not married in the commonly accepted legal sense? How might you react to such a relationship if: (a) you were just viewing it from the outside; (b) you were one of the partners; (c) you were a parent whose daughter or son was involved in such a relationship?
4. In a group, develop several skits in which you can contrast the addictive and facilitative relationship. Include as many of Peele's characteristics as possible. Role-play one of these for the class.
5. In a group, develop several skits involving communicative events such as male-female encounters, boss-secretary, professor-student, parent-child. Now role-play these with alter egos (someone standing behind each character saying what that character really wanted to say, like the example on pages 248–251) to show how deceitful communication can be. Put in some surprise endings.
6. Males and females can have many different types of relationships. Some of those most common are: father-daughter, mother-son, brother-sister, and husband-wife. In a group, list as many other male-female relationships as you are able, then attempt to differentiate between and among them, on the basis of normative behaviors and acceptable behaviors.
7. In a group, determine what it is about the sixties and seventies that has made it more accepting of relationships between people that previously were considered unacceptable. For example, has this era developed new views concerning (a) homosexuality, (b) bisexuality, (c) communal living, (d) unmarrieds living together, (e) childbirth before marriage, and (f) freer sexual relationships outside marriage? List aspects that are reflective of this culture's response to these relationships and results. What are the present norms? How are these changing norms being reflected in our culture?
8. In a group, list ten aspects of this culture that have allowed the "equality of the sexes" to flourish. Why did such a feeling take so long to permeate the thinking of our society? What occurrences helped to bring it out or about? Does it seem to be increasing in strength or decreasing in its attraction to individuals of both sexes? Are there certain segments of this

society where there is no equality of the sexes? Why is this the case? Are there things which will prohibit *total* equality of the sexes in our society? What might they be?

THOUGHT QUESTIONS

1. Discuss the relationship among the sources of self-evaluation and the need to be free, norms and codes, and one's values.
2. Differentiate between sexual needs and love needs.
3. Discuss the growth of a human relationship (friendship, marriage) using an analogy to plant growth or physical growth involving (a) facilitators, (b) nonfacilitators, (c) a combination of the two.
4. Differentiate between addictive and facilitative relationships.
5. Discuss the problems involved if one expects one person to fulfill all his or her needs and desires. What does this say about monogamous marriages?
6. What part do the following human characteristics play in human relationships: (a) self-esteem, (b) self-assertion, (c) self-realization, (d) self-transcendence?

RESEARCH QUESTIONS

1. Investigate the hierarchy of needs (p. 202) to see what the basis for this hierachy is. On what level should one place sexual needs? Why?
2. There are many sex manuals (the how-to-do-it-and-have-more-fun type) on the market today. In contrast to these there are books which emphasize that good sex results from good relationships. Compare the approaches of two or three books from each of these two groups in terms of focus, humanistic qualities, game playing, and long-range predictions for the relationship.
3. Investigate the role of self-esteem in healthy human behavior, focusing on its importance, its development, and its relationship to one's self-concept.
4. As a group project conduct a survey of 100 males and 100 females to find out what they think about the following concepts: (a) sex for fun, (b) sex for love, (c) sex for babies. Formulate your own questions, tabulate your data, and write a report.
5. As a group project conduct a survey on and around your campus to determine the feelings on the equality of the sexes. Ask questions like: Do you feel men and women should be allowed to hold the same jobs across the board? Do you feel women should be given special medical leave each month? Would you mind having a woman as a supervisor on your present job? How long before a woman is president of the United States? Will the

situation in which the survey is taken make a difference: (a) face to face, (b) telephone, (c) same sex as respondent, (d) if respondent has to sign name, (e) when males and females are both present?

REFERENCES

Bach, George R., and Deutsch, Ronald M. *Pairing* New York: Peter H. Wyden, 1970.

Barksdale, Lilburn S. *Building Self-Esteem.* Los Angeles: The Barksdale Foundation for Furtherance of Human Understanding, 1972.

Bartell, Gilbert D. *Group Sex: An Eyewitness Report on the American Way of Swinging.* New York: Peter H. Wyden, 1971.

Bem, Daryl. *Beliefs, Attitudes, and Human Affairs.* Monterey, Calif.: Brooks/Cole Publishing Co., 1970.

Berne, Eric. *Games People Play.* New York: Grove Press, 1964.

————. *What Do You Say after You Say Hello?* New York: Grove Press, 1972.

Buhler, Charlotte, and Allen, Melanie. *Introduction to Humanistic Psychology.* Monterey, Calif.: Brooks/Cole Publishing Co., 1972.

Christie, Richard, and Geis, Florence L. *Studies in Machiavellianism.* New York: Academic Press, 1970.

Coelho, George V.; Hamburg, David A.; and Adams, John E. *Coping and Adaptation.* New York: Basic Books, 1974.

Fensterheim, Herbert, and Baer, Jean. *Don't Say Yes When You Want to Say No.* New York: David McKay Co.,1975.

Frankl, Viktor E. *Man's Search for Meaning: An Introduction to Logotherapy.* New York: Washington Square Press, 1963.

————. *The Doctor and the Soul: From Psychotherapy to Logotherapy.* New York: Alfred A. Knopf, 1965.

Harris, Thomas A. *I'm OK — You're OK.* New York: Harper & Row, Publishers, 1969.

Keys, James. *Only Two Can Play This Game.* New York: Julian Press, 1971.

Luft, Joseph. *On Human Interaction.* Palo Alto, Calif.: National Press Books, 1969.

Maslow, Abraham H. *Motivation and Personality.* New York: Harper & Row, Publishers, 1970.

Masters, William H., and Johnson, Virginia E. *The Pleasure Bond: A New Look at Sexuality and Commitment.* Boston: Little, Brown & Co., 1974.

McCary, James Leslie. *Freedom and Growth in Marriage.* Santa Barbara, Calif.: Hamilton Publishing Co., 1975.

Mebane-Francescato, Donato, and Jones, Susan. "Radical Psychiatry in Italy: 'Love Is Not Enough,'" in *Radical Psychology,* edited by Phil Brown. New York: Harper & Row, Publishers, 1973.

Peele, Stanton, with Archie Brodsky. *Love and Addiction.* New York: Taplinger Publishing Co., 1975.

Ravich, Robert A., and Wyden, Barbara. *Predictable Pairing.* New York: Peter H. Wyden, 1974.

Reik, Theodor. *The Need to Be Loved.* New York: Farrar, Straus & Co., 1963.

Rokeach, Milton. *The Nature of Human Values.* New York: The Free Press, 1973.

Rubin, Theodore Isaac. *Compassion and Self-Hate.* New York: David McKay Co., 1975.

———. The Winner's Notebook. New York: Pocket Books, 1969.

Shostrom, Everett L. *Man, the Manipulator: The Inner Journey from Manipulation to Actualization.* New York: Bantam Books, 1968.

Steiner, Claude. *Scripts People Live: Transactional Analysis of Life Scripts.* New York: Grove Press, 1974.

Thoreau, Henry David. *Walden.* New York: The New American Library, 1960.

Toffler, Alvin. *Future Shock.* New York: Random House, 1970.

Viscott, David. *How to Live with Another Person.* New York: Arbor House Publishing Co., 1974.

Webster, Murray, Jr., and Sobieszek, Barbara. *Sources of Self-Evaluation: A Formal Theory of Significant Others and Social Influence.* New York: John Wiley & Sons, 1974.

Epilogue

Never, "for the sake of peace and quiet,"
deny your own experience or convictions.
                                    Dag Hammarskjold

You have now gone through some 260 pages of text, seventeen inventories, and numerous activities and exercises. We hope you have profited by it and that you will continue to think about what you have experienced. If you choose to become (or continue to be) a humanistic communicator, we wish you a positive outlook on all your experiences. If each of us continues to seek a deeper knowledge of ourself and others, perhaps we will inspire this same kind of humanistic behavior in others.

It might be interesting now to go back over your inventories and see if you have changed from your original positions. Remember, only you can know who you are and where you are going. You bring your own meaning to events. To think differently from others is neither good nor bad; it is only how you feel about it that matters. As you develop and mature into a fully functioning person, you will find a greater harmony and satisfaction within yourself. This will enable you to behave as you want to and to allow others the same freedom.

The integration of your self-actualizing behavior with the awareness of your social embeddedness can only make you a more complete person. In understanding yourself and others you must consider the whole person. Thus we must emphasize again the importance of having an unconditional positive regard for the person. U Thant came to the same conclusion but from a different perspective when he said:

I feel more strongly than ever that the worth of the individual human being is the most precious of all our assets and must be the beginning and the end of all our efforts. Governments, systems, ideologies and institutions come and go, but humanity remains. The nature and value of this most precious asset is increasingly appreciated as we see how empty organized life becomes when we remove or suppress the infinite variety and vitality of the individual.*

Or as Pablo Casals so succinctly put it: "The main thing in life is not to be afraid to be human."

Be human. It's your most unique characteristic.

---

*Quoted by May H. Weis in "NGOs — Who and What Are They?", *The Humanist*, July-August 1975, p. 46.

Index

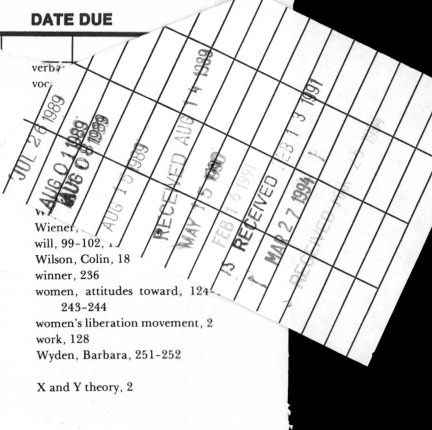